WILLIAM
The
CONQUEROR

The Kings & Queens of Medieval England

A series of scholarly yet accessible biographies of England's medieval monarchs.

Published

David Bates, *William the Conqueror*
Michael Hicks, *Richard III*
W.M. Ormrod, *The Reign of Edward III*

Titles commissioned

Douglas Biggs, *Henry IV*
Michael Hicks, *Edward V*
Ryan Lavelle, *Aethelred II*
Emma Mason, *William Rufus*
A.J. Pollard, *Henry VI*

WILLIAM THE CONQUEROR

David Bates

TEMPUS

Illustrated edition published 2001

PUBLISHED IN THE UNITED KINGDOM BY:

Tempus Publishing Ltd
The Mill, Brimscombe Port
Stroud, Gloucestershire GL5 2QG

PUBLISHED IN THE UNITED STATES OF AMERICA BY:

Tempus Publishing Inc.
2 Cumberland Street
Charleston, SC 29401
(Tel: 1-888-313-2665)

Tempus books are available in France, Germany and Belgium
from the following addresses:

Tempus Publishing Group
21 Avenue de la République
37300 Joué-lès-Tours
FRANCE

Tempus Publishing Group
Gustav-Adolf-Straße 3
99084 Erfurt
GERMANY

Tempus Publishing Group
Place de L'Alma 4/5
1200 Brussels
BELGIUM

British Library Cataloguing in Publication Data.
A catalogue record for this book is available from the British Library.

ISBN 0 7524 1980 3

Typesetting and origination by Tempus Publishing.
PRINTED AND BOUND IN GREAT BRITAIN.

CONTENTS

List of illustrations

Unless otherwise credited, all pictures are from the Tempus Archive.

Preface

This book is a biography of a man whose victory at the Battle of Hastings on 14 October 1066 brutally and dramatically changed the course of Britain's history. The conquest of England inevitably plays a large part in the story, but this is most definitely not a book about the Norman Conquest. Rather it is an attempt to describe and make sense of William's career, and to interpret his formidable personality and the attributes and policies which made him successful. Throughout it is emphatically a book about a man who not only became King of England, but who was also Duke of Normandy and from 1063 Count of Maine.

The book has been written without footnotes. There are therefore a large number of debts to the work of gifted scholars which cannot be properly acknowledged. I hope that those who recognize here the fruits of their endeavours will accept this general acknowledgement of how much I owe to them. A short bibliographical essay has been included to draw the reader's attention to the most important recent scholarship. One specific mention must, however, be given to Marjorie Chibnall's edition and translation of the *Historia Ecclesiastica* of Orderic Vitalis, a marvellous source whose reading and rereading has been an inspiration throughout the writing of this biography. Orderic is really the unsung hero of this book. Like him, I have tried to be fair, neither praising excessively, nor criticising too severely. I would also like to acknowledge the stimulus of attendance at the Battle Conferences on Anglo-Norman Studies organized by R. Allen Brown and of a single annual conference of the Haskins Society in Houston. Contacts and friendships formed on these occasions have been of great significance in helping to shape my thinking on William.

My mother's gift of a word processor has greatly assisted the task of writing. The book has been read in manuscript by Kenneth Fryer and Elisabeth van

Houts who have made numerous helpful suggestions. I have been helped at specific points by friends, colleagues and students, Maylis Baylé, Matthew Bennett, Jean-Michel Bouvris, Susan Davis, Véronique Gazeau, John Gillingham, Lindy Grant, Bob Higham, John Kenyon, Vivienne Miguet, Jinty Nelson, Mark Presneill and Emily Tabuteau. I am grateful to Lydia Greeves of George Philip for commissioning this book, and for some criticisms of an earlier draft which helped towards the production of a significantly better text of the book I wished to write. Jane Edmonds has seen the manuscript through to publication and has suggested numerous improvements, as well as being a notable provider of encouragement. My wife Helen has read all the book in its several drafts, discussed numerous aspects of it with me, and been a constant source of support and counsel. My debt to her exceeds all others. My children Jonathan and Rachel have encouraged and have shown their usual patience and understanding through school holidays shared with William the Conqueror; Jonathan has helped with the maps and Rachel has always insisted that the text should be readable.

Preface to the illustrated edition

I am grateful to Jonathan Reeve for suggesting that this book could be republished. The text is, with very minor amendments, exactly the same one which was first published in 1989.

Maps

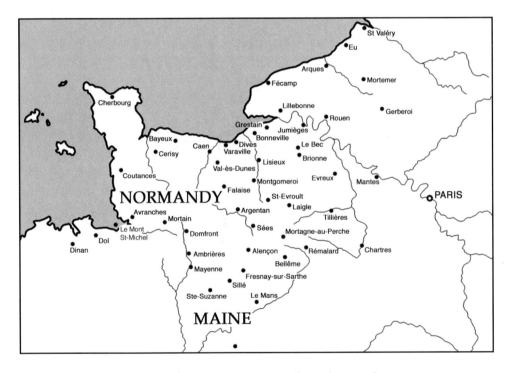

Map 1 – Northern France in the eleventh century

Map 2 – England and Northern France in 1066

Introduction

William the Conqueror was Duke of Normandy from the eighth year of his life in 1035 until his death on 9 September 1087. His rule in Normandy before 1066 was an outstandingly successful one, but it was his victory at the Battle of Hastings on 14 October 1066, and his subsequent coronation as King of the English in Westminster abbey on Christmas Day 1066, which catapulted him to immortality and made him one of the most important of all England's kings. We need only reflect on the 1986 celebrations of the 900th anniversary of the making of Domesday Book, with the many exhibitions, conferences and television programmes, to appreciate how we can still contemplate in awe and wonder one of William the Conqueror's greatest achievements. And across the Channel, modern visitors to Normandy find themselves constantly confronted by reminders of William's life, and of the heroic age of the Normans with which he is so intimately associated. These reminders are not just monuments, but also the names of streets, bars and shops. At Rouen, for example, the chief town of Normandy both then and now, it is currently possible to cross the River Seine by the Pont Guillaume Le Conquérant, to walk along the Rue Guillaume Le Conquérant, and drink in the Bar Le Conquérant.

From our vantage-point a little over 900 years later, William's career is important above all because his victory at Hastings began the last successful invasion of these islands. Dependent on whether they regard the Norman Conquest as a good thing or not, different historians have interpreted his life in different ways, and from vastly different perspectives. For example, in the later twelfth century, Wace, a Norman who was a canon of Bayeux cathedral, produced a giant poem in French, the *Roman de Rou*. Although the poem supposedly celebrated the achievements of all the Norman dukes, it is in fact dominated by William's

11

career and the Battle of Hastings. However, fifty years earlier in the same century in England, the monk William of Malmesbury, who was of Anglo-Norman parentage, was more ambivalent, accepting that William's victory at Hastings was a manifestation of God's will, yet regretting that it had happened; the battle was 'a fatal day for England, a sad disaster for the dear kingdom'. Between the twelfth century and the present, William has been portrayed as anything from a bloodthirsty tyrant to the true founder of the British constitution. An entire book could indeed be devoted to the opinions which have been expressed about William. Because of his importance, it is also inevitable that fallacies and fictions about him should have arisen. In the author's experience, a particularly amusing one is the way in which a modern visitor to the castle at Falaise may be shown the room where William is reputed to have been born, in a building known to have been built about one hundred years after the event. It is of course fascinating to dwell on such errors and on past opinions. They at least show, however, how significant a figure William was and how difficult, if not impossible, it is to make an objective assessment.

While writing this book, I have often wondered why we in Britain were, with a few exceptions, largely silent about William's career and achievements during the year 1987, the 900th anniversary of his death, whereas Normandy was awash with pageants, exhibitions and other reminders of the great man's life during the same year. To take this line of thought a little further, why should Normandy be so interested in the man and his successes, whereas England's celebrations were so blatantly devoted to Domesday Book a year earlier? Is it that we can conveniently integrate Domesday Book, as 'our earliest public record', into this island's heritage, whereas William the Conqueror, as a foreign invader and a conqueror, makes us feel uncomfortable? Is it that – at a time of low national morale and uncertain identity, when our government is putting a new stress on nationalism, and when our schools and universities are being invited to concentrate more fully than they have done on English history – we wish to insulate ourselves against the disturbing facts that the army which won the Battle of Hastings was a French one and that we have to look outside these islands for a major component of our heritage? I am not sure whether these speculations are entirely valid. But I certainly think I detect an insidious insularity when I sit through major conferences on Domesday Book whose participants have apparently made little or no effort to search the Norman documents for keys to that great record's contents and making; when I read essays from my students who obviously unconsciously believe that England is the centre of the universe because they can write about 'the English possessions in France' in the eleventh and twelfth centuries; and when I hear and see these same sentiments repeated in television programmes and historical publications as prestigious as *The Cambridge Historical Encyclopaedia of Great Britain and Ireland*. If the British (or perhaps more accurately the English) are becoming self-deluding about the nature of their heritage, then there is ample justification for reminding ourselves who William the Conqueror was, and where he came from.

A more prosaic, but no less important, reason for writing about William is that it is around twenty-five years since the last serious attempt at a biography was published. A lot has been written since then to increase our understanding of William's life and times, and of eleventh-century society in general. What follows is, however, primarily a personal view which draws on the researches of other scholars, and incorporates discoveries that I have made during a considerable number of years of research into William's career. It is woven around the theme that we cannot understand William's life unless we try to understand the society in which he lived, and it is based on the conviction that an accurate record of his career and achievements has to take full account of his rule in Normandy before 1066 and has to accept that after 1066 his task was not just to consolidate his conquest of England, but to govern separate territories on both sides of the Channel. Although the story is built up as strictly as possible from the contemporary, or near-contemporary sources, it is often necessary to sound a warning that we must always read these sources carefully, and often sceptically. Above all, it is highly questionable how far we can accept at face value most of what was written in Normandy in the eleventh century about the justice of William's government and the moral rightness of his claim to the English kingdom; a lot is propaganda which is only one side of the whole story. At the very heart of my account of William's career is the thesis that he was essentially a Norman duke who also became King of England. The central point is that William was a typical eleventh-century ruler whose preoccupations were fundamentally those of a Frankish territorial prince who gained additional lands, and that this fact is outstandingly evident in the way in which he ruled his various territories after 1066.

The view of William which will emerge from this biography is of an extremely effective ruler, who was not an especially appealing man. The mature William was an outstanding soldier, a very capable general and a warrior who led by example. He possessed great fortitude and acted with an unbending insistence on his own authority. He took very seriously the contemporary ideal that a ruler should keep the peace within his lands, do justice firmly, punish savagely, and protect the Church. This approach to government was that of a typical eleventh-century ruler and of a man firmly rooted in the times in which he lived, whose ideas were limited by the conventions of his age. Yet his ruthlessness and shameless manipulation of facts to justify dubious enterprises have a considerable and saddening modernity about them. His methods of government were brutal and in modern terms probably corrupt. He was rigid, puritanical and intolerant, and his most noticeable faults were cruelty and avarice. He was religious by the standards of an eleventh-century layman. He had in several major respects the ability to think on a large strategic scale, as is evidenced above all by his organisation of the conquest of England, and he had that mixture of intelligence, will-power and charisma which could persuade others to follow him on hazardous enterprises. In short, he is best regarded as an authoritarian ruler of a typical early medieval type. He was a brutal and highly successful opportunist and an outstanding example of an eleventh-century warrior chieftain whose essentially violent life has been given a veneer of legitimacy and respectability by the contemporary churchmen who wrote about him. His political achievement was unquestionably a massive one. It is to a very high degree doubtful whether so great a feat as the Norman Conquest of England could have been accomplished without this remarkable man's extraordinarily strong personality at its heart.

One

SETTING THE SCENE

The eleventh-century duchy of Normandy was the springboard for a movement of expansion which took the Normans to many parts of the then known world. The Norman Conquest of England, for example, should not be seen merely as the subjugation and colonisation of the English kingdom, but also as the creation of a base from which other Normans were to extend their power into other parts of Britain during the later eleventh and twelfth centuries. Also in the eleventh century, another group of Normans secured military and political domination over southern Italy and the island of Sicily, while during the same period yet other Normans took part in pilgrimages and in wars against the Moslems in Spain, and some made a major contribution to the First Crusade of 1096-1100. Their military trademark was the mounted knights who have been made familiar by the scenes of warfare portrayed on the Bayeux Tapestry, magnificently disciplined shock troops, normally capable of defeating less adept contemporaries, like the English, Welsh and Scots, in open warfare.

This great era of Norman activity has left some prodigious memorials, like the architectural remains which symbolize their domination over northern France, Britain and southern Italy. William the Conqueror's own monument is surely the town of Caen within his duchy of Normandy, with its great abbey church of St Etienne and its castle. In southern Italy, there are many splendid reminders of the Normans' presence, while in England we can still see cathedrals such as Durham and Norwich, and castles such as the Tower of London or Chepstow. For a number of reasons, historians have tended in recent years to look at this Norman expansion and at the so-called Norman achievement in an increasingly critical and analytical way. For example, until the publication of a book by Professor R.H.C. Davis entitled *The Normans and their Myth* in 1976, there was almost universal acceptance of the idea of the Normans as a race with unique military abilities. However, it is now appreciated that this was a thesis substantially developed by twelfth-century Normans who wrote after the great victories had been achieved, and that it was therefore a myth created by a people who had already succeeded, rather than evidence which can be used to explain success. In 1982, my own book, *Normandy before 1066*, stressed as the fundamental causes of Norman expansion a mixture of violence and social change within Normandy. It further argued that historians of the Normans and Normandy should concentrate on social and economic changes rather than accepting simplistic notions about Norman national and racial character.

As a consequence of these and other publications, there has been considerable recognition that military expansion and social mobility were widespread characteristics of eleventh-century French society, and not simply of Norman. Or, to put this another way, the Normans were merely the leaders of sections of a much larger migration of peoples which involved men and women from many parts of France. When we look more closely we see that Normans were not, for instance, the dominant group on the First Crusade or in Spain, and that even in one of their greatest conquests, southern Italy, the proportion of Normans to other Franks was probably around one in four, while Flemings, Bretons and others took a prominent role in the settlement of Britain. The expansion can be explained by structural social change within the warrior aristocracy of the French kingdom, at whose heart were the ambitions of numerous adventurous, ambitious warriors and the personal qualities of a number of great war leaders who provided direction and inspiration. As far as understanding William's career is concerned, a major consequence of putting the Norman achievements in their French context is that there is no longer any predetermined reason for his success: he was part of an eleventh-century historical process in which a number of French warrior leaders made extensive conquests because there was a supply of warriors ready to follow them; he most certainly should not be associated in any way with a supposedly unique Norman genius for war and conquest. William was in reality one of several eleventh-century French territorial princes who had successful careers as conquerors, and it is important therefore to put his life against the background of their achievements.

The origins of the duchy of Normandy lay in an early tenth-century settlement by Vikings around the town of Rouen and the River Seine. The leader of these first settlers, Rollo, our William's great-great-great-grandfather, was given authority in the lands he controlled by a grant from the then King of the Franks, Charles the Simple, a ruler who claimed authority over a kingdom roughly equivalent to modern France. The agreement between them is usually known as the Treaty of Saint-Clair-sur-Epte, after the place on the border of the two men's lands where they met. The much larger region which we call Normandy was subsequently created through a mixture of force and diplomacy by Rollo and his successors, who led expeditions outwards from their base near Rouen, and imposed their authority on fresh waves of Viking settlers, as well as on Frankish natives. By the early eleventh century the territory they had conquered was of the same extent as the eleventh- and twelfth-century duchy of Normandy, and was generally called 'Normandy' (*Normannia* or *terra Normannorum*, the land of men from the North) by contemporaries. By the standards of a medieval society, it was economically quite prosperous; its chief town, Rouen, was, for example, renowned as a trading centre, and must in many ways have resembled that other great Viking and post-Viking commercial town, York, about which we are now learning so much from archaeological excavations. Its ruler in the early eleventh century, Duke Richard II (996-1026), William the Conqueror's grandfather, was also the first man regularly to use the title 'Duke of the Normans'.

Richard II was held in high esteem as a warrior and a Christian ruler by those eleventh-century historians who wrote about him. He was also the last Norman ruler to maintain relations with the Scandinavian peoples from whom he and his warrior aristocracy were descended. Historians continue to debate the extent and longevity of Scandinavian influence within Norman society. Most would, however, accept that by Richard's time Normandy was in general terms distinguished from the neighbouring Frankish regions only by its unique origins. The Normans remembered, and sometimes paraded, their Scandinavian past. But they spoke French and were governed in a way which was in all essential characteristics French. They had converted to Christianity and Richard's reign was in fact a time of major developments in the Norman Church, since he summoned the religious reformer William of Volpiano to preside over a reorganization of four out of the five abbeys which then existed in the duchy. A splendid indication of how far the eleventh-century Normans differed from their Viking ancestors is of course the Battle of Hastings itself, where the descendants of the tenth-century Viking settlers in Normandy fought as a thoroughly Frankish cavalry force and defeated an English army dependent in considerable degree on Viking military methods. In the case of the eleventh-century Normans in general, as well as in the specific personal case of William the Conqueror, therefore, we are looking at men who were culturally French and whose political outlook equally was essentially Frankish.

A central feature of Normandy's tenth-century evolution was that it became an autonomous, self-governing territorial principality, within which the duke's authority was in practice supreme. The fact that the original Viking settlement had been theoretically subject to the authority of the King of the Franks caused both Rollo and his successors, down to and beyond Richard II, to become vassals of the kings and to regard their duchy as a constituent part of the kingdom of the Franks. However, this habitual relationship of lord and vassal became increasingly devoid of meaning and the actual power of the King of France within Normandy steadily dwindled away to nothing. The change was not simply a consequence of initiatives taken by the Norman rulers, but rather was part of a general development throughout tenth-century France which is often described as 'the rise of the territorial principalities'. Its result was that the effective power of the French king retreated until it was limited to a small region around Paris and Orléans, while authority similar to that exercised in Normandy by Richard II also passed to other major territorial rulers such as the Counts of Flanders, Anjou and Brittany. The frontiers of the principalities controlled by rulers of this type were ill-defined and fluid; each one had a central core, but otherwise they expanded and contracted with the military power of their rulers. In the areas between the major principalities there was land controlled by lesser powers, such as, to the south of Normandy, the Counts of Maine and the lords of Bellême, who tried to manipulate the rivalries of the greater powers around them.

An awareness of the political geography of northern France is essential background to an understanding of William's career. It is also crucial to appreciate that the first decades of the eleventh century were notable for incessant wars between princes in which Duke Richard II normally took the side of the French King Robert the Pious (996-1031). The course of events at this time was, however, dominated by formidable warriors like Count Fulk Nerra of Anjou (995-1040) or Count Odo of Blois-Chartres (996-1037). Count Fulk began a notable expansion of the lands ruled by the counts of Anjou – continued by his son Count Geoffrey Martel (1040-60) – which gave them control over lands stretching from the southern frontiers of Normandy in the north to Poitou and the Saintonge in the south, and from near Nantes in the west to Tours in the east. The buccaneering Count Odo also expanded his lands and, in the course of a turbulent career, laid claim to two kingdoms. The arrogant self-confidence of these rulers' aggressive campaigns, as well as the essential instability of French society at this time, are contextual matters which cannot be over-emphasized. The young William the Conqueror was born within a well-established and essentially Frankish territorial principality, but also into a very troubled and uncertain world, where princes and nobles were engaged in a ruthless competition for power, where violence and unrestrained aggression were central to the way of life of the aristocracy, and in which threats and opportunities existed on all sides.

A final factor to which attention must be drawn is the tenth- and early eleventh-century relations between Normandy and the kingdom of England. Their geographical proximity meant that there was a long-standing interest in Normandy in major events across the Channel, and also close relations at many levels. There is, for example, clear evidence of economic and cultural contacts in the tenth and eleventh centuries. In addition, the two lands shared a common Scandinavian heritage, which was founded on the extensive settlement in both of peoples of Scandinavian origin. There were marriages between the two lands' ruling families, of which the most important for our purpose is the one in the late tenth century between Duke Richard II's sister Emma and the English King Æthelred the Unready. At the time of this marriage both Normandy and England were sucked into the vortex of the raids which culminated in Cnut's conquest of England in 1016. Their roles in these events were, however, radically different. The English kingdom, having conquered its erstwhile Viking predators during the tenth century, became a prey to this second murderous wave; the long reign of King Æthelred the Unready (978-1016) is essentially a tale of disaster and final collapse. Normandy, however, ruled by a count and an aristocracy descended from Scandinavians, initially welcomed the new intruders. In or around the year 1003 Richard II even went so far as to make a treaty which permitted the Danes to dispose of loot, gathered in England, in Normandy and gave them free use of Norman harbours. However, after King Æthelred had fled, with his wife and three children, to Emma's brother Duke Richard in 1013, the children, who included the future King Edward the Confessor, were left behind when their parents returned to England; Æthelred to defeat and death, and Emma, somewhat later, to marry her family's supplanter, King Cnut (1016-35). Edward and his brother and sister thereafter lived under the protection and patronage of a number of northern French princes. The prominent part taken by the Norman dukes in providing a refuge for the exiles was the basis from which eleventh-century Norman historians developed the thesis that the Norman dukes were King Edward's consistent supporters and that Edward eventually promised William the Conqueror the succession to the English kingdom out of gratitude.

The Social Context

Medieval states, be they kingdoms, counties, duchies, or other units, were usually governed by a single source of authority, a man who bore the title of king, count or duke. For this man's success, leadership, and above all leadership in war, was of paramount importance. It is a basic fact of the sociology of medieval western Europe that the stability of kingdoms and territorial principalities was essentially dependent on their having a ruler whose personality commanded respect. England's medieval history illustrates this general point exceptionally well with several outstanding examples of the successful warrior chieftain in Richard the Lionheart, Edward I or Henry V, as well as of the weak and/or tyrannical ruler, like Stephen, John or Edward II. A ruler's military abilities were especially important in the eleventh century which, as has already been emphasized, was an exceptionally violent period in western Europe's history. Princes like Counts Fulk Nerra and Geoffrey Martel of Anjou or Count Odo II of Blois-Chartres were dominant personalities similar to the successful English kings mentioned above, and one or all of them might well have provided a 'role-model' for the young William to emulate.

All rulers of this early medieval period were theoretically unrestrained by any constitutional or legal limitations over the way they governed. They wielded immense arbitrary power and could dispense favour and disfavour at will. Contemporary political theory regarded a ruler such as a King of England or a Duke of Normandy as being responsible for the upholding and enforcement of law, but not necessarily as being answerable to it. He was not supposed to act unjustly, but in practice he could choose his favourites and deprive others of patronage and reward. However, when it came down to the practicalities of government, a ruler had to be relatively circumspect in order to balance loyalties and command the respect of his aristocracy. He had to be a good lord to his followers by being generous to them, by respecting their rights, and by protecting their lands. If he failed to do these things, he faced discontent and possibly rebellion.

A ruler like William was required by contemporary ideals to be always accessible to his subjects. In battle, this meant that he should be seen to be providing an example, something at which, as we shall see, William was outstanding. Accessibility was also of fundamental importance in peacetime. An anonymous late eleventh-century writer criticized William's grandfather Duke Richard II for shutting himself away from his people, and told how the duke had to be brought to his senses to resume the behaviour expected of a medieval prince. A portrait drawn of the way of life of William's great-grandson, King Henry II (1154-89), by Walter Map is surely also appropriate to William himself:

> Whatever way he goes out he is seized upon by the crowds and pulled hither and thither, pushed whither he would not, and, surprising to say, listens to each man with patience, and, though assaulted by all with shouts and pullings and rough pushings, does not challenge anyone for it, nor show any appearance of anger.

Privacy would have had a very small place in William's life.

In the eleventh century there were no capital cities in the modern sense of the term, and the civil service or bureaucracy which assisted government was minimal in both its size and activity. Throughout his adult years, William was constantly on the move around the territories he ruled. In Normandy his chief residences were at Fécamp, Rouen, Caen, Bayeux and Bonneville-sur-Touque, while in England after 1066 he made use of the palaces of the Old English kings at Winchester, Westminster and Gloucester. Occasionally he attended the dedication ceremony of one of the splendid abbeys or cathedrals which were being built in Normandy during his reign. At times he presided over large assemblies at major residences when his great vassals, that is, the nobles and churchmen of Normandy and England, gathered around him, bringing with them companies of their own vassals. In England after 1066, such assemblies were often the occasion of a ceremonial crown-wearing. Whether in England or Normandy, the assemblies provided the opportunity for discussions of policy, and of present and future wars; for William to hear disputes between his greater subjects, confirm charters, and preside over councils of bishops and abbots. They might also provide the moment when the army was brought together: William's vassals would then themselves simply bring with them contingents of warriors, and a force which is unlikely to have been more than one or two thousand strong would set off on campaign – the much larger army of the Hastings campaign is of course unique. The highly personal nature of William's authority made these gatherings extremely important factors in government. The household and the court were the true centre of power, patronage and favour, where the big decisions were made, where great disputes were settled, and William's favour and ill will were dispensed.

Between the great gatherings at his chief residences, William often lived much less splendidly during his and his companions' journeys around his dominions, when they were obliged to live off the countryside. More will be said in later chapters about the rudimentary, but well-organized, apparatus of central and local officials who supported William's itinerary; here we need only note that there are many references in Domesday Book to the ancient food rents which made an essential contribution to the upkeep of the royal court and that William's itinerant court was a considerable employer of personnel to judge by the numerous references in the documents to cooks, swineherds and the like. When not on campaign, William would probably on a typical day have heard Mass in the morning, hunted until lunchtime, then perhaps returned to the chase and/or other martial exercises until he and his followers feasted in the evening. This was a rough existence, the life of a crude, unlettered soldier, always surrounded by men of similar accomplishments and interests. He lived among a military household, whose members also included some chaplains and clerics, and often his sons and the women of his family.

Although eleventh-century government demanded great personal skill on a ruler's part, the actual institutions which supported it were rudimentary. In Normandy, as well as in England after 1066, William's household was staffed by a number of officers – stewards, butlers, marshalls, and the like – who appear in most royal and princely courts of the period. There was a chamber within the household for counting and storing money, and by 1066 probably a permanent treasury at Rouen, with a similar, rather larger treasury at Winchester after 1066, which had been inherited from the Anglo-Saxon kings. English local government, with its sub-divisions of shires into hundreds and wapentakes, was a more complex affair than Norman, but the chief local officials, the *vicomtes* in Normandy and the sheriffs in England, were essentially similar officials; both administered justice and collected revenues in the territories over which they had jurisdiction. In Normandy, and later in England, counts (or earls as they are usually called in England) were sometimes given responsibility for the defence and organization of a sensitive region. Revenues came from ducal and royal lands, from the profits of justice, as well as from long-existing customary rights like tolls and the Norman taxes of *bernagium*, a levy in oats taken throughout the duchy, and *gravarium*, an obscure general tax. In England there was the Danegeld, the first truly general tax of western Europe, which had a much greater potential for raising large sums of money than Norman taxes, along with a well-organized national coinage from which the kings drew considerable profit. The written word played a notable part in administration in both Normandy and England, although society had not yet evolved to the stage of trusting documents as evidence in legal disputes. These would commonly be resolved by recourse to an ordeal which supposedly revealed God's judgement; ordeals by battle, carrying a hot iron bar, or immersion in water were the most popular.

Eleventh-century society is commonly described as a 'feudal society'. We probably do best to regard 'feudalism' and 'feudal society' as terms which have been invented in modern times to make the study of the Middle Ages more difficult! The essential point for our purpose is that William was the leader of a landholding warrior aristocracy, within which all manner of arrangements, including the crucial one whereby one man agreed to perform or provide military service for another, were organized on the solemn basis of the relationship between lord and vassal. This relationship frequently involved the granting of land to the vassal in return for service and loyalty. In Normandy in the first half of the eleventh century – and indeed in northern France in general – feudal society was not a schematized pyramid, with a king at the top, some great lords beneath him, and other men who might be called knights beneath them. Nor indeed was it the system of tenure and law which evolved in the twelfth century. Rather it consisted of numerous personal relationships, which could cut across one another, and which might involve many and varied obligations. A wealthy member of the Norman aristocracy would certainly acknowledge William as his lord (*dominus*) and render him service, including providing a contingent of warriors when requested. But this lord might also become the vassal of other lords for other property which he held. Such multiple relationships would normally impose no more stress on their participants than do the numerous personal and professional obligations which most of us inevitably enter into during our modern-day lives.

The significance of so-called 'feudal' relationships would wax or wane according to how often the obligations they involved were performed. Given the importance of custom as the legal foundation of early medieval society, it was crucial that a service be regularly performed, since what was remembered was considered to be legal. A simple illustration of this maxim in practical operation is provided by the vassalage of the Duke of Normandy to the King of France, which although performed by each successive Norman ruler to each successive king, had, by the eleventh century, largely become a formality because no services of any significance had been given for many years. For understanding William's career, the crucial point to grasp in all this is that lordship and vassalage were a kind of social cement through which the powerful in society made arrangements which we would now recognize as contracts, agreements or treaties. The involvement of lord-vassal relationships with the holding of land, which in the eleventh century was the basic source of wealth and power, meant that they usually had a continuity over generations, because a man inheriting his father's, or other relative's, lands would usually negotiate a way to become the vassal of that relative's lord. This continuation of vassalic relationships meant that they sustained and reinforced existing social, territorial and political structures by keeping individuals and families in relatively unchanging relationships with one another. However, the creation of new lord-vassal relationships occurred in response to changes in the distribution of land and power. In the eleventh century the number and power of a lord's vassals were a sort of barometer of his own social standing.

A final factor to consider is the all-pervasive Christian Church. Its significance lies in the general emphasis on conformity and the presence everywhere of its institutions. It imposed a framework of ideas which theoretically governed the way in which people lived and died; its influence was inescapable. Its major constituents were large bishoprics and abbeys which were usually wealthy landowners. Its foundations were the countless village churches which are frequently mentioned in medieval charters. It is important to appreciate that in spite of the Church's all-pervasiveness, most medieval people were not especially pious. Medieval society was as much a society of saints and sinners as any other.

The result of the breakdown of the French kingdom into territorial principalities was that rulers of William's type had taken over what were previously royal prerogatives and had come to dominate and rule the Church within their lands, choosing bishops, and appointing abbots to the monasteries they and their predecessors had founded. Kings and dukes were indeed often thought of as religious dignitaries; a king such as the French King Robert the Pious (996-1031) presided at ecclesiastical councils, pronounced on matters of doctrine, and is even said to have performed miraculous cures. An early twelfth-century writer saw kings and bishops as jointly sharing in the government of the Church, and justified this state of affairs on the grounds that a king had been annointed with holy oil at his coronation. The papacy, a feeble institution in the first half of the eleventh century, exercised little real authority and scarcely ever intervened in the local churches of Christendom. When the papacy did begin to assert its innate reserves of authority over Christian society from the middle of the century onwards, it sent shock waves through the structures of western political society. William himself would almost always have been surrounded by churchmen who could remind him of his responsibilities for protecting the Church within his own lands, and who would tell him about the heavy burden of sin which his violent lifestyle entailed, and for which he ought to make amends by generous benefactions to the Church. These factors would have a considerable influence on the policies he followed.

Bishops in Normandy and England in the eleventh century were political figures, frequently present at court. The head of the Norman Church, the Archbishop of Rouen, was often a relative of the reigning duke. He presided over six suffragan bishops whose cathedral churches were situated at Avranches, Bayeux, Coutances, Evreux, Lisieux and Sées. At the start of the eleventh century there were only five monasteries in Normandy, but this number increased enormously as the century advanced, a pattern which was general throughout most of the medieval West. After 1066 William of course also took on responsibility for the much more extensive apparatus of the English Church, with its two archbishoprics of Canterbury and York, its numerous bishoprics and monasteries, and its vast number of village churches.

The Sources for William's Life

The biographer of any medieval character is inevitably hampered by the relatively small amount of available source material. There are many central facts which we do not know and cannot know. We gain only the briefest glimpses of William's domestic life and personal habits. We do not know the size of the armies he led, and we can barely guess how he assembled them. It is only very occasionally that we know where he was on a particular day. The criticism of medieval sources is a highly sophisticated business, requiring great skill in handling texts which are almost all written in Latin. But for those who wish to make sense of the medieval period, a general awareness of the difficulties involved in unravelling the complex evidence is essential. The large regions of ignorance which confront us should not be a reason to despair; the source material is ample enough to construct a reasonably full picture of both William's personality and his policies, and its gaps supply a challenge to the intellect.

A problem which arises as soon as we start to use the sources is that the eleventh- and twelfth-century writers on whom we have to rely saw historical events as the expression of God's purpose, which sometimes made them reinterpret their subject to fit an apparent pattern. One simple example of this is the treatment by Orderic Vitalis and William of Malmesbury, two early twelfth-century writers on whom we have to place great reliance, of the fate of Waltheof, the last Englishman to hold the office of earl, who was beheaded in the year 1076 after a rebellion against William. Both noted Waltheof's apparent involvement in a conspiracy against William, but both also thought that because miracles occurred at his tomb, he must have been innocent. Orderic even went as far as to suggest that the misfortunes suffered by William in his later years were a result of Waltheof's unjust execution. A writer describing such events today would probably be sceptical of the miracles, and would certainly not make any connection between them and the question of Waltheof's innocence or guilt. This preoccupation with the religious framework of events also explains why our sources are profoundly indifferent to the material conditions in which people lived; their main concern was with the ultimate fate of someone's soul and whether he gave succour to the Church and the poor.

The most important eleventh-century histories dealing with William the Conqueror's life were written by the Normans William of Jumiages and William of Poitiers. The first William was a monk of the Norman abbey of Jumiages, who completed his *Gesta Normannorum Ducum* ('The Deeds of the Dukes of the Normans') in 1070-71. The second William was at one time William the Conqueror's chaplain and also an archdeacon of the Norman cathedral church of Lisieux. His *Gesta Guillelmi Ducis Normannorum et Regis Anglorum* ('The Deeds of William, Duke of the Normans and King of the English') was completed by around 1077. William of Jumièges's history is much the shorter in its treatment of William's reign. It is written in a careful, but limited, Latin style. William of Poitiers's, in contrast, is the work of someone exceptionally well-read in the Classics, and determined to show off his learning in a rhetorical and sometimes verbose way. Both wrote with the purpose of praising and justifying William's actions, and Poitiers, in particular, presented many of William's actions through images of stereotyped Christian rulership. William of Jumièges stated his intentions in the following way:

> If anyone wishes to criticize a man chained to sacred learning of presumption or any other fault for producing such an account, let him know that the motive of this little work is in my opinion not unworthy, for the qualities of outstanding men, both in secular and ecclesiastical affairs who are well regarded in the eyes of God, should be brought to the attention of the living.

A writer who sets out to use his subjects to portray the 'qualities of outstanding men' is certain to choose his facts selectively, because he wants to display their virtues. The same considerations apply even more to William of Poitiers, whose much more detailed work is obviously biased in William's favour. The beginning of his history is lost, but his theme is established early on in a passage which deals with the murder of Edward the Confessor's brother Alfred:

> You (i.e., Earl Godwine of Wessex, the father of King Harold) contemplated and were pleased to do something which is detestable according to the morals and laws of peoples the furthest removed from Christianity. The most unjustified misfortunes inflicted on Alfred brought joy to you, whereas to decent people they brought tears. But William, the most glorious duke, whose actions we will with God's help set before future generations, killed Harold, your offspring most like you for his cruelty and treachery, with an avenging sword.

While in another place he says:

> It sometimes happens that the good actions of kings, princes and other magnates, not having been truthfully reported, are condemned by men of goodwill in future ages, while misdeeds which should in no way be copied are taken as exemplars for usurpation and other evils. As a result, we hold it our bounden duty to record as truthfully as possible how this William, whom we are commemorating in writing and whom we wish both in the present and the future to be pleasing to all and displeasing to none, was to take possession of the principality of Maine, as of the kingdom of England, not simply by force, but also by the laws of justice.

William of Poitiers was therefore writing a justification of William's acts; a work which was in some senses propaganda. Both he and William of Jumièges were composing within a literary model which was common in the eleventh century. Neither made any pretence of trying to write objective history as we understand it. There is usually no counterweight to their testimony, so it is generally impossible actually to prove that they are liars. However, there is a distinct feeling, above all with William of Poitiers, that he is often giving us much less than the truth and that in many situations there is a story which he chooses not to tell. It is on occasion our duty to try to reconstruct this hidden version.

The most informative later source is the marvellous *Ecclesiastical History* written between the early twelfth century and 1141 by Orderic Vitalis, a monk of the abbey of St-Evroult in southern Normandy. Orderic had been born in England in 1075 of a French father and English mother. His history began as an account of the history of his own monastery, but developed into a grand, diffuse and rambling history of the Normans. The range of his interests and the vividness with which he presented his material are truly remarkable. So too is his desire to tell an accurate and unbiased story, although it has to be recognized that his information was not always accurate. His contribution is particularly valuable for the last years of William's life, but it is always important on account of the mass of information he supplies, and because he makes more effort than any other writer to give a balanced appraisal of William's character and actions. Also essential is the history written by another monk, William of Malmesbury, who, like Orderic, was of mixed Anglo-Norman parentage but who, unlike him, wrote in England. His *De Gestis Regum Anglorum* ('On the Deeds of the Kings of the English') was completed around the year 1125. He also was concerned to present a truthful account, although with a weakness for anecdote and gossip. His and Orderic's profound interest in William's times stemmed from the momentous importance of the Norman Conquest of England, which had started a process of change which was still being worked through during their lifetimes.

There are many other sources which make major contributions to our understanding of William's life, such as the *Carmen de Hastingae Proelio* ('The Song of the Battle of Hastings'), the Bayeux Tapestry and the Anglo-Saxon Chronicle. The *Carmen* is a poem probably written within three years of the Battle of Hastings, although some scholars doubt this. The Bayeux Tapestry is of course especially important for its visual content and for its portrayal of the Norman invasion of England. The Anglo-Saxon Chronicle survives for this period in three versions, now known as 'C', 'D' and 'E', and it is particularly valuable because it presents events from the point of view of the defeated English; its tone is sombre and regretful. More will be said about all three when they become especially relevant to the story. The sources also include charters, documents which were usually written to record transfers of property. The texts of some of them still survive on their original parchment, but the majority exist only as later copies, while a few are forgeries. The originals can be wonderful affairs, written in good, clear handwriting on parchment, and apparently splattered with crosses written on behalf of consenting witnesses. The fact that they were attested by people present when William confirmed them makes them especially valuable for their information about William's court. They are also important as a source of knowledge of his itinerary and his methods of government. For England after 1066, and for studying William's wealth, there is finally the incomparable, if mysterious, survey known as Domesday Book. This great record contains an account of England's resources; it is of outstanding importance for an understanding of how William controlled and organized his conquered kingdom. But despite the apparent objectivity of its statistics, it too presents problems of bias, since it was a record produced on William's orders to portray the Norman version of the legitimacy of the Norman Conquest. Here, as elsewhere, a biographer of William the Conqueror has to confront the difficulties that the source material is not only small in quantity but was often written by insiders who were committed to supporting or justifying William's deeds and policies.

Two

BOYHOOD AND YOUTH

We do not know the exact date of William's birth. The closest we can come is to deduce that he was born either in the autumn of the year 1027, or perhaps early in 1028. His place of birth was Falaise in Lower Normandy. His father was Robert, the second son of Duke Richard II, who succeeded his elder brother, Richard III (1026-27), as Duke of Normandy on 6 August 1027. His mother was Herleva, the daughter of an undertaker of Falaise. At William's birth, Robert would have been in his early twenties. Herleva's age is unknown; her death some time after 1050 suggests that she was of approximately the same age as her lover.

The meeting of Robert and Herleva took place when Robert was controlling the district of southern Normandy known as the Hiésmois on behalf of his brother Duke Richard III. He had been given this responsibility by their father Richard II shortly before his death in 1026. Since Falaise was within the Hiésmois the meeting with Herleva clearly occurred during one of Robert's visits to the castle there. This meeting and William's birth were soon to become the subject for some romantic storytelling. Even a relatively sober historian like the early twelfth-century William of Malmesbury wrote what are surely fabulous tales. He said, for example, that Robert first saw Herleva when she was dancing and that he came to love her passionately. He also mentions that while Herleva was pregnant she dreamt that her insides were stretched out to cover Normandy and England and that at birth the baby took hold of the rushes spread on the floor and held them firmly; seeing this the midwife hailed it as an omen and said that the boy would be a king. Another version of the meeting of Robert and Herleva has him spot her while she was washing clothes in a stream. These are of course simply the earliest of the legends which were to develop around the obscure birth of a great man. The truth is that we know very little about William the Conqueror's birth.

William's eleventh-century biographers tried to conceal his illegitimate birth. Herleva's name is not mentioned by either William of Jumièges or William of Poitiers, and the only specific reference to her before 1100 is in a charter of the year 1082. However, the evidence indicates that the relationship between William's parents was more than a casual sexual liaison, since her relatives were advanced to positions of some importance at court. It is possible that the couple had a second child, a daughter named Adelaide, whose exact parentage is unknown but who was certainly William's sister. Later, Herleva was married to Herluin de Conteville, a lord of moderate means with some land on the south bank of the Seine estuary. The marriage was a convenient means in eleventh-century society of providing for a woman who had risen to some social eminence. Its date is uncertain, but a reasonable guess is that it took place during Duke Robert's lifetime, probably a little before he set off on his fatal pilgrimage to Jerusalem in January 1035.

Initially William's prospects were not especially good. At the moment of his conception, his father was not even Duke of Normandy and may not have been expected to become so. Even when Robert was duke, there must have been a presumption that he would marry; he was after all still only about thirty when he died on pilgrimage. It would have been conventional for him, like all contemporary rulers, to have entered into a marriage consecrated by the Church. Even though the domestic arrangements of the Norman rulers had continued to reflect their non-Christian Viking origins and had often disregarded Christian etiquette, the succession by a bastard to the duchy was unlikely in the eleventh century. The Burgundian historian Rodulf Glaber, who is usually well-informed on Norman matters, even suggests that Robert was briefly married to a daughter of Cnut, King of England. If legitimate children had been born from this or any other marriage, William would probably have been pushed to one side, whatever the strength of the bond between Robert and Herleva. As it was, the unmarried Robert consistently recognized William as his son during his reign as duke, and shortly before leaving for the Holy Land in January 1035, he had the leading Norman magnates swear fealty to him and accept him as his heir, and then had the bequest confirmed by his overlord, the French king, Henry I (1031-60). These arrangements, which were typical eleventh-century behaviour, created the probability that William would succeed if his father failed to return.

Herleva's two sons by Herluin de Conteville, Odo and Robert, later respectively Bishop of Bayeux and Count of Mortain, were to be closely associated with William's adult career. This patronage of his two half-brothers suggests that William was close to his mother. So too does his generosity to Herluin de Conteville, who rose from being a minor lord to a magnate with lands throughout Normandy in the years before 1066, and also the fact that William entrusted his own bride to Herleva's care. Herleva's death occurred in an unknown year, probably soon after 1050, and she was buried at the abbey of Grestain, which her husband Herluin had founded in a beautiful setting near the River Seine. Almost nothing now survives of this monastery and her tomb has disappeared. As far as relations between father and son are concerned, the only recorded incident available to us is when Robert took his son to the abbey of Préaux, which a vassal had founded, where he witnessed the founder's son having his ears boxed to help him remember a grant of property. In the last years of his life William tried to have his father's bones returned to Normandy, an act which looks more like the sentimentality of an elderly man than a gesture of affection. But William's father's pilgrimage and death certainly had an impact on his son, for when William founded an abbey in 1063 it was dedicated to St Stephen, a saint uncelebrated in Normandy until Duke Robert acquired one of his fingers at Jerusalem. This relic was sent back to Normandy and formed the basis of a major cult. The evidence suggests that at the least William always venerated his father's memory.

Duke Robert's reign was an unsettled and rather undistinguished period in Norman history. The circumstances of his succession were somewhat suspect: his elder brother Richard III, against whom Robert had rebelled, died after reigning for one year, and it was suggested by some contemporaries that he had been poisoned. After his succession Robert was almost immediately faced by wars against the two most prominent political figures of his father Richard II's time, Archbishop Robert of Rouen and Bishop Hugh of Bayeux. Both were churchmen, but they were also large landowners who had enjoyed great political power. Robert defeated Bishop Hugh and compromised with Archbishop Robert. Also during the first years of Robert's reign, there was throughout Normandy much seizure of property belonging to the Church, a symptom of a society in which lawlessness was prevalent. In addition, Robert had to deal with problems around Normandy's frontiers, fighting wars against the Count of Brittany and the lord of Bellême. Both had apparently encroached on Norman territory, a clear sign that this was a phase in the struggles between the various territorial princes of northern France when Normandy was relatively weak. Finally, there was a social and political revolution which was eventually to have profound consequences for the government of the duchy. Robert permitted, or had to submit to, the seizure of offices in the ducal household and in local government by great landed families. Of especial importance was their takeover of the position of *vicomte* throughout much of Normandy, an office whose holders were the chief local officials of ducal government, with responsibility for the financial and judicial administration of a specific region of the duchy. With the benefit of hindsight historians can see that this process represented the rise of many of the families who were to be William the Conqueror's companions and who were later to take a leading part in the conquest of England. But the immediate consequence was that a Duke of Normandy had to rule in collaboration with these families, or not at all.

Robert's rule in Normandy was probably more that of an umpire between contending factions than of a duke who was genuinely in control of his duchy. The disorder was never sufficient, however, to prevent him from continuing some of the traditions of his father's reign and maintaining a basis of authority which his son inherited. For example, he founded a new monastery at Cerisy in Lower Normandy and the reforming monks who had become prominent in the Norman Church under Richard II continued to be so. Like his father, Robert was an ally of the French kings, and in 1033 he welcomed and gave support to King Henry I, who had been driven out of his lands by a rebellion. This act may have had important consequences; it was perhaps out of gratitude that King Henry confirmed William's right to be his father's heir. Robert also gave positive assistance to the English exiles, the brothers Edward and Alfred, who had first taken refuge in Normandy in 1013. They continued to frequent his court and even on occasion witness charters. We are told by William of Jumièges that Robert even attempted to invade England on their behalf, but the story is hard to believe because the fleet was 'diverted' to Brittany where it just happened to assist one of Robert's campaigns. We should not, however, underestimate Robert's commitment to Edward's and Alfred's cause. The obviously warm friendship between the duke and Count Drogo of the Vexin, the first husband of the two brothers' sister Godgifu, indicates a closeness between the families which must have been a major influence on Edward's decision to promise the succession to Robert's son William.

Early in the year 1035 Duke Robert departed on the pilgrimage to Jerusalem from which he never returned. When the news of his death reached Normandy, the young William, who was still only in his eighth year, succeeded to the duchy. Despite the unsettled period during his father's reign, he inherited what was still a well-established principality, with a distinguished recent past in Richard II's time. But the seizures of property and offices during Robert's reign, and the rivalries that they had inevitably engendered, had almost certainly made Norman society inherently unstable. And in addition it is almost a truism of the medieval period that when a young boy rules there will be turmoil. After 1035 such personal and political security as William might have enjoyed in the first seven years of his life were devastated as his duchy was plunged into chaos and civil war.

Minority

The first landmark in William's minority is the death in 1037 of the duchy's elder statesman, Archbishop Robert of Rouen, a brother of Duke Richard II, and with him, apparently all possibility of political stability. After this, aristocratic families in several regions of the duchy began to fight one another and the ducal household itself became an arena for violent feuding. William's whereabouts are rarely known during the first twelve years of his reign. Orderic Vitalis tells us that his life was at times in danger and that his mother's brother Walter slept with him and often concealed him for safety in poor men's houses. A sign of how precarious his circumstances were is that at some date in the early 1040s, when he was at Le Vaudreuil on the River Seine to the south of Rouen, his steward Osbern was murdered in William's bedchamber while the young duke slept. The perpetrator of this deed was a son of Roger I de Montgommery, a man whose fortunes had advanced under Duke Robert. Osbern's followers subsequently took a suitably bloody revenge. Clearly the young William was quite unable to control events within his own household, let alone stop the feuds which were taking place throughout the rest of Normandy.

Two guardians, Count Gilbert of Brionne and Count Alan of Brittany, were nominated at different times from among William's relatives to act as his guardians and to be responsible for his political and military upbringing. Both were slaughtered by rivals in the early 1040s. To judge by the witness lists of the twenty-five or so ducal charters from this period, the dominant figures around the young duke for much of his minority were his two uncles, Count William of Arques and Archbishop Malger of Rouen, both sons of Duke Richard II. These two men were later to be chased from office by the adult William, and the reputations of both were as a result blackened by William's apologist William of Poitiers. Yet Count William, who became Count of Arques soon after 1035, defended church property and sponsored a respectable appointment to a bishopric during his years of power. Archbishop Malger, who had succeeded Archbishop Robert after 1037, organized a council of churchmen which, although poorly attended, at least condemned the evils of the times. William's leading counsellors may have been more supportive and effective than the like of William of Poitiers would have us think.

Although it is impossible to arrange the events recorded by the sources in a fully-convincing chronological order during William's minority, it is at least obvious from William of Jumièges's history that a number of attempts were made to assert ducal authority. Among these was William's order to a reluctant Norman castellan to hand over the castle of Tillières, which was close to the frontier of the lands of the French king, to Henry I. The motive appears to have been to appease Henry's anger against those Normans who had given asylum to some of his enemies. William is also said to have led a successful campaign against a noble named Thurstan Goz, who had attempted to set himself up as an independent power in the castle at Falaise. It is, however, unlikely that the teenage William did anything more than go along with these ineffective demonstrations, and, as an apprentice soldier, improbable that he took any meaningful part in the fighting. It is obvious that the duke and his remaining supporters had lost real control over the province he was supposed to rule and that such security as existed was provided by the local domination exercised over their own regions of influence by aristocratic families. These were times of quite dramatic violence; in a crime which shocked even contemporaries, the southern Norman lord William Giroie attended a wedding feast given by one of his lords, William de Bellême, and left cruelly disfigured, without ears, eyes and genitals.

The first major turning point in William's fortunes is the battle fought at Val-ès-Dunes to the south-west of Caen in 1047. This was a truly decisive moment since defeat would have meant deposition. William's chief opponent was Count Guy of Brionne, the son of a daughter of Duke Richard II who had married a Burgundian count. Guy was therefore Duke William's cousin and near contemporary. He had returned to Normandy during William's early years and, at some time in the early 1040s, after the murder of Count Gilbert of Brionne, who was one of the young William's guardians, had acquired the major castle of Brionne in central Normandy. This and other properties gave substance to his ambitions and made him claim the duchy on the basis of his legitimate kinship with the ducal house. He is known to have attracted a great deal of support in western Normandy and to have been favoured by the citizens of Rouen, with the result that the revolt became so strong that William was obliged to seek assistance from his overlord, King Henry I. A later, possibly legendary, account by the poet Wace tells of William narrowly escaping capture and death at Valognes, which is near Cherbourg and deep in enemy territory; then making an epic ride to safety at Falaise, and afterwards travelling to meet King Henry at Poissy near Paris. After their conference Henry led an army into Normandy which fought with William's supporters against Guy and the rebels at Val-ès-Dunes. The brief contemporary accounts of the battle tell us only that it was a closely contested affair and that most of the Normans fought against William. William of Poitiers, whose boastfulness on William's behalf can be irritating, praises William's personal contribution, but says nothing significant about the course of the battle. Wace, who knew the battlefield well, and had many connections with the descendants of the participants, records that one of the rebels, Ralph Taisson, changed back to William's side, and that after a hard struggle, William's enemies were forced back, many of them dying by drowning as they tried to cross the River Orne.

King Henry I was undoubtedly William's saviour in 1047. He was of course a lord coming to the rescue of a vassal in difficulties. But this probably does not fully explain an intervention whose main motivations may well have been a mixture of gratitude to William's father, who had saved him from his enemies in 1033, and an appreciation of wider political conditions in northern France. In the face of the rising power of the formidable Geoffrey Martel, Count of Anjou (1040-60), who had recently made a major territorial gain by capturing the town of Tours, Henry badly needed allies, and probably hoped to re-establish the traditional alliance between the King of France and the Dukes of the Normans which had been so strong in Richard II's time. By aiding William in his hour of need, he may have thought that he had done so.

The 1030s and 1040s were an exceptionally volatile period in Norman history; they were, for example, a major phase in the migration of warriors to southern Italy to take part in the conquests there. The period of William's minority was not, however, entirely devoid of achievements and positive developments within Normandy. They included a significant phase in the growth of the abbey of Le Bec, which was founded in *c.*1034 and which later became of outstanding importance in the history of the Anglo-Norman Church. The celebrated Lanfranc of Pavia became a monk there in the early 1040s. Several other abbeys were founded during this period, and the successors of the men who had been prominent in the monastic reforms of Richard II's reign were still at their posts. Ducal government was in disarray, but it had not ceased to exist; the *vicomtes* and other members of the aristocracy often made themselves responsible for local order. Politically, the most important development of all within Normandy was a consolidation of the local power of the aristocracy. The takeover of offices in the duke's household and of the position of *vicomte* in Duke Robert's reign was reinforced by the construction of earthwork castles and the subjugation of previously free landholders into vassalage. The full nature of these changes has always been difficult for historians to grasp, but it is a reasonable conclusion that their effect was to make the most powerful members of the Norman aristocracy even more powerful. If ducal authority was ever to be effective again, it was essential that it come to terms with this transformation.

There is no evidence from William's later life to suggest any acquaintance with letters, and it is unlikely that he received much of a formal education during the troubled times of his minority, even though a tutor named Ralph the monk does appear in one charter. As we saw earlier in this chapter, two of William's guardians were killed. Nevertheless, someone must have taught him the military skills appropriate to a young aristocrat of his age. For the other requirements of government in these primitive times, he probably needed only to look around him and learn from the examples set by great

Norman lords or by the Counts of Anjou such as Fulk Nerra (995-1040) or Geoffrey Martel (1040-60). It is likely that the cruelty and ruthlessness later so evident in his character probably originated in the range of brutalizing experiences he underwent during the second decade of his life.

After Val-ès-Dunes, William, who was around twenty years of age, was able to become more assertive. His first major act appears to have been the proclamation of the Truce of God throughout his duchy at a ceremony held near Caen to which saints' relics were brought. The Truce had evolved in southern France in the latter part of the tenth century with the purpose of controlling unlicensed violence. In its Norman version, warfare was prohibited at certain times in the week and the duke's army was given special privileges for subduing illegal fighting. We can reasonably start the account of William's effective reign as duke from this point.

Three

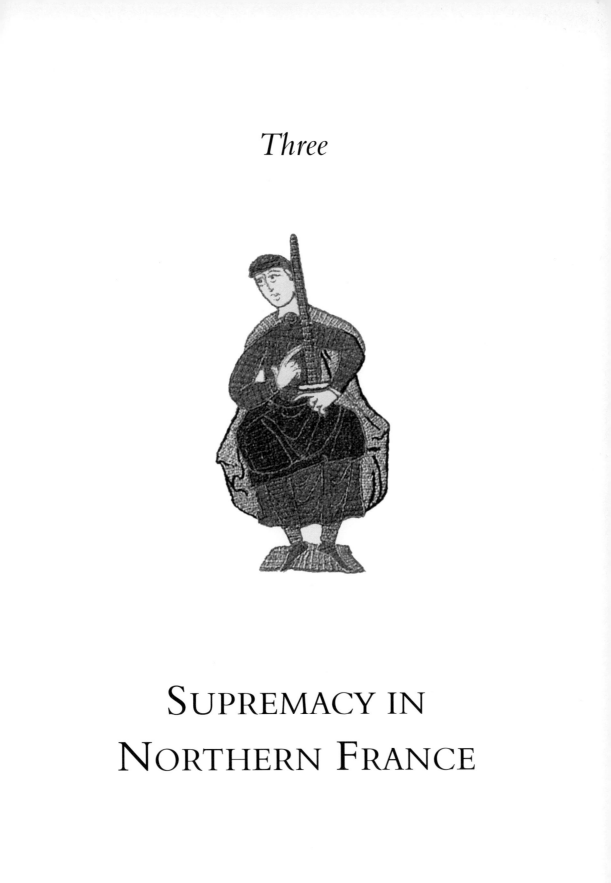

SUPREMACY IN
NORTHERN FRANCE

Between 1047 and 1066 William established himself as Duke of Normandy, achieving dominance over the Norman aristocracy and, after a long struggle, over Normandy's northern French neighbours as well. We cannot fully know what William's policies and tactics were during this period. However, it is obvious that much that he undertook was predetermined by circumstances, since the 1050s were dominated by a battle for survival during which Normandy was invaded twice. It is also clear, however, that during this very same period, William was in the process of creating the opportunities which he later seized to take him to greatness. William's fundamental goal throughout these years appears to have been to try to undermine the power of the Count of Anjou to the south of Normandy. Security in northern France was manifestly always his first objective, even if he did also do such things as accept Edward the Confessor's offer of succession to the English kingdom.

An important, but ultimately inexplicable, phenomenon is the vehemence of the opposition which William aroused almost from the outset of his career. The two foremost rulers in northern and north-western France, King Henry I and Count Geoffrey Martel of Anjou, both men with considerable worldly experience, formed an alliance in 1052 which events show was in large measure directed against William. This occurred at a time when his achievements did not apparently merit such treatment. We can only conclude that from his early twenties, William must have been widely feared and hated.

Initiatives and Setbacks

William consolidated his success at Val-ès-Dunes during !048 and 1049, and in late 1049, probably as a quid pro quo for King Henry's support at Val-ès-Dunes, he led a Norman force to join the French king's army for a campaign against Count Geoffrey Martel of Anjou. The aim of the expedition was obviously to try to reduce the dominance over western and central France which the count was building up through his conquests of parts of Aquitaine and the Touraine. It achieved a notable success in the capture of the castle of Mouliherne near Angers. William's personal bravery during the war is praised by William of Poitiers, who mentions a particular exploit in which the duke at the head of four knights was able to defeat and put to flight an enemy troop of fifteen.

This campaign is our last reference in the sources to active co-operation between William and King Henry before the dramatic realignment of power brought about by Henry's decision to ally with Count Geoffrey Martel against William. Several important events took place in the period from 1049 to 1052 which must have contributed to this. In October 1049 the question of William's betrothal to Mathilda, daughter of Count Baldwin V of Flanders, was discussed at an ecclesiastical council held at Rheims by Pope Leo IX. Quite apart from its immediate significance, this council was a landmark in the history of the medieval West. A pope had not crossed the Alps for many years. Leo's direct intervention in the affairs of the French Church and kingdom initially produced a good deal of mayhem, with cosy local arrangements being disrupted as the pope began a campaign to bring moral reform to the lives of both clergy and laity. Bishops were threatened with deposition and one, so an account of the council tells us, was struck dumb when he tried to deny accusations that a colleague had purchased his bishopric. The general significance of the Council of Rheims is that for the rest of William's life, papal authority became a powerful and occasionally intrusive presence which needed to be handled carefully in a way which had not previously been necessary.

At the council William's projected marriage was condemned, probably on the basis that it was thought to be within the prohibited degrees of kinship. Scholars have long thought that William defied this papal ban for almost ten years, before eventually obtaining agreement to a marriage which had in fact taken place in either 1050 or 1051 through a settlement which included the foundation of two abbeys at Caen. It has recently been suggested, however, that the papacy relented at a much earlier date, probably shortly after the council. The reasons for this suggestion are that the source which describes the date of the lifting of the ban is late and demonstrably untrustworthy; that relations between William and the papacy were otherwise consistently good during the 1050s, and that two Norman ecclesiastics, Lanfranc, Prior of Le Bec, and Geoffrey, Bishop of Coutances, visited Rome in 1050. It is also an important point that no scholar has even been able to discover why the relationship between William and Mathilda was sufficiently close to cause the initial ban. The prohibition was probably a setback which was quickly negotiated away. Mathilda was brought to Normandy by her father, and was received by William's mother and step-father. She and William were married at Eu on the duchy's north-eastern frontier. A son, Robert, the first of many children, was born relatively soon after the marriage.

Considering the uncertainties of his parentage and the insecurities of his youth, William had made a magnificent match in marrying Mathilda. Her family, the counts of Flanders, ruled the most impressive territorial principality of northern France and were related to both the German emperors and the kings of France. The marriage signalled Normandy's return to its usual place among the leading French territorial principalities; the fact that it took place at all indicates that William was speedily restoring ducal authority, since a prince as powerful as Count Baldwin would not have entrusted his daughter to someone whose future was significantly at risk. The marriage also shows that William was now ploughing his own political furrow in contravention of his supposed alliance with King Henry I. In particular, in allowing Norman bishops to attend Pope Leo's council at Rheims and by his negotiations with the pope, he is likely to have offended the king, who had tried to obstruct the council by preventing bishops from attending.

The next significant information about William's activities in France is his first independent campaign against northern French enemies during the years 1051-2, when he attacked and captured the castles of Alençon and Domfront from Count Geoffrey Martel of Anjou. Alençon was situated within Norman territory and Domfront was just over the frontier in Maine. The two castles had formerly been held by the lords of Bellême as vassals of Duke Richard II. In the early 1050s the current chief of the Bellême family was Ivo, who was also bishop of the southern Norman diocese of Sées. Since the late tenth and the early eleventh centuries the family had accumulated possessions which straddled the Norman frontier, and had in consequence entered into relationships of vassalage with the Norman dukes and other neighbouring lords. At some date before 1051, Bishop Ivo had definitively thrown in his lot with Count Geoffrey and had formed an alliance with him, thereby abandoning whatever loyalty his predecessors had owed through vassalage to the rulers of Normandy. The consequence of this was that when Geoffrey increased his already extensive conquests by capturing Le Mans and acquiring domination over the county of Maine in 1051, a major power not only threatened the Norman frontier, but had an access route across it. Quite apart from trying to recover lost Norman territory, William therefore also had excellent defensive reasons for undertaking this campaign. The castles of Alençon and Domfront became bases from which Geoffrey could threaten to advance and establish an Angevin salient into southern Normandy as far north as Sées and Argentan.

William first tried a lightning strike against Domfront with a small force and was, so we are told, personally prominent at the head of the assault; William of Poitiers recounts how William at the head of fifty warriors beat off an enemy force of three hundred which tried to intercept him. Having failed to achieve surprise, William settled down to a war of attrition against the formidable stronghold, which was situated on a high rock. He surrounded it with four fortifications of his own. William of Poitiers – again – insists on William's great energy and vigilance as he travelled round his extended besieging army. He says that good discipline was maintained among the Normans and that William felt sufficiently secure to engage in a spot of hunting in the nearby forests during quiet periods in the siege, the earliest reference we have to a passionate interest of William's. At one stage Geoffrey Martel advanced towards Domfront with an army and the two forces went through the formal acts of defiance in preparation for a battle. But before one could take place, Geoffrey suddenly retreated. William of Poitiers attributes his withdrawal to terror induced by the sight of William's army, but a more likely explanation is a strategic appreciation that his hold over his vast lands would not suffer if the remote outposts of Domfront and Alençon were abandoned to William and that he had a great deal to lose by being defeated in a pitched battle.

After Geoffrey's departure the war ended swiftly and brutally. Aware that the Count of Anjou had left the region, William launched a surprise attack against Alençon, which is some thirty-five miles to the east of Domfront, and which was weakly defended. The brief siege included a famous and telling incident. The story appears first in a general way in the *Gesta Normannorum Ducum* of William of Jumièges, and was subsequently developed in the twelfth century when Orderic Vitalis began his historical work by making interpolations in the *Gesta*. Apparently the inhabitants of Alençon beat furs and pelts to mock Duke William by alluding to the fact that his ancestors, that is, his mother's family, had been undertakers. After capturing the place, William had the culprits' hands and feet cut off. Unsurprisingly this is the last reference in the sources to anyone making jokes about William's illegitimate birth. On learning of this act of savagery, Domfront is said to have surrendered out of fear.

Another important development took place in the spring of the year 1051 when Edward the Confessor, the son of King Æthelred the Unready, and since 1042 King of the English, sent a message to William that he was his choice as the next King of England. It is possible on the basis of an entry in the 'D' version of the Anglo-Saxon Chronicle that William visited Edward later in the same year to have the promise confirmed, although such a journey is intrinsically unlikely given William's absorption in the warfare around Domfront at the same time. As far as William was concerned, in the context of the year 1051 the offer of the English succession provided a potential

1. A fifteenth-century stained glass portrayal of Edward the Confessor, whose promise of the English throne to William was a major success for the young duke.

opportunity more than the certainty of a secure future. He would probably have recognized what is obvious to us, namely, that he could expect little positive support within England and that his claims would be opposed by the kingdom's most powerful family, which was led by Godwine, Earl of Wessex. We will look in more detail at the problems of the English succession in Chapter Five.

The alliance between King Henry and Count Geoffrey was in the process of formation during the early months of 1052, and was certainly in existence by 15 August 1052 when the two men were in each other's company at Orléans. The reasons for this turn-around are not entirely clear. William's successful defiance of Count Geoffrey must have made a powerful impression on his contemporaries, since the count had a reputation as an unscrupulous politician and was a great warrior who had defeated most of his neighbours in war. William had indeed shown himself ready not only to defy Geoffrey's encroachments into Norman territory, but to take positive steps to undermine

Angevin power in Maine; in 1051, for example, he had given asylum to Gervase de Château-du-Loir, Bishop of Le Mans, a bitter opponent of the Angevins. King Henry may have been shocked by William's independent attitude towards the Council of Rheims, and reconciled to an agreement with the apparently superior Count Geoffrey because the latter's recent divorce had made him abandon ambitions to the south and east of Anjou which had threatened Henry's security. It is also possible that the prospects opened up by Edward the Confessor's promise to William would have been a considerable worry to other powers in northern France; a duchy of Normandy which could draw on England's resources could easily and dramatically tilt the balance of power between the various rulers. Whatever the explanation, the danger presented to William's position in Normandy by the alliance is obvious, since the balance of forces in northern France was now very definitely weighted against him. He was indeed so disconcerted by the development that he even travelled to meet with King Henry on 20 September 1052, but with no discernible result. The recapture of Alençon and Domfront was an important gain, but it is an achievement which should not be overestimated, since William made no attempt to follow up his victory, and presumably felt it beyond his resources to do so.

The Struggle to Survive

Fresh problems surfaced for William during the siege of Domfront. One of the most influential figures of the minority, his uncle, Count William of Arques, slipped away during the siege and raised a rebellion based on his castle at Arques in north-eastern Normandy. William of Poitiers provides the only contemporary explanation for Count William's revolt, telling us that the count had been disloyal from William's earliest years and that he now planned to exclude ducal authority from the lands to the east of the River Seine. Given Count William's record of apparently loyal service throughout William's minority, this explanation of events is inherently unconvincing. It is more likely that he had taken offence at some aspect of William's conduct since the victory at Val-ès-Dunes – perhaps his increasing reliance on advisers of his own choosing, a topic which will be examined in the next chapter. As the revolt developed, it became clear that Count William had assembled a formidable coalition from among the most powerful of the territorial rulers with lands adjacent to Normandy's eastern frontier, including Count William's brother-in-law, Count Enguerrand of Ponthieu, Eustace, Count of Boulogne, and Ralph, Count of Amiens and Valois. William's rule over the duchy of Normandy was put in even greater peril when King Henry and the Count of Anjou decided to use the opportunity to launch an invasion.

There must have been a time-lag between the sieges of Alençon and Domfront and William becoming fully aware of Count William's intentions, since the duke was apparently in the Cotentin in the far west of Normandy when he heard of Count William's defiance. He then reacted quickly, moving with remarkable speed to shut the rebel up in his castle of Arques, to the extent, according to William of Poitiers, that the horses of almost all William's companions dropped from exhaustion during the ride eastwards. On the journey, he revitalized a reluctant besieging force which had set out to Arques from Rouen, then invested the superbly situated castle, and, having narrowly failed to capture it, built a fortification to blockade the lower slopes of the hill on which it stood. The rapid advance had the effect of disrupting whatever plans William's enemies may initially have devised because it isolated one of them before the others were ready. The coalition's attempts to relieve Arques were beaten off, and one of its chief members, Count Enguerrand of Ponthieu, was killed in a skirmish near Arques on 25 October 1053. William of Arques was eventually obliged to surrender on humiliating terms which involved forfeiting his lands and leaving the duchy. As a result of his allies' setbacks, an army which King Henry had led into the duchy left shortly after the surrender of Arques.

This success did not, however, end the crisis, since, either late in 1053, or early in 1054, King Henry and Count Geoffrey returned with substantial forces, despatching into Normandy two armies which are said to have contained warriors from many regions of France. One of them, commanded by the king himself and Count Geoffrey, advanced via Evreux in the direction of the duchy's chief city, Rouen. William led the Norman army which blocked its path. The second army, consisting of men from north-eastern France, crossed the Norman frontier near Mortemer, intending presumably also to advance on Rouen. But early in February 1054 this second force was intercepted and defeated by an army commanded by a coalition of magnates from Upper Normandy loyal to William. His allies' discomfiture was announced to King Henry through a herald and his army left Normandy rather than risk battle. As a result, he and William made a short-lived peace, and there was a significant pacification of Normandy's easterly neighbours which greatly increased William's security. In particular, Enguerrand's successor as Count of Ponthieu, Guy, was captured, and released only after signing a treaty of friendship which included an agreement to provide military service. However, the victory was far from total; another enemy, Count Ralph of Amiens and Valois, remained hostile and is known to have launched at least one later raid across the Norman frontier in c. 1061.

After Mortemer, William again took the military initiative to the south of Normandy, pursuing once more his well-established policy of trying to weaken the Count of Anjou's grip on Maine. He built a castle at Ambrières, a few kilometres south of Domfront, as a bridgehead into Maine, and beat off a relieving force led by Count Geoffrey Martel himself. William's efforts had not, however, greatly harmed his chief enemies, and Geoffrey and King Henry were able to launch a second invasion of Normandy in 1057. They advanced through the Hiésmois. To do this they must have crossed the Bellême lands, thereby indicating that Bishop Ivo of Sées was still Count Geoffrey's ally. Henry's and Geoffrey's forces are known not to have been as large as in 1053-4, but they were still sufficiently formidable for William to avoid committing himself to a pitched battle. The invaders' strategy is obscure. They advanced up the course of the River Dives to the coast, ravaging the countryside as they went; trying perhaps to tempt William into battle on unfavourable terms. As it turned out, however, it was the duke who seized the initiative, shadowing his enemies until they were crossing the estuary of the Dives near Varaville – where the river was then much wider than it is nowadays – waiting until the advancing tide had split their army, and then pouncing to shatter the rearguard while the rest watched helplessly from across the river. William's generalship appears to have been of a high order because, as on a number of other occasions, he had refrained from action until the time was right. Henry I and Count Geoffrey left the duchy, never to return.

The Battle of Varaville was something of a landmark in the rise of William's fortunes; Normandy was never again invaded during his lifetime. It produced some immediate gains. Bishop Ivo of Sées abandoned his Angevin connections and made a deal with Roger de Montgommery, one of William's closest companions and one of the greatest nobles of Normandy, whereby Roger was made heir to the lordship of Bellême through the rights of his wife, who was related to Ivo. In 1058 William launched an offensive against King Henry I's lands, recovering the castle of Tillières, which had been taken out of Norman hands during his minority, and capturing the castle of Thimert, some twenty-four kilometres (fifteen miles) beyond Normandy's frontier. However, the enterprise was not a resounding success for, by 1060, Henry I had invested, and was trying to retake, Thimert. What finally and definitively changed the balance of power in northern France was the deaths of King Henry and Count Geoffrey Martel within a short time of one another in 1060. Henry was succeeded by a young boy, his son Philip, who came under the protection of William's father-in-law, Count Baldwin V of Flanders. A peace treaty was agreed between Philip's advisers and William, and a little later Philip confirmed William's designation of his son Robert as the heir to Normandy, just as Philip's father had once agreed to William's own designation. Robert in all probability became Philip's vassal. 'Normal' and peaceful relations had thereby been re-established between Normandy and the King of France. In Anjou, Count Geoffrey's death was followed by the weak rule of his nephew Geoffrey the Bearded and subsequently a disputed succession between Geoffrey and his brother Fulk Rechin, which incapacitated Angevin power for more than a decade.

The First Conquest

William's great success in the period between 1060 and 1066 was the conquest of Maine, the first major expansion of Norman territory accomplished under his rule. He launched his invasion of the county soon after the death on 9 March 1062 of Count Herbert II of Maine (1051-62), justifying it on the basis of an agreement, reported only by William of Poitiers, by which the count had become William's vassal and had agreed to marry one of his daughters. Herbert had also apparently promised that his county would pass to William if he died without heirs. The background against which William of Poitiers placed his account of this agreement was the long-standing lordship of the Counts of Anjou over Maine, and, in particular, the power exercised by Count Geoffrey Martel after he had strengthened his domination over Maine in 1051. According to Poitiers, Count Herbert had fled from Geoffrey's tyranny and had then made the agreement with William. He added the extravagant assertion that the Norman dukes had once been the overlords of Maine.

William of Poiters' case is in fact notably vague in several crucial places. He does not, for example, name the daughter whom Herbert was supposed to marry, and there is no actual evidence that any betrothal ever took place. His suggestion that Count Herbert fled from Geoffrey Martel's tyrannical rule is contradicted by good evidence from elsewhere which shows the two men co-operating in the county's government, and his idea of Norman overlordship over Maine has no foundation other than a possible grant to Normandy's earliest Scandinavian settlers in 924 which never took effect. His statement that Herbert on his deathbed repeated the promise that his county would pass to William may be credible but, even if it happened, its validity has to be dubious since it cannot have been confirmed by the Count of Anjou who was accepted by all sides as overlord of Maine. It also cut across the good hereditary claims of living relatives of Herbert's father, Count Hugh IV (died 1051). To an outsider attempting to be objective, William of Poitiers' arguments look like chicanery attempting to justify what was essentially an act of opportunism. In all probability, Count Herbert may, at some moment when his relations with Count Geoffrey were uneasy, have made some kind of promise to William to try to secure Norman support. But this certainly did not give William any absolute right to the succession.

William invaded Maine soon after Count Herbert's death on 9 March 1062. His army encountered energetic resistance from the men of Maine who had offered the succession to Walter, Count of the Vexin – the husband of a sister of Count Hugh IV – and had sought support from Geoffrey Martel's successor, Count Geoffrey the Bearded. In the circumstances, William preferred to ravage the countryside and capture castles, with the general intention of terrifying his opponents into submission, rather than launching a direct attack on Le Mans, the chief city of the county. From his point of view, this was an economical way to campaign since it avoided committing too many men to a hazardous attack on a well-fortified town. Le Mans was gradually isolated within Maine as the surrounding castles were captured. When the expected help from Anjou failed to materialize, Count Walter and most of his supporters submitted, and William and his army entered Le Mans.

The subsequent deaths of Count Walter and his wife Biota raise important questions about William's political methods. Neither William of Jumièges nor William of Poitiers refer to these deaths, with the former not even mentioning Walter at all and the latter merely noting his submission. But Orderic Vitalis in Book III of his *Ecclesiastical History*, which was completed by *c.*1125, records what he describes as a rumour that Walter and his wife were poisoned by their enemies. In Book IV, also completed in *c.*1125, he puts a much more specific assertion into a speech made by one of Wlliam's enemies, namely, that William murdered the couple while entertaining them at Falaise. Impressed by this tale, several modern historians have offered an additional motive for William wanting Walter out of the way because he was a son of Drogo, Count of the Vexin, and of Godgifu, sister of King Edward the Confessor, and brother of Ralph, Earl of Hereford (died 1057), and could therefore have been a rival for the English succession.

There is, however, insufficient evidence to prove William's guilt. The case against him is based entirely on hearsay and circumstantial evidence. Orderic treats the accusation as a rumour and as the opinion of one of William's enemies; he does not commit himself to accepting the story. Additionally, there is no contemporary evidence to support the idea that either Walter or his deceased brother Ralph of Hereford had any aspirations to succeed King Edward. William's and Walter's fathers had been close friends and had died together on pilgrimage; such sentimental considerations are, however, unlikely to have carried much weight with William. The most notable aspect of the problem is the fact that William, even if guiltless, should be thought capable of murder for political gain. When we leave behind the cosy, sycophantic world of William of Poitiers, we discover that some thought of William as a man able and willing to perpetrate the most ruthless of acts.

The conquest of Maine was completed by the capture of Geoffrey de Mayenne's castle at Mayenne, a place of great strategic importance since it was directly to the south of Domfront and therefore vital for Norman communications with Le Mans. William's army deliberately used fire to spread panic among the garrison, which William of Poitiers thought would otherwise have been defeated only by being starved out. The fact that Geoffrey was not deprived of his lands and castle after such a determined defiance is an important commentary on the way in which William set out to rule his new conquest. There was no massive Norman takeover in Maine, and William did little more than receive the fealty of the men of the county, place a garrison in Le Mans, and strengthen the fortifications there. He was also careful to foster the installation of supporters in prominent positions in the Church. As a result, when the incumbent of the bishopric of Le Mans died in 1065, he was replaced by a member of the Le Mans cathedral clergy named Arnold, who had the additional recommendation of being a Norman from the region of Avranches, and whose election was probably influenced by William. Finally, William sought to confer as much legitimacy as possible on Norman rule in Maine by allowing his son Robert to do homage to Count Geoffrey the Bearded of Anjou at a ceremony at Alençon shortly after the conquest had been completed; in the eleventh century all Counts of Maine had been vassals of the Counts of Anjou.

William's final campaign in northern France before 1066 was an attack on Brittany in either 1064 or 1065, which completed the creation of a curtain of friendly or acquiescent powers around the Norman duchy's borders. A participant in this campaign was the future King Harold of England who took part in the expedition in the course of the visit to Normandy during which he promised to assist William's succession to the English kingdom (see Chapter 5). The purpose of the campaign was to punish Count Conan II of Brittany for some recent raids which he had made across Normandy's western frontier. William utilized a rebellion in eastern Brittany to advance to Dol, Rennes and then to Dinan, where the Bayeux Tapestry shows Conan surrendering. He then returned to Normandy, stopping at Bayeux where Harold swore his famous oath to accept William's kingship in England.

This expedition completed the process whereby all major powers in the immediate vicinity of Normandy's borders were either cowed into accepting Norman domination or were persuaded to enter into more active alliances. To the east of Normandy, Count Eustace of Boulogne, who had given succour to Count William of Arques' rebellion, became an ally and later played a prominent part in the Hastings campaign. In the same region, Count Guy of Ponthieu was a vassal, members of whose family also took part in that expedition. To the rear of both was the powerful principality of Flanders, ruled by William's father-in-law, Count Baldwin V. Also to the east the buccaneering warrior, Ralph, Count of Amiens and Valois, had abandoned his alliance with the French kings and become William's friend, probably after succeeding to the county of the Vexin after his cousin Count Walter's death in 1063-4. This new collaboration was apparently cemented by a life lease to Ralph of Gisors, which was on the Norman frontier with the Vexin, and by Ralph sending his second son Simon to be educated at William's court. To the south of Normandy, the lordship of Bellême was now friendly and Maine had been conquered. All this represents a remarkable achievement on William's part, and an enormous change in fortune since the early 1050s.

An outstanding factor in William's success in the period up to 1066 was his generalship. His campaigns appear to have been carefully measured affairs, and in particular the way in which his wars to the south of Normandy in the 1050s concentrated on the subjugation of accessible castles suggests a secure grasp of what was practicable. It is notable how often he appears to have surprised his opponents and caught them off balance either on the battlefield, as at Varaville, or at sieges such as Alençon or Arques. It is also remarkable how often he was prepared to use brutal methods like fire and mutilation to achieve a quick result. When he invaded the lands of his enemies, he devastated the countryside in an attempt to provoke battle by cutting off his adversaries' supplies, a well-established and regularly practised medieval military tactic. By 1066 we are clearly dealing with a commander who thoroughly understood the contemporary arts of war, and whose generalship has a measure of brilliance about it. He was a battle-hardened warrior trusted by his men, a crucial factor when it came to attracting soldiers from all parts of France to take part in the invasion of England. In political terms, however, we need to keep a clear sense of perspective on William's achievements. He had come an enormously long way since the battle of Val-ès-Dunes in 1047. But it is very important to recognize that his supremacy in northern France in 1066 was in many fundamental respects an artificial one which was likely to be transitory, since it was based on the weakness of the French king and the Count of Anjou. The future was not necessarily going to be easy.

Four

NORMANDY BEFORE 1066

The dominance William built up over the Norman aristocracy, his reputation as a ruler who supported and fostered the Church, and Normandy's supremacy over its northern French neighbours were all crucial to his being able to conquer and then successfully organize the English kingdom. The break in the warfare with northern French enemies provided the opportunity to assemble, unhindered, a large army for the invasion, while good relations with Normandy's aristocracy meant that it supplied the core of this force. The inner circle of magnates who were William's closest advisers and companions in pre-Conquest Normandy reaped the largest rewards in England after 1066 and played a central part in the redistribution of English land. William's protection of the Norman Church was influential in persuading the papacy to support the 1066 expedition and it provided a model for his post-1066 government of the English Church. Normandy before 1066 is in many significant respects a blueprint for England after 1066; an understanding of it is crucial to everything which followed.

The early sources present two very different images of William's government in Normandy. On the one hand he is portrayed by his contemporary apologist William of Poitiers as always just and justified, religious, a great warrior, and a protector of the Church and the poor. On the other hand there are stories in the early twelfth-century Orderic Vitalis of ruthlessness, impulsiveness and injustice. In dealing with the downfall of Count William of Arques and his brother Archbishop Malger of Rouen in 1053 and 1054 respectively, for example, William of Poitiers blackened both men's characters, suggesting that Count William's treachery was longstanding and that Archbishop Malger was lazy, self-indulgent and disobedient to the papacy; Duke William was entirely in the right, they in the wrong. In contrast, in passages in his interpolations into the Gesta Normannorum Ducum of William of Jumièges and in Book III of his Ecclesiastical History, Orderic charged William with vindictiveness and with listening to his closest advisers to the detriment of justice, and suggested that a fair trial could not be obtained in his court. At one point he observed that the predecessor of William's half-brother, Robert, as Count of Mortain, was deprived by William of his office and extensive lands for trivial reasons. He also tells us that Abbot Robert of St-Evroult thought it safer to flee Normandy than stand trial on a charge of making jokes about William, even though he was innocent.

Orderic's opinions are especially important because most of them are included in one of the earliest sections of the Ecclesiastical History, compiled before he had decided to embark on his great history of the Normans, and before his treatment of William's reign came under the influence of William of Poitiers. Orderic was not unbiased, since he was writing of men who were friends of his abbey of St-Evroult. His account does, however, add a dimension of realism which is absent in William of Poitiers. It is impossible, for example, to accept Poitiers's verdict on Count William and Archbishop Malger because both had supported Duke William loyally during the troubled times of his minority and had made some attempt to mitigate the troubles. A likely explanation for their revolt is that both had reacted aggressively as they were displaced at court by favourites of William's own age and kind or that they disapproved of his hazardous provocation of King Henry and Count Geoffrey Martel in the early 1050s. The basic difference between Orderic and William of Poitiers is not, however, one between an account of tyrannical, arbitrary rule and an uncritical eulogy. The two agree that William's rule brought peace and prosperity to mid-eleventh century Normandy; Orderic's underlying message is partly that William's rule was authoritarian, ruthless and partisan, but also that he was simply a ruler who exercised extremely effectively the arbitrary prerogatives inherent in his position.

All sources indicate there was an unprecedented expansion within Norman society as William's rule brought internal peace from 1047 onwards. The most obvious visible sign of this to us nowadays is church-building. For example, the two Norman bishops who were to obtain immense rewards from the conquest of England, Odo of Bayeux and Geoffrey of Coutances, both began the construction of new cathedrals before 1066 and assembled clergy for their cathedral chapters. Most of the great aristocratic families founded new abbeys in the period after 1050; among the most powerful of the Norman magnates, William fitz Osbern founded two monasteries at Lyre and Cormeilles, while Roger de Montgommery established three at Troarn, Almenèches and Sées. The most remarkable development of all is probably the rise of the abbey of Le Bec from poverty and obscurity into an intellectual centre which attracted scholars and students from many parts of Europe. Le Bec's story can be traced in the life of the first abbot, Herluin (the *Vita Herluini*), although the greatest single cause of achievement was the presence of the famous teacher and theologian Lanfranc. Material taken mainly from charters provides plentiful evidence of economic expansion elsewhere in society, such as the creation of new rural settlements called *bourgs* and the growth of towns.

William's successes were supported – crucially – by consistent good health and dynastic security. A charter mentions that William was once seriously ill while staying at Cherbourg at a date some time before 1063, and that he promised to endow three canons in the collegiate church there on his recovery. There is otherwise no reason to doubt that he enjoyed excellent health. His and Mathilda's marriage was exceptionally fertile and by 1066 there were seven children, of whom three were sons. The succession was therefore assured, and there was not likely to be that jostliing between rival factions which often occurred when there was no definite heir. In or shortly before the year 1063, William took the routine precaution of formally designating his eldest son Robert as the heir to Normandy and having the great nobles swear to be faithful to him.

William and the Norman Aristocracy

In essence, William's most significant success within Normandy before 1066 was to persuade his duchy's aristocracy to participate in his projects and support his rule. This group, whose propensity for aggressive military expansion had taken some of its members to southern Italy and other places from the late-tenth century onwards, became convinced that it was in their interests to serve William. Consequently, the great Norman lords whose ambitions and rivalries had fuelled the civil wars of the duke's minority brought their contingents of soldiers to his court and let them fight his wars. As a result, as William's court and household became the heart of Norman aristocratic society, he built up formidable powers of control within his duchy. There was, for example, a considerable increase in the number of men who acknowledged William as their lord, and over time his authority grew so great that it even affected the terminology with which contemporary documents described the relationship between the duke and his vassals. Prior to William's reign, it was common to say that a particular warrior or noble was a *fidelis* ('faithful man') of the duke, whereas, under William, the same situation was increasingly described in terms of the duke being the *dominus* ('lord'). His power eventually included the right to prohibit the building of fortifications of any significant size within Normandy and to take over a noble's castle for his own use.

Just how remarkable William's powers were is shown by the fact that they were frequently disregarded after his death; we only know about his rights over castles from an inquest of 1091, usually known as the *Consuetudines et Iusticie*, which sought to establish what the customary powers of the Norman duke had been during William's reign. The same inquest also recorded that William had had the right to take a magnate's son, brother or nephew as a hostage for his good conduct.

The first stage in the development of William's power was the punishment and final defeat of the rebels of Val-ès-Dunes. One prominent rebel, Nigel, *vicomte* of the Cotentin, was exiled and another, Grimoult du Plessis-Grimoult, imprisoned; the former was eventually restored to his lands and office in 1054, but the latter died a prisoner in chains. William of Poitiers tells us that the citizens of Rouen were punished for supporting the rebellion. However, William's chief enemy at Val-ès-Dunes, Count Guy, was able to shut himself up in his castle at Brionne and hold out there for a long period of time, perhaps, according to Orderic Vitalis, for as much as three years. David Douglas, the renowned modern historian of ducal Normandy, took Orderic's statement literally and suggested that William's power was so reduced by this rebellion that he lost control over Rouen and eastern Normandy until after the siege was over. Such a drastic reduction of his authority for so long a period seems unlikely, however, given that William undertook major projects during these years such as assisting the French king's campaign against the castle of Mouliherne and marrying Mathilda, and in the light of the fact that a known ally, Roger de Beaumont, appears as *vicomte* of Rouen in the year 1050. Most probably, William spent little more than the year 1048 and perhaps some of 1049 terminating Guy's resistance and clearing up after the revolt. Count Guy then went into exile and never returned to Normandy. William of Poitiers suggests rather implausibly that William was prepared to forgive him, and that it was Guy's choice to leave the duchy.

The creation around William of a close-knit group of very powerful men drawn from the leading families of the duchy and from the duke's own family began in the years after Val-ès-Dunes. William fitz Osbern and Roger de Montgommery, who were undoubtedly William's closest advisers and associates during the period up until 1066, attested charters regularly from around the year 1050 and were mentioned by William of Poitiers as having been prominent in William's army at the siege of Domfront of 1051. Thereafter they were more frequently in William's company than any other Norman magnates. Roger de Beaumont was also especially important, while other members of William's inner circle included Bishop Geoffrey of Coutances, Hugh de Montfort-sur-Risle, and William de Warenne. The duke also appointed his half-brother Odo, one of the two sons of Herleva and Herluin de Conteville, to the bishopric of Bayeux, in either late 1049 or early 1050, while his other half-brother Robert was given the position of Count of Mortain in around the year 1060, with lands mainly in south-west Normandy and responsibility for Normandy's frontier where it touched the counties of Brittany and Maine. These men were all of roughly the same age as the duke and can be seen almost as his companions in a common enterprise. The group's co-operation also suggests that William's rule possessed remarkable healing powers, since Roger de Montgommery's brother had killed William fitz Osbern's father during the wars of the duke's minority.

An important feature of these developments is that, with the exception of his two half-brothers, William's closest associates were all drawn from long-established, powerful families who had usually done exceptionally well out of the disorderly times of his father's reign and his own minority. William very definitely did not attempt any kind of social revolution by advancing men of lesser social status to positions of power; even the rewards given to his brothers were not unusual, since early medieval rulers were expected to provide for their families. It was in fact a central feature of William's rule to accept and make no effort to reverse the political and social changes which had emerged in the two decades before Val-ès-Dunes. He acquiesced in the transfer of *vicomtés* and offices in the ducal household into the hands of great aristocratic families and set out to co operate with them. No effort that we know of was made to budge, among others, William fitz Osbern from the stewardship in the duke's household which his father had held, or the likes of Roger de Montgommery or Hugh de Montfort from the *vicomtés* held by their fathers. Similarly, although William of Poitiers does say that some castles built during William's minority were flattened, the castles which the major families of the duchy had built were left alone, usually to be used as the chief residences of the families, despite the requirement of the custom in the *Consuetudines et Iusticie*.

The key to William's system after 1047 was the selective application of powers which traditionally and uncontestably belonged to a Norman duke. Thus, for example, the power to prohibit the construction of fortifications was a right proclaimed by French kings as far back as the ninth century and one presumably exercised by William's predecessors up until the time of troubles between 1026 and 1047. From this base of established custom, William's relations with the Norman aristocracy were constructed around a system of patronage out of which some men did very well indeed. Roger de Montgommery, for example, was clearly allowed to fight private wars against members of the Bellême family in southern Normandy, in order to prosecute his wife's claim to the Bellême inheritance, because his ambitions coincided with William's own. Count Robert of Mortain was also apparently allowed to acquire territory to the south of his county for himself. The ducal right to take over castles appears to have been shared with William's favoured families and could act to their advantage, as when Roger de Mortemer offended William after the Battle of Mortemer and his castle at Mortemer was passed into the custody of William de Warenne. In the same way, William's powers as protector of the Norman Church could be turned into a source of patronage, as, for example, when Roger de Montgommery was given custody of the collegiate church of St Martin of Ecajeul founded by Stigand de Mézidon. An anecdote in a charter indicates how this system might have worked for lesser men, when a minor landowner named Ralph Cardon is said to have been able to placate William's anger against him through the intervention of Count Robert of Mortain; at the same time Ralph made a grant to the abbey of Grestain which was under Robert's patronage and protection.

William's general expectation appears to have been that members of the Norman aristocracy would participate in the maintenance of his authority. Those who did, received generous rewards. Those who did not were frequently treated harshly. As well as Count Guy of Brionne, Count William of Arques, Count William Werlenc of Mortain and Archbishop Malger of Rouen, men as powerful as Ralph de Tosny, Hugh de Grandmesnil and Arnold d'Echauffour were sent into exile, although, with the exception of Arnold, they were all subsequently allowed to return and were readmitted to favour. Orderic's catalogue of William's unjust acts includes the suggestion that Arnold d'Echauffour was exiled on the sole word of Roger de Montgommery and that an exposed frontier castle was entrusted to Hugh de Grandmesnil on Roger's malicious advice. Although the Normans have a reputation for their freelance military adventures, it would appear that William discouraged such activity and insisted that his vassals take part only in warfare licensed by him; Baldric, son of Nicholas, a renowned soldier who went to Spain without obtaining William's permission, had his estates confiscated. However, for all the ferocity of William's regime, it usually operated within the conventions accepted by eleventh-century aristocratic society; disinheritance and the permanent confiscation of estates, for example, were normally punishments inflicted only on William's relatives, whereas for members of other families, exile tended to be temporary and disinheritance almost unknown. It is clear that William placed a high premium on loyalty and service. His great achievement within Normandy was to mould aristocratic ambition and enterprise to fit in with his own purposes.

Institutions, the Church, and the Town of Caen

In institutional terms, William's achievement was a conservative one, since he worked mostly within the existing governmental and administrative structures. Like any early medieval ruler, he travelled constantly around his duchy, staying sometimes at the major residence at Caen, which he had had built, or at older palaces which he had inherited from his predecessors, or at other places where he and his entourage could be accommodated. When he confirmed charters on his travels we are given an occasional rare glimpse of spontaneous behaviour. One of these documents describes William confirming a grant at La Hougue in the far north of the Cotentin, while feasting in the company of several of his magnates, when a forester named Hugh disputed the grant. William, in what looks like a piece of play-acting, tried to strike Hugh with a pig's bone. Another charter mentions monks from the non-Norman abbey of St-Florent of Saumur questioning William's understanding of a grant he had made, and being told that

> We are Normans, and we understand such things because they should be done in that way, and therefore, with God's consent, we will do them.

As with earlier Norman rulers and with other eleventh-century territorial princes, it is difficult to think of William having anything worthy of being called an administration at his disposal before 1066. This point is conclusively and exceptionally well illustrated by the surviving ducal charters, of which around 150 survive from the period between 1035 and 1066, occasionally as originals or early copies, but mostly as copies made by medieval clergy, later historians or lawyers from lost originals. Some of the charters were complex confirmations of numerous grants made by one or more of William's vassals, written on large sheets of parchment. Others were much simpler. All original ducal charters that survive from Normandy before 1066 were written by their beneficiaries and presented to William for confirmation. Having approved the contents, he sometimes drew his personal cross on the parchment; one (see Plate 4) not only has William's cross, but also what must be a delightful specimen of the autograph cross of his eldest son Robert, then perhaps around seven years of age. More often, however, the crosses were drawn by the scribe who wrote the charter.

Finance came from the traditional revenues which had been collected on behalf of William's predecessors, such as the tolls, *gravarium* and *bernagium*, which were described in Chapter One. They were paid into the chamber (*camera*) which was within William's household. We know very little about the chamber, except that it must have been a very basic financial organization – no more than a rudimentary treasury of receipt. This continuity does not, however, mean that William was not significantly richer than earlier Norman rulers, since all the signs are that the duchy's increasing economic prosperity brought greater wealth into William's household than had been normal under his predecessors. Revenues from tolls in eleventh-century Normandy appear to have grown at what could have been a dramatic rate, at least judging by a unique statistic which records that proceeds received by the Bishop of Coutances from tolls at St-Lô rose from £15 to £220 after the bishop had had a new settlement established there. William certainly profited from such developments and an increase in ducal wealth is clearly indicated by the growth in the number of household officials who occur in the witness lists of charters.

William also built up a close collaboration with the Church during the period between 1047 and 1066. The proclamation after Val-ès-Dunes of the Truce of God, which prohibited private warfare at certain times, was an early display of the alliance between duke and clergy that was to become a keystone of William's rule in both duchy and kingdom. The punishment of infractions of the Truce was made the bishop's responsibility, but the specific exemption given to the duke's army from the Truce's prohibition of warfare between Wednesday evening and Monday morning shows its central importance to keeping the peace. As his power grew, William increasingly took on the traditional ruler's role of the protector and governor of the Norman Church, presiding at several ecclesiastical councils, of which the most notable were at Lisieux in 1054 and 1064 and at Rouen in 1063. He also began to reshape the Norman Church by appointing his own men to bishoprics when they became vacant; among his earliest appointments was of course his brother Odo to the bishopric of Bayeux. The deposition of his uncle Malger from the archbishopric of Rouen in 1054 was followed by the appointment of

Maurilius, a non-Norman from Rheims, a saintly man whose good qualities show William's determination to have capable and respectable men in the highest positions in the Norman Church. But, as with the laity, churchmen who displeased William were treated as disloyal subjects; before 1066, for example, at least one abbot was driven out of office, and an abbey as renowned as Mont Saint-Michel had lands taken away because it was suspected of involvement in the Val-ès-Dunes revolt. William before 1066 showed himself to be a generous benefactor and protector of the Church, but it must be remembered that this role was in many respects just an aspect of ducal authority. As time passed, this power eventually grew so great that by the last years of his reign it was normal for William's permission to be required for the foundation of a new abbey.

In ecclesiastical matters, William clearly depended a great deal from the late 1040s on the Italian Lanfranc, who became his closest ecclesiastical adviser throughout the 1050s and 1060s, and was later to be his choice for the crucial post in England of Archbishop of Canterbury in 1070. Lanfranc, who was born in Lombardy, already had an established reputation as a teacher and theologian when he came to Normandy in the early 1040s, hoping to attract pupils in a province with no great reputation for learning. Instead, a spiritual crisis led him to seek monastic seclusion in the then impoverished abbey of Le Bec. He gradually emerged from retirement during the 1040s and attended Pope Leo IX's Council of Rheims of 1049, taking part in the negotiations which made William's and Mathilda's marriage acceptable. He resumed teaching and also took a leading role in the doctrinal debates of the 1050s and 1060s around the eucharistic heresy of Berengar of Tours. At an unknown date, probably around 1047, he offended William and was almost driven into exile. But thereafter the collaboration between the two men became a close one. From William's point of view, the availability of such a learned and able man, whose intellect and knowledge were respected throughout western Europe, must truly have seemed to be a godsend. It and William's personal support for the Church in Normandy ensured that there were cordial relations with a succession of popes after the difficulties about William's and Mathilda's marriage had been negotiated away. The friendship with the papacy was put to practical use in 1054 when a papal legate deposed William's uncle Malger from the archbishopric of Rouen and was to be extremely important in the events of 1066.

The most spectacular remains of William's rule in Normandy still visible to us are in the town of Caen. Although there was certainly a settlement there in Roman times, and it can be shown to have been a growing urban centre by 1025, it was William's initiative alone which raised Caen to the status of the second town in the province after Rouen. A large fortified residence was built on a rocky spur at what is the centre of the modern town and two abbeys were founded by William and his wife Mathilda in *c.*1059 and *c.*1063, perhaps as a penance to atone for their marriage having been prohibited by the papacy. William's foundation, St-Etienne (i.e., St Stephen's), was a monastery and Mathilda's, La Trinité, a convent for nuns. As with the castle, construction began in the later 1050s, and an abbot, the renowned Lanfranc, was appointed to St-Etienne in 1063. La Trinité, presumably well-advanced but as yet incomplete, was consecrated in the presence of a great assembly of Norman magnates on 18 June 1066. The personal significance for William and Mathilda of the two churches is shown by their decisions to be buried in them.

Nothing can now be seen above ground of William's palace in Caen. But major excavations in the 1960s under the supervision of Michel de Bouard have given an impression of what it looked like. The circumference of its outer wall was similar to that of the existing castle. None of the eleventh-century masonry can be confidently located in the surviving wall, but it is certain that William's residence had a stone wall, probably with a continuous walkway around the inside. The square towers which can be seen now were twelfth-century additions. There was a tower-gate entrance in the north-west corner similar to the one which survives at Exeter, and probably two other entrances in the south and east. Within the walls the excavation found traces of a hall, approximately 18 metres by 6 metres, along with a chamber and a chapel. This domestic accommodation was typical of princely residences of the time and the hall may indeed have been similar to that built by William fitz Osbern at Chepstow. But in comparison with what William and his sons later built in England – for example, at Westminster and Winchester – the scale of the accommodation is small. The conquest of England had the general effect of making the Normans plan their buildings on the grandest possible scale, and William's son Henry I clearly thought the buildings at Caen inadequate. As well as raising the walls, he added a new hall which still stands, albeit much restored (the so-called *Salle de l'Echiquier*) and a keep whose foundations are visible after the excavation. This said, the creation of William's residential complex at Caen was an enormous enterprise, given the ditches which would have had to be dug in the north and east and the great length of the wall. The large area within the ramparts contained numerous private houses, some of which were on the spur before the castle was begun.

The remains of the two Caen abbeys are much more substantial than those of William's palace. They rank among the great monuments of

Romanesque architecture. St-Etienne in particular is a church of considerable originality. Its choir was rebuilt in the thirteenth century and the stone vaulting over the nave and transepts was installed in the twelfth century – a remarkably early date for such vaulting. Otherwise what we can see now is still essentially the church begun for William in the 1050s and substantially completed during his lifetime. Its massive, plain west front with its two towers – the spires date from the thirteenth century – was to provide a model which often recurs in great English churches. The stark simplicity of this façade can look functional, but the nave is a masterpiece, its bareness emphasizing a wholeness and symmetry entirely uninterrupted by intrusive decoration. Monumentality and height are achieved by making the second triforium stage almost as tall as the arcades of the nave. The moulding of the nave piers anticipates the smooth lines of twelfth-century Gothic and appears to be radically different from the square forms of earlier Romanesque. The appearance of space in the nave of St-Etienne was a major architectural development and was often imitated in England, for example, at Blyth and Southwell.

By way of contrast with St-Etienne, La Trinité is more complex architecturally. Its choir, the upper stories of the nave and the crypt are all now thought to have been rebuilt in the late eleventh and early twelfth centuries. It is a more completely Romanesque church than St-Etienne, but there is less of Mathilda's church to be seen than there is of William's. The bases of the towers and the arcading of the nave are the most obvious features of the original church which are still visible. The superb capital sculpture in choir and crypt, in many ways the crowning glory of the Romanesque La Trinité are products of the generation after the death of the founders.

The splendour of both churches must have been enhanced after 1066 with injections of English wealth, and it is impossible to know for certain what William's and Mathilda's original wishes were. But we can be sure that they intended to develop 'their' town of Caen on a grand scale and that the plans were laid and the work begun long before the conquest of England. Finally, it is important to recognize that William's Caen was not simply a display of military architecture or piety – although it was of course both of these things – but above all one of power. It served the practical purpose of demonstrating William's authority to all, and it emphasized the magnificence of William's authority in a way which was to be repeated and developed in England. Caen also displayed William's power in western Normandy where his predecessors had traditionally been weak and where the rebellion defeated at Val-ès-Dunes had been concentrated. The splendour of the surviving Caen churches is an apt tribute to the 'golden age' in Normandy's history which William's reign represents. The town shows that William was significantly more powerful than any previous Norman duke.

Five

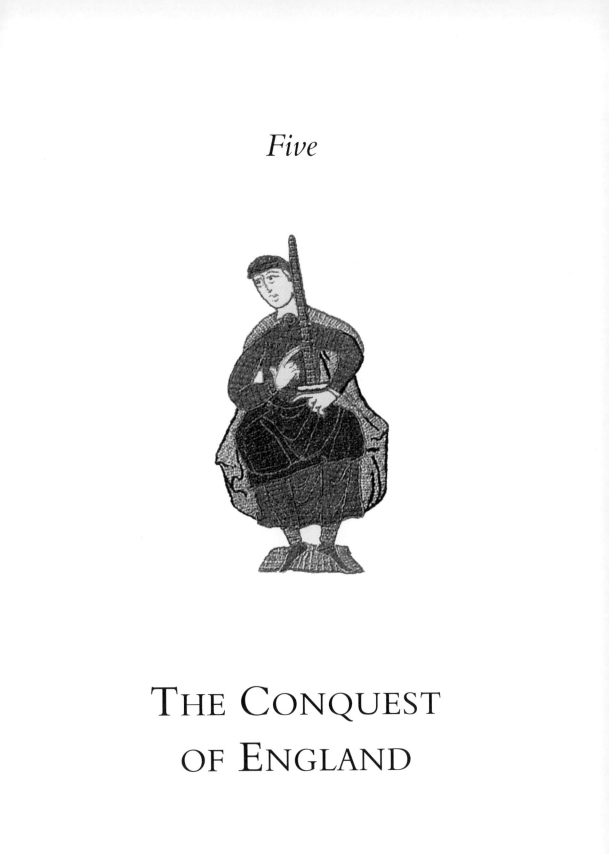

THE CONQUEST
OF ENGLAND

The united kingdom of the English was a creation of the tenth century. The process of unification began with the conquest of most of what we now call England by the Vikings in the later ninth century. Their victories eliminated the major kingdoms of Mercia and Northumbria, as well as lesser ones such as East Anglia, and left Wessex under Alfred the Great as the solitary surviving independent English kingdom. Alfred's descendants were able gradually to subjugate the districts under Scandinavian control to their authority during the first half of the tenth century, a process which has reasonably been called 'the Wessex Reconquest', and which concluded when the last Viking King of York, one Eric Bloodaxe, was driven out in 954.

This Wessex-made kingdom of England was a strong and powerful monarchy. Its kings were wealthy and impressive rulers, although their authority was never especially strong in northern England where they held little land and where there had been relatively heavy Scandinavian settlement. Alongside the monarchy, the English Church also became an effective, unitary body in the tenth century, as a result of the movement usually referred to as the 'Tenth-Century Reform'; numerous monasteries were founded and the quality of the clergy reformed, processes which were supervised by the kings. The central and local institutions of the monarchy were well-developed by contemporary standards. Particularly impressive features were the single national silver coinage which was changed at regular intervals from the 970s onwards; the presence of a central secretariat for the production of documents in the king's name; the existence of organized local communities and courts within shires and their sub-divisions known as hundreds; and the occasional capacity of the kings to legislate for the conduct of these communities and to intervene through emissaries in their routine. There was a procedure for raising an army and a navy for the kingdom's defence, and, even in the face of disaster, the monarchy was sufficiently powerful to mastermind prodigious feats of administration, like the great Danegeld. This was a national tax of a kind unknown in western Europe, which was first levied during the reign of Æthelred the Unready (978-1016) to pay off the invading Danish armies.

The kingdom of the English was prosperous by the standards of the time. Its population is usually estimated to have been 1,500,000-2,000,000 people, although this is a guess based on very inadequate statistical information, and is probably too low. There were towns of some size at London, York and Winchester, with populations in the first case of around 25,000 people and in the latter two of 10,000, and many other communities of significant importance. The northern frontier with the kingdom of the Scots remained undefined, while the majority of the princes who ruled the various regions of Wales usually acknowledged the overlordship of the English king, even if they also occasionally launched raids into western and midland England. The extensive Scandinavian settlement in the wake of the Viking invasions and, paradoxically, the kingdom's wealth were its two greatest weaknesses, since they made it attractive to invaders, and especially to Scandinavian ones. In the later tenth century, a new, massive wave of attacks from across the North Sea began. They culminated in 1016 in the conquest of England by Cnut, King of Denmark, who thereby replaced the Wessex dynasty of English kings.

As we saw in Chapter One, the origins of William's direct interest in the English succession lay in the flight to Normandy of the family of King Æthelred the Unready. From this starting point, William of Jumièges and, above all, William of Poitiers, developed the theme that the Norman dukes were the future King Edward the Confessor's consistent supporters and that Edward eventually promised William the Conqueror the succession to the English kingdom out of gratitude. The two authors' exaggerated deployment of this idea on occasion crosses the line between truth and falsehood. It is impossible to believe, for example, as William of Poitiers asks us to do, that the support of the fourteen-year-old William was instrumental in persuading the English to accept Edward as king in 1042. In practice the Norman rulers, assailed by political problems in northern France and aware that England was controlled by Cnut (1016-35), who was also King of Denmark and from 1028 King of Norway, did little more than give a refuge to a young man who was essentially a landless adventurer without prospects. Richard II made no military demonstration on Edward's behalf that we know of and the most that can truthfully be said of William's father, Duke Robert, is that he was a generous host who may well have been personally close to Edward and his family. Edward continued to be a welcome guest in Normandy during William's minority, and was probably at Rouen in 1041 when he was summoned to return to England. He certainly owed his political survival to the Norman dukes, but in 1042 it was changing political circumstances in England, notably the childlessness and early death of Cnut's son King Harthacnut, which made Edward King of the English, a position which he then occupied until his death on 5 January 1066.

There is broad agreement among scholars that Edward promised the succession to William during the year 1051. The exact course of events at this time and afterwards is, however, difficult to disentangle since the promise is mentioned only in the Norman sources and does not appear in the English ones. It is likely that it was conveyed to William in April 1051 by the Norman Robert of Jumièges, whom Edward had recently appointed to the archbishopric of Canterbury. What Edward was doing, and what his exact policy towards the English succession was, are topics which historians have long discussed without ever reaching full agreement. The belief that he was consistently pro-Norman throughout his reign, and that his consistent purpose was to secure William's succession, is old-fashioned, but not entirely abandoned. It has also been suggested both that he was a devious politician playing off contenders in England, Normandy and Scandinavia against each other and – very differently – that he was not truly in control of his court which was in fact dominated by the most powerful English noble family, that of Earl Godwine of Wessex, whose sons included Harold and Tostig, and whose daughter Edith was Edward's queen.

A reasonable explanation of the confusing evidence is that the promise to William and the exiling of the Godwine family, which took place in 1051, represent Edward's bid for freedom. At this point Edward was powerful enough to send Godwine's youngest son and a grandson to William as hostages. He was assisted in this by a general wish among the English aristocracy to avoid civil war. However, after the Godwine family's triumphant return by force in 1052 his capacity to manoeuvre became greatly reduced and he probably accepted that William's succession was unlikely. Godwine's family thereafter seized positions of power, and after Godwine's death in 1053 Harold succeeded him as Earl of Wessex. In 1055 Tostig was given the great earldom of Northumbria, and other brothers, Gyrth and Leofwine, were subsequently given the earldoms of East Anglia and Kent respectively. Under their influence, a mission was despatched to Germany in 1054, which, according to the twelfth-century chronicler incorrectly identified as 'Florence of Worcester', went on Edward's orders and set in train the negotiations for the return from Hungary of his nephew Edward the Exile. In strictly hereditary terms, this Edward had far and away the best claim to be England's next king, and, when he died in 1057, shortly after reaching England, he left a young son who inherited his claim. In these circumstances William could not look forward to further assistance from King Edward with any optimism. With hindsight, it is obvious that the key to the events which occurred during the fifteen years after the promise was made in 1051 is the fact that William took the bequest seriously.

The next significant event in the story occurred either in 1064 or 1065 when Earl Harold's visit to France presented William with a marvellous opportunity

2. The Bayeux Tapestry: Edward the Confessor talks to Harold, Earl of Wessex. The Tapestry's caption EDWARD REX gives no clue as to their conversation. Is Edward sending Harold to Normandy to promise the succession to William? Or is he warning him against a dangerous personal visit?

which he exploited ruthlessly. As with so much of the background to 1066, the exact reasons for Harold's journey are controversial. For William of Poitiers the explanation was simple; Harold came to Normandy to confirm Edward's promise of the succession. There is, however, no direct confirmation of this in a contemporary English source, and later in the eleventh century it was said in England that Harold went to secure the release of the two hostages given in 1051 and was tricked by William. This version first occurs in a history written by a Canterbury monk named Eadmer and seems to be supported by the Bayeux Tapestry, which was made in England, in all probability at Canterbury, and appears to represent an admonishing King Edward telling a humbled and flustered Harold 'I told you so' after his return from Normandy. The problem is that the Norman sources tell a coherent and plausible story, but that they had good reasons to be economical with the truth. We shall probably never know exactly what happened. It is nonetheless hard to believe that Harold can have voluntarily gone to Normandy to confirm the promise to William, and equally

4. Harold's party crosses the Channel to the land of Count Guy of Ponthieu.

3. Harold prays and then feasts at his hall at Bosham (Sussex), before embarking on the sea.

hard to believe that Edward, by this stage surrounded at court by Harold's family, really had the power to send the earl to Normandy if Harold did not wish to go. There is a lot to be said for Eadmer's view that Harold went to Normandy on a personal mission which William, ever the opportunist, exploited superbly.

Whatever the reasons for Harold's journey, once in France, he first was captured by Normandy's north-eastern neighbour, Count Guy of Ponthieu. William had him rescued and taken to Rouen and then, according to William of Poitiers, to Bonneville-sur-Touque. There Harold became William's vassal, swore an oath to assist William's succession to England and promised to place Dover and other fortified places at his disposal. William then took Harold on his campaign into Brittany against Count Conan II. The English earl is said to have distinguished himself on this campaign, during which the Bayeux Tapestry shows him going through a ceremony resembling knighting at William's hands. It also clearly shows Harold swearing an oath to William at Bayeux on the return journey from Brittany. This contradiction between the

5. Harold lands and is immediately taken into custody by Count Guy.

6. Guy and his men take Harold to Guy's castle at Ponthieu. On the far right a man draws attention to the arrival of emissaries from William of Normandy.

Tapestry and William of Poitiers on the location of the oath might be thought to cast doubt on the general truthfulness of both accounts, especially as Orderic Vitalis, writing in the twelfth century, placed the oath at Rouen. But the differences can probably be explained in terms of a treaty and oath of fealty at Bonneville, which was a ducal residence near Lisieux where William of Poitiers was an archdeacon, and a religious ceremony involving an oath on relics at Bayeux. Orderic, over half a century later, may simply have been baffled by conflicting traditions. It is likely that Harold reluctantly swore the oaths because he believed himself to be in some danger, and probably because he behaved that later developments would invalidate them. They represented a masterly stroke on William's part to implicate King Edward's most powerful subject in his plans and laid the basis of the argument that when Harold took the English crown in 1066, on the grounds that the succession had been bestowed on him by Edward the Confessor on his deathbed, he was guilty of perjury.

8. William is shown receiving messages from Guy, who then brings Harold to William.

7. *The journey and arrival of William's messengers. Turold, the foreshortened figure, may well be a tenant of Bishop Odo of Bayeux and one of the indications that Odo was the Tapestry's patron.*

How valid was William's claim to be Edward's heir? William of Poitiers, who discussed the matter at length, believed that William was Edward's rightful heir because the promise invalidated all later bequests. This was a strong argument, although, both in practice and in law, not the overwhelming one which William of Poitiers made it out to be. Succession to the English kingdom had become something of a lottery in the eleventh century; force of arms or decisive action had made Cnut king in 1016 and Harold Harefoot's succession in 1035 also required a coup. When there had been a peaceful succession in the tenth and eleventh centuries, three factors had generally made a man acceptable for kingship; a blood relationship to previous kings, designation by the reigning king, and acceptance by the English nobles. William in reality had only the second of these in his favour, for since civil war followed Edward's promise in 1051, such consent as might have been given by the English nobles at that time was of dubious quality. When William of Poitiers suggests that Archbishop Stigand of

9. *William receives Harold from Guy.*

10. *William and Harold converse in William's palace at Rouen. On the right is one of the Tapestry's most mysterious scenes involving a lady named Ælfygfu and a priest. The man baring his genitals hints at a sexual scandal.*

Canterbury, Earl Godwine of Wessex, Earl Leofric of Mercia and Earl Siward of Northumbria actually agreed to William's succession he strains our credulity beyond acceptable limits. The three earls might have consented in 1051 but Godwine's cannot have been sincerely given. Archbishop Stigand's can only have been given in 1052 when he became archbishop; that is, after Godwine had returned to England in triumph – a most unlikely possibility.

Edward's apparent support for other candidates, such as Edward the Exile, King Svein Estrithsson of Denmark, and later Harold of Wessex, made William's claim one among many, and to an outsider it was not necessarily the best one. One weakness in William of Poitiers's argument for William, which was appreciated by Orderic Vitalis, was that it only took account of Harold's claims, and did not notice the claims on the basis of kinship of the young son of Edward the Exile, Edgar the Ætheling. Another factor is that in 1066 the English people clearly did not want William to be their next king. When

12. *Harold is shown rescuing warriors from the quicksands around Le Mont Saint-Michel, before the Normans capture Dol. Count Conan of Brittany is shown fleeing.*

11. William departs on a campaign into Brittany, taking Harold with him. The army is shown passing Le Mont Saint-Michel.

William learnt of Edward the Confessor's death on 5 January 1066, he would quickly have appreciated that the king's deathbed request to Harold gave Harold's kingship a considerable degree of legitimacy and that Harold was the popular choice. If William wanted to be King of England he had no alternative but to prepare to invade.

Preparations for Invasion

The subject of the organization and conduct of the Hastings campaign has attracted many historians over the years and a vast literature has resulted. The sparseness of the sources means that numerous aspects are uncertain and many are controversial. We do not know, for example, how many troops William had in his army. Also the credibility of a major source, the so-called 'Song of the Battle of Hastings' (the *Carmen de Hastingae Proelio*), has been

13. The Normans are shown attacking the castle at Dinan, which eventually surrenders.

14. *Conan's submission is followed by an important scene in which William knights Harold, before the army returns to Bayeux. In contrast to William of Poitiers, the Tapestry displays Harold as a heroic figure.*

doubted by Professor R.H.C. Davis. In a book devoted to William, it is unnecessary to go deeply into these controversies. We can concentrate on what is known of William's personal contribution. It can at least be said, however, that some sort of consensus (against which some would argue very strongly indeed) accepts that William's army numbered 7000 men, and that my own view is that on the *Carmen* Professor Davis has not proved his case and that it can be used as a source for the battle.

According to the early sources, the first stage of William's preparations was a setpiece council, which William of Malmesbury located at Lillebonne, and at which William is supposed to have persuaded the faint-hearted among the Normans that the risks of invading England were worth taking. Discussion is said to have focussed on Normandy being exposed to outside attack during William's absence, on the likely destruction of all that had so far been achieved, and on the difficulties of the enterprise. This great debate, described first by William of Poitiers, looks like an artificial literary contrivance, rather

16. *Harold is shown reporting back to Edward. The previously upstanding Harold is here shown hunched and disfigured, suggesting perhaps that he already intends to break his oath to William.*

15. *Harold takes his fateful oath to William at Bayeux, before returning to England.*

than an authentic record of what happened; Normandy was after all more secure than it had been for several decades and after Harold's oath to William, England, and the expedition to conquer it, must have been talked about avidly by every Norman warrior worth his salt. Given that William's army eventually contained men from Flanders, Brittany and even Aquitaine, it is obvious that the campaign had been long planned and well publicized. However, the holding of such an assembly was an important occasion in formal, and possibly ritual, terms, giving William the opportunity to commit his followers to a dangerous project and prepare everyone for the risks ahead. It shows him consulting with his vassals, as a good lord was required to do, and is a tribute to his skills in man management.

The charters and Orderic show William at his palaces at Rouen, Fécamp, Caen, Bayeux and Bonneville-sur-Touque during 1066. The witness lists of the charters in particular demonstrate that he was meeting regularly with his chief men throughout the months before sailing to England, and suggest a

17. *Scenes placed in reverse order show Edward's death, his discussion with his followers, including perhaps the bequest of the kingdom to Harold (the caption is not specific) and his burial in Westminster Abbey.*

18. The crown is offered to Harold and his coronation follows. The appearance of the comet is portrayed as a source of consternation to Harold. Ghostly ships predict the invasion.

series of rallies to encourage and organize the preparations; William fitz Osbern and Roger de Montgommery were the only lay magnates to be frequently in their duke's company, whereas many other important men appear only on one occasion. During his progress around his duchy, William also entertained great lords from other parts of France who were planning to join the invasion: the Poitevin Aimeri, vicomte of Thouars, was certainly present at some stage, while Eustace, Count of Boulogne, was in the duke's company when he was at Bayeux. Precautions were taken for the uncertain times ahead by naming Mathilda as regent in Normandy, to be supported by Roger de Beaumont and Roger de Montgommery. William's son Robert, who had been accepted as his heir to both Normandy and Maine, is known once to have acted in his father's place by confirming a charter, but at this stage there was no question of him having any actual power. William also continued with the routine business of governing his duchy during this period, appointing a new abbot for the monastery of St-Evroult while at Bonneville.

20. Ships are built in preparation for the invasion.

19. A ship crosses to Normandy taking news of Harold's coronation. William is shown in council. The cleric on the right could be Bishop Odo.

Extensive diplomatic preparations were made in the course of 1066. An embassy was sent to Rome, which persuaded Pope Alexander II to give the invasion his blessing and a papal banner. This story has the authority only of William of Poitiers, but attempts to dismiss its credibility have never been entirely convincing. The arguments used in Rome by William's emissaries are not known, but were presumably those later recounted by William of Poitiers; namely, Edward the Confessor's promise, Harold's perjury, and the fact that Harold had been crowned by Archbishop Stigand of Canterbury, a prelate whose status was regarded as irregular by Pope Alexander and his cardinals. A reference in a letter of 24 April 1080 written by Pope Gregory VII (1073-85) who, as Archdeacon Hildebrand, had been prominent in papal counsels in 1066, suggests that he had been one of William's supporters and that the mission had not been entirely favourably received in Rome:

21. Supplies are assembled.

22. *William is shown embarking on the sea.*

> I believe it is known to you, most excellent son, how great was the love I have always borne you, even before I ascended the papal throne, and how active I have shown myself in your affairs; above all, how diligently I laboured for your advancement to royal rank. In consequence I suffered dire calumny through certain brethren insinuating that by such partisanship I gave sanction for the perpetration of great slaughter.

The anxieties are likely to have been about whether a campaign to remove Harold, which was probably going to cause many deaths, was justified. In the end, however, the Norman embassy carried the day, although in present-day eyes, at least, the fact that Harold's case went unrepresented before the papacy is strange. William's approach to the pope demonstrates a considerable awareness on his part of the possibilities of the current political climate in Rome. The practice of sponsoring military expeditions with a papal banner

24. *Disembarkation of men and horses.*

23. The fleet crosses the Channel to Pevensey. The horses on board the ships should be noted.

was a very recent development, which was designed to increase the papacy's authority; William was notably astute to ask for one. Through it he achieved a remarkable coup which immediately transformed a buccaneering enterprise into a legitimate assault on a usurping king. According to William of Poitiers, William also made treaties with the Emperor Henry IV, who was King of Germany, and Svein Estrithsson, King of Denmark, although the latter subsequently proved to be disloyal.

The culmination of the preparations appears to have been the dedication of Mathilda's abbey of La Trinité of Caen on 18 June, an occasion surely staged as a symbolic preliminary to the great venture. Sadly no description of this religious ceremony survives, simply a charter which shows that most of the major figures in Norman society were present. Above all the dedication was a religious occasion, with Archbishop Maurilius of Rouen and four out of his six suffragan bishops in attendance, along with eight abbots, including the heads of almost every monastery of which the duke was the direct patron. The

25. William's army moves up to Hastings. The troops are shown seizing supplies.

26. These scenes show food being prepared for a meal.

new church of La Trinité, as we saw in Chapter Four, is unlikely to have been completed, but adequate buildings must have existed for the proper observance of the monastic rule. On the day of the ceremony William and Mathilda gave their young daughter Cecilia, then around seven years of age, to be a child oblate at the abbey.

By July the invasion fleet had assembled in the estuary of the River Dives and at nearby harbours in western Normandy, where it remained for about a month, perhaps unable to cross on account of contrary winds. It then moved up the coast to St-Valéry-sur-Somme in Ponthieu, from where a shorter crossing was possible, some of William's men meeting their deaths by drowning on the way. The fleet finally set sail on the night of 27-28 September, landing at Pevensey after dawn, having anchored for a while in the middle of the Channel. An uneventful crossing was ensured by the departure of an English fleet which had remained at sea until 8 September when its provisions had run out. Torches attached to the masts maintained contact

28. The proximity of William's army is reported to Harold. The burning of the house illustrates the strategic ravaging of the region around Hastings which William used to lure Harold into battle.

27. *On the left William is shown at dinner, with a bishop (presumably Odo) blessing the food. William is then shown in discussion with his two brothers, with Odo apparently doing the talking. On the far right is shown the construction of a motte-and-bailey castle at Hastings.*

between the invaders' ships, although at one stage William's may have drifted away. A few ships became detached from the main fleet and landed near Romney.

A series of anecdotes provided by William of Poitiers shows how William sought to sustain morale during these tense preliminaries. He is said to have maintained good discipline throughout the time in the Dives estuary and to have prohibited looting. He ordered that the deaths which had occurred during the voyage from Dives to St-Valéry be kept secret. At St-Valéry he had the relics of St Valéry brought out of the local church in order to move in procession behind them, and later he imparted a sense of urgency to the less enthusiastic by being impatient to leave when the wind was at last favourable. On the crossing he hid anxiety when his ship became separated from the others by eating a good breakfast, including spiced wine. Another source tells us that William's ship for the voyage had been given by the Duchess Mathilda and was called the *Mora*. It seems to be represented on the Bayeux Tapestry as

29. *The massed cavalry of William's army is shown advancing to battle.*

30. William is shown questioning a certain Vitalis (probably another of Odo's associates) about the whereabouts of Harold's army.

a typical square-rigged Viking ship with a cruciform banner at the masthead, a carved lion's head at the prow, and a child on the stern who is holding a horn to his lips and pointing towards England.

The Hastings Campaign

The circumstances facing William's army when it arrived in England had been both eased and complicated by recent events. In 1065 the people of Northumbria had rebelled against their earl, Harold's brother Tostig, and had had him replaced by Morcar, a member of the family of the Mercian earls. Tostig was exiled and seems to have thought that Harold, by not fighting on his behalf, had let him down. He threw in his lot with Harold's enemies, and ravaged the English coast. He may have negotiated with William, but failed to make an agreement with him. He eventually joined Harold Hardraada, King of Norway,

32. William is shown encouraging his troops as they ride into battle.

31. A scout reports to William about Harold's army. Careful reconnaissance was obviously a significant factor in William's eventual victory.

with whom he invaded northern England in the late summer of 1066. William benefited from these English divisions and at Hastings faced an English army weakened by absenteeism and by weariness after the long march to and from northern England, where King Harold had had to lead it to defeat and kill Harold Hardraada and Tostig at the Battle of Stamford Bridge on 25 September. Although this undoubtedly assisted William's cause, it is a telling commentary on the uncertainties of the entire Norman campaign that when he landed at Pevensey on the morning of 28 September he would not have known whether he was going to have to fight the English or the Norwegian Harold. After Stamford Bridge Harold moved rapidly south, reaching London by 6 October.

After landing, the Norman army moved from Pevensey to Hastings. William's strategy was evidently to stay near the coast, consolidate, and draw his enemy on into a battle which he hoped would be decisive. Earthwork castles were thrown up at Pevensey and Hastings and the surrounding countryside was devastated, partly for supplies and partly to try to force

33. The combined infantry and cavalry of William's army advance. It is noticeable that the majority of horsemen wield their lances as spears rather than charging with them in couched position.

34. The French cavalry and densely packed English infantry clash. The portrayal of a sole English archer is often seen as indicating that Harold's hurried march to Hastings required him to leave crucial troops behind.

Harold to join battle to stop the pillaging. The effects of this destruction are still evident in Domesday Book, compiled twenty years later; the Bayeux Tapestry shows a house being burnt, possibly with a woman and child inside it, while the *Carmen* mentions the seizure of women and children. William's strategy of staying near to where his army had disembarked had the advantage of keeping his lines of communication as short as possible and permitting a retreat to his ships. To have advanced into England would have invited being cut off and being vulnerable to a war of attrition. In the prelude to the Battle of Hastings it was Harold who could dictate the military terms, since he could either advance quickly or hold off and assemble larger forces. But William's tactics, which were of a kind often used by medieval commanders, put psychological pressure on Harold, who could be portrayed as caring insufficiently about the sufferings of his subjects. William and his men used the time available while they waited to gain a good knowledge of the local terrain through their scouts.

36. The turmoil of battle with warriors on both sides being cut down.

35. These scenes portray the deaths of Harold's brothers, Earls Gyrth and Lesfwine.

Harold's army advanced rapidly from London and reached the area of present-day Battle by 13 October. His force lacked the warriors of the northern earls, Edwin and Morcar, and contained very few archers, but it was probably larger than William's and it contained crack troops who had taken part in the defeat of Harold Hardraada and Tostig. Harold's aim was to achieve surprise by the speed of his advance. William countered by keeping his soldiers fully armed through the night of 13-14 October and marching them to what was to be the battlefield in the early morning of 14 October. By doing this, he out-generalled Harold by attacking while the English were still tired from their march and before they had deployed their resources to full effect. As is obvious from a visit to Battle, Harold occupied a strong defensive position up on the ridge, but, as the contemporary sources make clear, his soldiers were squashed in there, and vulnerable to the Normans' mobile and well-organized cavalry because they lacked the room to manoeuvre. As on several earlier occasions in his career, William had perceived the opportunity for an early strike and moved quickly.

37. On the left a group of poorly armed English defend a hill, while on the right Bishop Odo (possibly not directly involved as a combatant) is shown encouraging troops.

38. On the far left William raises his helmet to dispel a rumour that he had been killed. This was a crucial moment in the battle after which the Normans are shown advancing.

The Battle of Hastings lasted throughout most of the day and was hard fought. It was finally settled by Harold's death in the later stages, but this must have come after the English army had been progressively weakened by the Normans' disciplined cavalry tactics. This fateful day for the English kingdom soon became a topic for the myth makers and we cannot be entirely sure that the exploits which are credited to William are always true. William of Poitiers tells us that before the battle William mistakenly donned his chain mail reversed towards the left. This could have been a premonition of ill luck, but he laughed it off, saying that God would decide, and that such superstitious omens did not bother him. During the exchange of ambassadors before the battle began, he is said to have offered to settle the matter by single combat with Harold and to have promised Harold that he would hold his father's estates if he accepted William as king. This looks like ritual posturing. An incident which is mentioned by Poitiers, the *Carmen* and the Bayeux Tapestry is William's removal of his helmet in order

40. The scene of Harold's death continues on the far left. He may also be the warrior who is cut down. After this the English turn to flight.

39. *The English forces are now in disarray. On the right a warrior grasping an arrow through his head could well represent Harold, shot through the eye.*

to rally his troops, an episode which Poitiers associates with the spread of a rumour that William had been killed. After dispelling this fear, William harangued his men and led the recovery himself, charging forward wielding his sword and cutting down several of the enemy. This was probably the moment at which the Normans came nearest to defeat, and at which William's personal leadership changed the course of events. William is also said to have had three horses killed under him. In brief, the sources portray William as the archetypal medieval warrior-king, who led by example and whose safety was crucial to the morale of his men.

The Bayeux Tapestry, which was made for William's half-brother, Bishop Odo of Bayeux, most probably before 1077, was typical of all early medieval art in not seeking to give an accurate likeness of its subjects. We can, however, be reasonably confident in accepting its general presentation of William's dress and equipment as not being significantly different from that of his companions. He is shown as wearing the same kind of three-quarter length tunic and cloak as other important Normans. His special authority is

represented either by a special sword or lance, as in the council of war before the battle where he bears a sword held vertically in front of him. In the battle itself his armour consists of the typical conical helmet with nose guard and the normal coat of chain mail, and is distinguished only in that the chain mail covers the entire leg, a feature shown only for a few, presumably very prominent men. During the battle his authority is displayed by his

41. *The Tapestry continues to display the fleeing English, but its end is lost. It is likely that it concluded with William's coronation.*

carrying a kind of club or mace. He does not hold the kite-shaped shield which is the usual equipment of the mounted Norman warriors on the Tapestry, suggesting that he mostly stayed behind the main line of troops, giving orders and support, but able to move forward in emergencies.

In the immediate aftermath of victory William refused an offer of money from Harold's mother to give her son a Christian burial, on the grounds that his actions had led to many deaths. Instead Harold was buried on the seashore. William of Poitiers thought William's decision an appropriate act of mockery for a man who had tried insanely to fight God's will. William also left the bodies of the English unburied, and organized the burial only of his own side's dead. Again his contemporary apologists thought this justified; the English had opposed a just cause and had supported a tyrant who deserved death. The act was in any case a normal one among medieval commanders; Poitiers does note that the English were allowed freely to bury their own casualties and with some justification thought this a generous gesture. William may even have later relented about Harold, who was subsequently reinterred in the church he had founded at Waltham. But the date of, and William's part, if any, in this transfer are not known.

King of the English

William kept his army at Hastings for about a week after the battle. He then moved slowly around south-eastern England via Romney, Dover and Canterbury to reach Southwark and the southern end of the single bridge across the Thames on the site of modern London Bridge by late November. On the journey his troops burnt both Dover and Southwark. At London Bridge he evidently decided that it was not possible to force a crossing and therefore led his forces on a long, rapid march in early December around the south and west of London through Surrey, north Hampshire and Berkshire before crossing the Thames at Wallingford. During this time, a detachment was sent to Winchester, the ancient capital of the English kingdom, to secure its surrender and that of Queen Edith, who was not only Edward the Confessor's widow, but also the late King Harold's sister. The campaign had sapped the English will to resist and, at Wallingford, the major English submissions began. Archbishop Stigand of Canterbury was the first to give in. Others did so at Berkhamstead, including the city of London itself.

William's tactics in the months after Hastings were a mixture of caution and respect for military necessity, governed always by the underlying purpose of putting ever-increasing pressure on those English who might be predisposed to continue resistance. To begin with he had obviously hoped that there would be a rapid, general surrender while he was still at Hastings. When there was not, he moved at a pace commensurate with feeding a large army and used the submission of towns to take tribute to pay his troops. His army suffered from dysentery and he himself was afflicted by an illness somewhere near Canterbury. On the march around London, he allowed his forces to ravage the countryside, another brutal campaign whose effects can be traced from signs of devastation in Domesday Book. It is likely that William for some time took seriously the continued English efforts to resist. The city of London and the remaining English leaders had elected a new king, Edgar the Ætheling, the son of Edward the Exile, a boy of perhaps fourteen years, whose position was sufficiently respected for the monks of Peterborough to seek his approval for their choice of a new abbot. In this context, William's relatively slow march around Kent was an advance designed to permit a large army to feed itself off the countryside and to allow the English to absorb gradually the lessons of defeat. The much more rapid encircling of London which followed was clearly intended to produce submissions by isolating the city and the English leaders in it through what must have been a terrifying display of superior military power.

William of Poitiers tells us that after the English submissions at Wallingford and Berkhamstead William consulted with his Norman advisers before agreeing to a coronation. Since the whole point of the expedition had been the acquisition of the English kingdom, it is unlikely that William had the doubts that Poitiers suggests he had. What was surely happening was that William was once more ratifying what had been achieved and preparing for an uncertain future by consultation with his most important companions. The implications of victory must have been becoming starkly obvious. The kingdom had been gained only after an arduous and costly campaign, and an army of conquest had now to be transformed into an army of occupation. Henceforth William was going to have to rule territories on both sides of the Channel and his way of life and that of his aristocracy were going to change dramatically. Kingship was above all a serious business. One was annointed with holy oil and acquired mystical qualities which a mere duke did not possess. William of Poitiers says that the Normans were unanimous that William should take the crown.

William's coronation took place in Westminster abbey on 25 December 1066 in the same church where Harold had been crowned and where Edward the Confessor was buried. There is controversy among scholars as to which ceremonial *ordo* was used to crown William, but no one doubts that he was crowned according to a rite which had been used to crown earlier English kings. The purpose was therefore to show continuity; to present William, Duke of Normandy, as the legitimate successor of an ancient line of kings. He was crowned by Ealdred, Archbishop of York, the senior acceptable representative of the English ecclesiastical hierarchy, given the papacy's known disapproval of Archbishop Stigand of Canterbury who had crowned Harold. William of Poitiers speaks of the presence of many English bishops and abbots, which is not impossible since we know from a reliable source that the bishops of the relatively remote dioceses of Worcester and Hereford had been present at the surrender at Wallingford. From the start William was trying to involve his new subjects in his rule as well as to stress continuity and legitimacy.

At the ceremony itself, Bishop Geoffrey of Coutances sought the assent of the Normans present. Their loud shouts terrified the guards outside the church, who, fearing an English uprising, promptly set fire to houses in the neighbouring city of London. Orderic adds more detail to this tale of panic and confusion by reporting that most of the congregation fled from the church and that the ceremony was completed by the bishops and clergy, with the new king trembling from head to foot. William's coronation was designed to allow him to assume the political and ideological role for which his proclaimed belief in his status as Edward the Confessor's heir had preordained him. Like the approval for the Hastings campaign obtained from the papacy, it was a magnificent example of how an act of violence for which there was no more than a debatable justification can be cloaked in legitimacy and moral right. However, although intended to be an act of continuity and reconciliation between conquerors and conquered, William's coronation was in fact a tense occasion conducted amidst close security. Fear at the possibility of rebellion, rather than joy at the accession of a new king, was probably the dominant emotion among all those gathered at Westminster on that Christmas Day.

Six

THE TRIUMPHANT KING

William stayed in England from Christmas 1066 until March 1067, during which time, according to William of Poitiers, firm discipline was maintained within the large army which had brought William victory. In this first short stay in his new kingdom, William received English submissions, and is said to have confirmed the privileges of the city of London, done justice, and made some laws. The document by which London's liberties were confirmed may well be a sealed writ in English, drawn up in the manner of similar documents from Edward the Confessor's reign, which still survives in the archives of the city of London. If it is, its traditional English form illustrates magnificently William's wish to emphasize continuity. But its being addressed to a port-reeve named Geoffrey, who was unquestionably a Norman, and to the burgesses of the city, both English and French, shows that the settlement of Frenchmen and Normans in England had already begun.

Another striking feature of these first weeks was the systematic despoliation of the accessible parts of conquered England. For William of Poitiers it was a virtuous act that large amounts of treasure should be sent across the Channel in January 1067 in spite of the bad weather; he says that a thousand churches in France, Aquitaine and Burgundy and other regions were the beneficiaries of William's munificence, and that the papacy received treasures worthy of Byzantium, as well as the war banner of the defeated King Harold. But the most common technique used to 'make' these gifts available appears to have been organized tribute-taking, masterminded by William himself. The money raised was also used to pay off his troops.

When William returned to Normandy in March 1067, he took with him several of the leading Englishmen, including the former 'King' Edgar the Ætheling, Archbishop Stigand, and the Earls of Mercia and Northumbria, the brothers Edwin and Morcar. The visit lasted until 6 December 1067. The spoils of victory were displayed to the Norman people, most notably when William celebrated Easter (8 April) in the old ducal palace at Fécamp amidst a great assembly attended not just by Normans, but also by nobles from France. According to William of Poitiers, all looked in wonder at the king's fair-haired English 'guests'. On 1 July William attended the dedication of the new abbey church of Jumièges by the River Seine, a magnificent building of which substantial ruins remain.

In England in the meantime his two regents, his brother Bishop Odo and William fitz Osbern, were starting to impose Norman rule on a kingdom where the spirit which had inspired massive English resistance in 1066 was still very much alive. The west and north were still largely unvisited by the Normans, and other regions were barely subdued. An attempt at an invasion by William's former ally, Count Eustace of Boulogne, who had been the second husband of Edward the Confessor's sister Godgifu, was beaten off with some ease by the Norman garrison at Dover; it may be that Eustace thought that English disaffection with the Normans gave him a chance of obtaining the kingdom. The Anglo-Saxon Chronicler wrote about this time in sombre and fatalistic language, describing oppression, castle-building and brutality. When William returned to England in December, bringing with him his old friend Roger de Montgommery, it was to confront turmoil. Unsurprisingly it was not yet thought safe for Mathilda to cross to England; she may in any case have been pregnant with an eighth child.

In early 1068 William marched into south-western England and besieged Exeter where Harold's mother had taken refuge. His army contained some English troops, who were presumably recruited on the basis of the prerogative of an English king to call out the shire levies. The citizens of Exeter had obtained aid from other regions of England, and refused to be overawed when William invested the town with a large army and blinded a hostage within sight of the walls. They held out for eighteen days and surrendered only when it was obvious that further resistance was pointless, but after they had inflicted heavy casualties on William's army. William then ordered the construction of a castle, the so-called 'Rougemont Castle', of which the gate can still be seen. Its custody was entrusted to a Norman noble, Baldwin, son of one of William's guardians in his youth, Count Gilbert of Brionne. But the town was otherwise granted lenient terms, at least to judge from Orderic's comments and the supporting evidence of Domesday Book which shows Exeter making the same payment to the king in 1086 that it had done in 1066. The policy was evidently to display Norman power through the castle and the castellan, but to try to show that in other ways life could return to normal under Norman rule. William then marched on into Cornwall, presumably to obtain more submissions, before returning to Winchester for Easter (23 March). A Breton named Brian was installed as Earl of Cornwall.

Mathilda was brought from Normandy to be crowned queen on Whit Sunday (11 May) 1068. Like William's, her coronation was performed by

Archbishop Ealdred of York. The witness lists of two charters confirmed at this time show a large and truly Anglo-Norman assembly gathered around the new king and queen. There were present the two English archbishops, Stigand and Ealdred, numerous English bishops and abbots, the English earls, Edwin, Morcar and Waltheof, and lesser English thegns such as Tofi, sheriff of Somerset, along with the great Norman figures, the king's two half-brothers, Bishop Odo and Count Robert of Mortain, William fitz Osbern, Roger de Montgommery, Count Robert of Eu, and Bishop Geoffrey of Coutances, and many others. The charters deal with the sort of routine matters that an established regime would expect to handle, namely, a grant of lands to the church of St Martin-le-Grand in London and the restoration of an estate to the cathedral church of Wells. William's reunion with Mathilda was also evidently a domestic success, since the last of their four sons, the future King Henry I, was born within a year of the coronation.

Whitsun 1068 marks the apogee of William's attempts to establish an Anglo-Norman state in England. Shortly afterwards, Earls Edwin and Motcar rebelled and at about the same time Edgar the Ætheling departed from court and took refuge with Malcolm III, King of the Scots (1058-93). According to Orderic the immediate cause of the revolt was Edwin's disenchantment with William, who had denied him genuine authority over his lands and had withheld a daughter whom he had promised to him in marriage. Orderic then says that the English rebels met with Welsh princes in an attempt to incite general rebellion, most especially in those regions not fully under Norman control. But it is obvious from the subsequent course of events that the English chiefs had acted without having evolved any coherent plan of campaign and that William moved with typical swiftness to ensure that one did not develop. He advanced to Warwick and built a castle there whose custody he subsequently entrusted to Henry, son of Roger de Beaumont. This cut Edwin's and Morcar's Anglo-Welsh force in the west Midlands off from the rebels who had risen against William in northern England. Edwin and Morcar therefore surrendered. The northern English are reported to have put on an impressive display of manliness, sleeping permanently out in the open, but neglecting the elementary military requirement of moving south. They sued for peace when William reached Nottingham, where another castle was established. The king took hostages from them and then moved up to York where another castle was built on the site of what is now called Clifford's Tower. These successes sent shock waves further north, since Bishop Æthelwine of Durham and at least one Northumbrian noble also submitted. The bishop was then employed on a mission to the King of the Scots – who had in any case done very little to support his allies – who indicated that he would not fight against William.

William's arrangements for the Midlands and the North are an obvious replica of those which he had instigated in the South-West. William Malet was made castellan of York and one Robert fitz Richard was given general responsibility for Yorkshire. More ambitiously Robert de Commines was sent to be Earl of Northumbria. This installation of Normans and other newcomers in the North marked a notable change from William's initial efforts to govern the North through the native northern English aristocracy; his first Earl of Northumbria, Copsi, had been killed in a local feud, while the second, Gospatric, had joined the 1068 rebels. Having installed some of has followers in the North, William travelled south by way of Lincoln, Huntingdon and Cambridge, again establishing castles at each place. These castles, close to the Humber and on the edge of the Fenland, were intended not only to overawe the inhabitants of eastern England, but also to anticipate a potential attack from Denmark, which by this stage William must have known to be likely. He then returned to Normandy in late 1068, taking Mathilda with him, having seemingly effected a great extension of his authority by two impressive progresses into the West and North.

The notion that William might be king of a kingdom whose aristocracy was a mixture of native English and French newcomers foundered during the two years between 1066 and 1068. In fact, it was doomed from the beginning because it was an impossible ideal. William was in truth trusted by very few Englishmen, and he in turn trusted very few of them. The enormous English support for Harold in 1066 indicates that William was basically just not wanted as king by the English. The 'honourable' imprisonment of the English chiefs taken to Normandy in 1067 coupled with the massive seizure of booty were understandable steps for William to take at the time, but they were hardly likely to win the trust and affection of his new subjects. The weakness of the foundations of William's power in northern England and the likelihood of a Danish invasion both provided very seductive temptations to revolt, to which many Englishmen succumbed. At the same time, William was also under overwhelming pressure to distribute lands to his Norman and French followers as rewards for their services and for reasons of security. The redistribution of Englishmen's property began in 1067 and 1068 with developments such as Bishop Odo being made Earl of Kent, William fitz Osbern, Earl of Hereford, and Roger de Montgommery and others being given blocks of territory in Sussex, each with a castle at its centre, to protect the lines of communication with Normandy (the so-called Sussex rapes). These examples were only the tip of the iceberg of the massive transfer of land to Frenchmen and their vassals which was beginning.

The psychology of these difficult times is well caught by William of Poitiers's tendentious suggestion that no Englishman was deprived of his land unjustly, but that security required that castles be placed in the hands of men whom William could trust. It is also apparent in Orderic's statement that while Earl Edwin rebelled because he felt that William had not treated him honourably, William did want to treat him well, but was talked out of doing so by his greedy Norman followers who coveted English estates. These were conditions in which no one could feel truly safe; the sheer violence of the times must have increased everyone's sense of insecurity, and, with the arrival of the Danes in 1069, the history of the Norman Conquest of England entered a new phase.

The Great Campaigns of 1068 to 1070

William's strategy for the north of England collapsed within a few weeks of his departure for Normandy in the autumn of 1068. The northerners saw the presence of the Norman castles as an intrusion and a provocation, and the small size of the Norman forces as an invitation to attack them; calculations probably based on the fact that William's English predecessors had rarely visited the North and that William would not therefore be any different. Also, Edgar the Ætheling was still active and he and a number of Northumbrian nobles joined the Yorkshire rebels. Robert de Commines and almost all his men were killed in Durham soon after their arrival; Robert fitz Richard and many of his men were also slaughtered; and William Malet and his followers were besieged and trapped in the castle at York. Methods which had effectively displayed William's authority in the South-West had failed dismally in the North. He therefore returned to England in early 1069 and moved swiftly north. He caught the rebels in York while they were besieging the castle, defeated them and allowed his army to sack the city. He then built a second castle, to the west of the Ouse, and returned to the South, leaving his closest lieutenant, William fitz Osbern, behind to tidy up. The king was back at Winchester for Easter (13 April) where William fitz Osbern joined him. This time Mathilda had remained in Normandy; she would in any case have been about to give birth to the future King Henry I.

In the period 1069-70 William's rule in England faced its greatest crisis. By Easter 1069 he must have been aware that a large invasion from Denmark was imminent. King Svein Estrithsson of Denmark (1047-76) had a claim to the English throne because he was the son of King Cnut's sister and the cousin of King Harthacnut (1040-42). He also claimed that Edward the Confessor had designated him as his heir shortly after his coronation. He therefore represented that longstanding Scandinavian interest in the English kingdom which had made Cnut, Harold Harefoot and Harthacnut kings between 1016 and 1042. By 1069 he had acquired a reputation as an effective ruler, and had apparently received many invitations from England to invade, and even gifts of money. A measure of how seriously William took the Danish threat is shown by the fact that he remained permanently in England until late in the year 1070, his longest absence from Normandy during his entire lifetime. It is also notable that he made no immediate effort to retrieve his authority in Maine which had collapsed in 1069 in the face of a local rebellion.

The Danish army which arrived in the summer of 1069 was essentially an expeditionary force, commanded by King Svein's brother Osbern and three of his sons, and presumably intended to prepare the way for Svein's own arrival later. It was nevertheless a large army which is said to have been carried in a fleet consisting of 240 ships. Its failure to make a landing at Dover, Sandwich and other places on the east coast points partly to the effectiveness of the coastal defences which William had organized, but must also reflect the likelihood that the Danes' plan was always to land in the North to establish a base for a full-scale invasion. Whatever the case, they eventually landed on the banks of the Humber and joined up with the rebels led by Edgar the Ætheling, William's nominee as Earl of Northumbria, Gospatric, and Waltheof, the son of Earl Siward of Northumbria (died 1055). The combined army then advanced to York and captured it on 20 September. William's enemies were thereby formidably concentrated but, on the other hand, they were in a remote part of the kingdom where supplies were limited because of the devastation of recent campaigns.

According to Orderic, whose account of these years is based on the lost concluding sections of William of Poitiers, William was hunting in the Forest of Dean while the Danes were moving up the east coast. After heating of the fall of York he moved north. His initial strategy appears to have been one of containment. In this he was helped by his enemies' reluctance to risk all in a decisive battle; it is possible that they were waiting for further reinforcements from Denmark and hoping meanwhile that, with much of northern England up in arms, William would not be able to make progress. The Danes fell back from York to the Humber where William's army and other Norman contingents were able to keep them cut off from the South.

At one stage a detachment of William's military household based in the castle at Lincoln defeated a force under Edgar the Ætheling which tried to push southwards, and later, troops under Counts Robert of Mortain and Robert of Eu launched a surprise attack and defeated some of the Danes. William himself is known to have made a diversion to Stafford to crush a local rebellion, but late in the year he took the major decision to seize the initiative and push north to complete the encirclement of the Danes. The major problem in doing this was crossing the River Aire near Pontefract which took three weeks of fierce fighting; William is said to have decided not to try to have a bridge built for the reason that this would signal his intentions and make his army vulnerable to attack, and to have preferred to wait until a defensible bridgehead could be established by force, which would enable his troops to ford the river under cover. After making the crossing, William pushed on to York, ravaging the countryside as he went. He spent Christmas in the midst of the ruins of the city, having, with his usual sense of the majesty of kingship, sent to Winchester for his crown and regalia in order to make an appropriate display of royal authority. The Danish army, now trapped on the banks of the Humber estuary and desperately short of supplies, made peace in return for money and permission to forage along the coasts. It agreed to depart in the spring.

Although the Danes had apparently been thwarted, William must have been keenly aware that three expeditions to York within eighteen months had not secured his authority over northern England. The region still had the potential to support further uprisings and to welcome other invaders. At Christmas 1069 William's English enemies had simply retreated into the hills, ready to re-emerge, they probably reasoned, after his predictable departure. However, instead of leaving, William marched north, dividing his army into small units whose job was to pursue the rebels into the hills and ravage the countryside. Peasants were slaughtered, crops in store burnt, animals killed, and tools and ploughs destroyed so that no seed would be sown for the next harvest. A Durham writer described infected corpses decaying in the houses and streets and survivors eating horses, cats and dogs and selling themselves into slavery. He said that no village was inhabited between York and Durham and that the land remained unploughed for nine years. Refugees are known to have travelled as far south as Evesham. Domesday Book, compiled sixteen years later, confirms that a terrible destruction had been inflicted on many parts of the county. At the River Tees, Gospatric and Waltheof surrendered. William then moved still further north, bringing ruin to areas of Durham and Northumbria as well, but here, forewarned, the peasantry left their houses in advance. William's purpose, brutally carried out, had been to ensure that the North could not support rebellion in the forseeable future.

In late January or February of 1070 William returned south across the Pennines to suppress a rising on the Welsh frontier. This was one of a number of revolts which had broken out at the same time as the Danish invasion, but the only one which was sufficiently serious to require William's personal attention; disturbances in Dorset and Somerset, for example, had been quelled by Bishop Geoffrey of Coutances and those in Devon and Cornwall, involving landings from Ireland by illegitimate sons of King Harold, by the citizens of Exeter. During his wintry crossing of the Pennines to Chester, William was apparently a great inspiration to his troops; he is said to have overcome all complaints about the severity of the conditions by sheer force of personality and to have used his great physical strength to assist lesser mortals across the difficult terrain. On this march the countryside was again ravaged and William's savagery did not even spare the saltworks at Nantwich, a valuable source of royal revenue, which had also not recovered by the time of Domesday Book. Castles were constructed at Chester and Stafford, after which the pacification of the Welsh border was mostly left to Roger de Montgommery who became Earl of Shrewsbury, Hugh d'Avranches who became Earl of Chester, and William fitz Osbern and his son Roger, who held the earldom of Hereford. By Easter (4 April) William had paid off his army and was at Winchester to meet legates sent by the pope.

The Final Subjugation of the English

The meetings with papal legates at Winchester and Windsor were a logical consequence of Pope Alexander's support for the invasion of 1066 and can reasonably be seen as a legitimation of William's victory by the highest religious authority on earth. The two legates with whom William did business at Winchester were the cardinals John Minutus and Peter. Also present was another legate, Bishop Ermenfrid of Sion, who had known William for many years, since he had first visited Normandy in 1054 to superintend the deposition of Archbishop Malger of Rouen, and was presumably a friend to William's policies. By Whitsun only Ermenfrid remained in England, the others having crossed to Normandy.

The accounts of these momentous ecclesiastical councils suggest that William and the cardinals presided together, even though it was often obvious that the churchmen were simply doing the king's bidding. The Easter council at Winchester began with William being crowned by the cardinals, a remarkable event, without precedent in English history. The council then proceeded to agree to some reforms for the moral and organizational improvement of the English Church and finally, to depose Archbishop Stigand of Canterbury and, after him, his brother Bishop Æthelmær of East Anglia. The cases of other bishops were also examined and some abbots were removed from office, a process continued at Windsor at Whitsun, when prelates from Normandy were appointed as replacements. The most significant of all these appointments was that of Lanfranc to the archbishopric of Canterbury. Thomas of Bayeux, a former pupil of Lanfranc and a protégé of William's half-brother, Bishop Odo, was appointed to the archbishopric of York in succession to Archbishop Ealdred who had died on 11 September

1069. The English bishops and abbots were treated in a variety of ways. Some were certainly regarded as political prisoners; Archbishop Stigand, for example, spent the rest of his life in chains at Winchester. Others were despatched to monasteries. The result of these changes was that only two bishops of English birth remained in office, and one of these, Siward of Rochester, was a very old man. Only the saintly Wulfstan of Worcester survived the purge along with several Lotharingians appointed by Edward the Confessor. Wulfstan's early twelfth-century biography suggests that he kept his office only because of divine miraculous intervention.

Between 1070 and 1072 William dealt with the remaining threats to his hold on England. In 1070 the Danes, far from having left as agreed, were strengthened by the arrival of King Svein Estrithsson. According to the Anglo-Saxon Chronicle, the English believed that he intended to conquer the kingdom. Svein sent a division of his army to the Isle of Ely to join the one remaining pocket of English resistance whose moving spirit was a Lincolnshire thegn named Hereward, a man later to be glorified in twelfth- and thirteenth-century legend. William's response was to negotiate with the Danish king, who departed for home later in the summer, presumably convinced that William was so well entrenched as to be invincible. Hereward was left isolated in Ely.

William crossed to Normandy in either late summer or early autumn to deal with some pressing problems, but in 1071 he returned not only to deal with Hereward, but also with the hapless Edwin and Morcar. They had apparently remained loyal during the Danish invasion, but had now rebelled again because they are said to have feared imprisonment. Edwin travelled around to rally support, but on his way to Scotland was betrayed and killed by three of his followers who took his severed head to William, an act of treachery to their lord on which William gave his verdict by banishing them. Morcar meanwhile had joined Hereward's band in Ely, against whom William now brought massive force to bear. The Isle was blockaded from the north by a fleet of ships, and on land was encircled on all sides. William's troops built a causeway which enabled them to attack from the west, a major engineering feat since the causeway is said to have been three kilometres (two miles) long. Hereward escaped, but Morcar was held in custody for the rest of his life, obtaining only a brief release at William's death in 1087. Most of the rebels were captured; some among them were imprisoned, while others were mutilated by blinding or having limbs removed before being allowed to go free.

Having crushed all his opponents in England, William led an army into Scotland, supported by a fleet, in the summer of 1072. His exact purpose is not known, but it is reasonable to think that he was aiming to end King Malcolm's protection of the English pretender Edgar the Ætheling and to stop the Scottish king interfering in the northern counties. The Norman army advanced beyond the Forth with the Scots retreating ahead of it. The two kings then reached an agreement, known as the Peace of Abernethy, whereby the King of the Scots became William's vassal and gave hostages who probably included his eldest son Duncan. King Malcolm also apparently agreed to expel Edgar the Ætheling from his court. The Scottish king had therefore recognized the legitimacy of William's rule and a measure of political stability had been brought to England's shattered northern regions. Nevertheless, in the far north William was still relying on native lords to represent his authority. Although the treacherous Gospatric, who had been reappointed to the earldom of Northumbria after his submission in 1070, was finally deposed in 1072, his replacement was another former rebel, Waltheof. With Waltheof, however, William made immense diplomatic efforts to ensure his loyalty, even marrying him to his niece Judith, the daughter of his sister Adelaide.

As far as Orderic Vitalis was concerned the devastation of northern England in 1069-70 was a sin which could not be forgiven:

> My narrative has frequently had occasion to praise William, but for this act which condemned the innocent and guilty alike to die by slow starvation I cannot commend him. For when I think of helpless children, young men in the prime of life, and hoary grey-beards alike perishing of hunger, I am so moved to pity that I would rather lament the griefs and sufferings of the wretched people than make a vain attempt to flatter the perpetrator of such infamy. Moreover, I declare that assuredly such brutal slaughter cannot remain unpunished. For the almighty Judge watches over high and low alike; he will weigh the deeds of all men in a fair balance, and as a just avenger will punish wrong-doing.

We would now treat the deliberate slaughter of so many non-combatants as a war crime, whatever political justifications can be adduced on William's behalf. The 'harrying of the North' is a clear turning-point in William's career as England's king, because it was manifestly around that time that he decided that England would be ruled almost exclusively by his French followers. It was in the same vein that in 1070 he had the monasteries of England plundered, removing the wealth which fearful Englishmen had stored in them. This really was the point of no return; many who might previously have hoped to resume normal lives were deprived of that hope. We are told that William did begin to try to learn the English language, but soon gave up. The years of brutal campaigning probably dissolved any affection he may once have felt for the land and its people, and after 1072 he spent very little time in England.

However, when all is said and done, the qualities which made William a great and formidable ruler are indelibly stamped on the years between 1066 and 1072. His campaigns during these years were prodigious military feats. One of his contemporaries, the elderly Lanfranc, could write to Pope Alexander II as late as the period between Christmas 1072 and 21 April 1073 of William as the indispensable talisman of the Norman achievement in England:

> I urge you to entreat God mercifully to grant long life to my lord
> the King of the English .... While the King lives we have peace of
> a kind, but after his death we expect to have neither peace nor any
> other benefit.

The Stabilization of Normandy and England

Throughout these years of activity in England, William was also responsible for the 'normal' business of governing Normandy. Subsequent to his long visit in 1067, charters show that he was again in Normandy during the later months of 1068 and the start of 1069 and then in late 1070 and early 1071. On the latter visit he is known to have discussed matters connected with his abbey of St-Etienne of Caen with the two papal legates who had previously been so helpful at the Winchester Easter council of 1070. The duchy was at peace during these years; the weakness of William's main northern French rivals, which had been of such crucial significance in the years leading up to 1066, continued into the early 1070s. Mathilda was usually responsible for government during William's absences, along with their eldest son and heir Robert. The first dangerous development came in 1069 when the Norman hold on the county of Maine was destroyed by a rebellion masterminded by Geoffrey de Mayenne, and the second in 1070 when quarrels began in Flanders among members of Mathilda's family.

William appears to have thought the events in Flanders sufficiently pressing to require an immediate intervention, although it looks as if he made less effort there than he might have done. William fitz Osbern was sent with a small force to assist the widow and young children of Mathilda's eldest brother, Count Baldwin VI, who were embroiled in a succession dispute with Baldwin's next eldest brother, Robert 'the Frisian'. However, fitz Osbern was killed and the countess's party defeated at the Battle of Cassel (20 or 22 February 1071). As a result, Robert the Frisian became Count of Flanders, with William apparently deciding that nothing more could be done. The change of rulers in Flanders meant that a previously friendly power was now hostile. In addition, the death of William fitz Osbern deprived William of the man who had been his closest colleague over twenty years, and who had acted as his deputy in both England and Normandy. We know very little about fitz Osbern's personality. Orderic says that he was 'the bravest of the Normans, renowned for his generosity, ready wit, and outstanding integrity', but he also says that he was 'the first and greatest oppressor of the English'. This second statement should be taken as a moral rather than a factual comment, which was intended by Orderic to explain God's judgement on fitz Osbern's family, who were soon to lose their lands in England. He was buried in Normandy at the abbey of Cormeilles which he had founded, and of which nothing now survives. His visible memorial has to be the great hall of Chepstow castle built at his command during the short period from 1067 to 1071 when he was Earl of Hereford.

After his Scottish campaign in 1072, William again crossed the Channel to Normandy, and in early 1073 took a large army of English and French warriors to Maine to restore Norman authority there. He followed his usual tactic of seeking to induce a rapid surrender by inflicting a great deal of damage. He advanced to Fresnay-sur-Sarthe in Maine, devastating the countryside as he went. At Fresnay the castle surrendered without putting up much of a resistance. While there William knighted Robert, the son of Roger de Montgommery, a coming-of-age which is a reminder that the generation which had accomplished the conquest of England was an aging one and that their children were growing to vigorous adulthood. From Fresnay William's army moved southwards to Sillé, which also submitted quickly, and then to Le Mans, which William encircled and threatened to sack if it did not surrender. The citizens handed over the keys of the city the next day and were given generous terms. The submission of the entire county of Maine took place soon afterwards. Although there had been no serious fighting, William made a gift of land to the cathedral church of St Julian in order to compensate for damage done to the building, which must then have been under construction; the existing nave is in fact still largely the nave of that church. The campaign was over by 30 March when William was back in Normandy confirming some charters for the Manceau abbeys of St-Pierre-de-la-Couture and St-Vincent of Le Mans at Bonneville-sur-Touque, in the presence of several of the chief churchmen of Maine.

A distant, but significant, development occurred on 30 June 1073 when a new pope was consecrated. Both William and Archbishop Lanfranc of Canterbury wrote to congratulate him on his election, and the cordiality of the exchange suggests that the friendship between William and the new pope's predecessor would be maintained, especially as the new pontiff, who took the name of Gregory VII, had supported the grant of the papal banner to the Normans in 1066. In reply, Gregory counselled William to continue on the path of righteousness and wrote that, 'we deem that you alone among kings cherish above all others what we have earlier written'. To Queen Mathilda he quoted the text that if a sinful husband can be saved by a faithful wife, a good one will surely be improved further. It is only in the zealous tone of Gregory's letter to Archbishop Lanfranc that there are signs that Greogry's sternness might be a source of future tension:

> Bishops, the very men who should be shepherds of souls, in their endless craving for worldly glory and the delights of the flesh are not only choking all holiness and piety within themselves, but the example of their conduct is luring their charges into every kind of sin. A man of your experience knows the danger to us if we do not oppose them, yet how difficult it is to resist them and restrain their wickedness.

William spent the whole of 1074 in Normandy after a brief visit to England in 1073 to disband his army. Charters from the year 1074 show him at Rouen in May, on one occasion at Lillebonne, and in November back at Rouen, each time carrying out routine tasks of government. The attestations of the charters show that some of William's closest associates were with him in Normandy for much of the year; Bishop Odo, for example, was in the duchy from at least May to December and Roger de Montgommery was also there for several months. In the same period, William also dismantled a menacing coalition by diplomatic means and finally neutralized the English pretender Edgar the Ætheling. Edgar had again been received in Scotland by King Malcolm in contravention of the Peace of Abernethy of 1072, and provided with ships and treasure to take up the offer by the French King Philip I of the use of the castle of Montreuil-sur-Mer. Montreuil, between modern Dieppe and Boulogne, was near enough to Normandy's eastern frontier to be a base from which to launch raids into Normandy, but the threat never materialized because Edgar's fleet was devastated by storms in the North Sea. He then returned to Scotland, and subsequently travelled through England to Normandy to submit to William. His surrender marked the end of an era, since there was no longer a native English claimant to hamper William. The king is supposed to have treated Edgar well, although the only specific evidence is his tenure in Domesday Book of two estates in Hertfordshire. He lived at court until 1086 when he went off to the Norman lands in southern Italy.

1074 is in many ways the high point of William's career. His absence from England for so long a period suggests that he was at last confident of his security there. The kingdom was left under the control of several major barons, of whom Richard ritz Gilbert, the elder brother of the castellan of Exeter, and William de Warenne were the most prominent. It was during his stay in Normandy that William was received into the confraternity of the great Burgundian abbey of Cluny, the most prestigious monastery in the whole of western Europe at this time. He thereby became a spiritual brother of Cluny, a benefactor for whose soul the monks would say regular prayers. Several other kings had a similar status.

William also appears to have refused invitations to intervene in the civil war developing in Germany. The chronicler Lampert of Hersfeld says that a false rumour spread in Germany that William was about to capture Charlemagne's old capital city of Aachen at the invitation of the Archbishop of Cologne. Another writer suggests that Henry IV, the King of Germany, sought William's aid. These stories are important because they show what men at this time thought William capable of achieving; it is noteworthy that although the rumour about the attack on Aachen was soon discovered to be without foundation, it was sufficient to make the German king abandon an expedition to Hungary and march instead to the Rhine. The German invitations must have been good ones to turn down. But throughout his career, William's ambitions, although large ones, were always securely grounded in practicability, and the German wars were both remote and irrelevant to his direct concerns. In 1074, the only clouds on William's horizon were the domestic tragedy of the death of his second son Richard in a hunting accident at some time between 1069 and 1074, the beginnings of domestic disharmony as quarrels started between him and his eldest son and heir Robert, and the first stirrings of the revival of the powers of the King of France and the Count of Anjou.

Seven

THE MAN AND HIS FAMILY

There is no contemporary portrait of William the Conqueror and we have only a slight notion of what he actually looked like. This is as should be expected, since early medieval artists had no interest in trying to produce a physical likeness of their subjects. The Bayeux Tapestry, for example, provides only a stylized representation of the king, and William's seal and the coins minted in his name all simply portray him in a manner intended to symbolize authority. The illuminated portrayals in twelfth-century manuscripts are all equally stylized. Subsequent ages have at times seen William in their own image, as in the celebrated eighteenth-century copy of a sixteenth-century portrait of William as a Renaissance prince which now hangs in the abbey church of St-Etienne of Caen. We can only hope in this case that proximity to the tomb inspired an empathy with his subject in the unknown artist!

William's tomb was first opened in 1522 and was said then to contain the skeleton of a large man with exceptionally long arms and legs. As a consequence of the tomb being despoiled by Calvinists later in the sixteenth century, only a single thigh bone survives now. This was examined in 1961 and again recently, and on this fragile basis it is thought that William was around 1.75 m (5 ft 10 in) tall, a remarkable height for a medieval man. Meagre as it is, this information does at least confirm the literary sources' statements that William was a man of exceptional appearance and strength. William of Poitiers, for example, related that Count Geoffrey Martel of Anjou believed William to be the greatest warrior on earth and that after an arduous foraging expedition during the Hastings campaign, William was still strong enough to carry back the hauberk (coat of chain mail) of an exceptional warrior such as William fitz Osbern, who was presumably exhausted by his exertions! William of Malmesbury illustrated the same point with the information that William's arms and shoulders were so powerful that he could draw a bow which other men could not even bend while spurring on a horse; a manoeuvre which would demand both great dexterity as a horseman and immense strength, since it would involve releasing the reins and controlling the horse only with

42. *William I, in a window at St Mary's Hall, Coventry, late fifteenth century.*

thighs and legs while wielding the bow. We also know that William became exceptionally fat in the last years of his life, with the size of his stomach becoming a matter for jest among his enemies. This corpulence looks to he an hereditary characteristic, since at least two of his sons also became fat; the apparently useful information that William was sparing in his consumption of food and drink appears in an early text, the *De Obitu Willelmi*, but the passage concerned has been shown to have been copied almost word for word from a ninth-century life. of the Emperor Charlemagne, and so may not be an actual description of William's appearance. One of its few independent passages does, however, indicate that William's voice was harsh and rough. He is generally said to have been majestic when sitting and standing.

The most celebrated, and also the most penetrating, assessment of William the Conqueror's character is the obituary which appears in the 'E' version of the Anglo-Saxon Chronicle. The author, an anonymous Englishman, had lived at court and had witnessed the king's doings. He praised his kingship and thought him more powerful than any of his predecessors. He brought peace and security: 'any honest man could travel over his kingdom without injury with his bosom full of gold, and no one dared strike another, however much wrong he had done him. And if any man had intercourse with a woman against her will, he was forthwith castrated.' The chronicler noted William's concern for Christianity and his encouragement of the Church: 'this country was very full of monks and they lived their life under the rule of St Benedict, and Christianity was such in his day that each man who wished followed whatever concerned his order.' He was gentle to good men who loved God, but immeasurably stern to those who resisted his will. He was 'a very wise man', but he was implacable and violent, and crushed all who opposed him. The greatest tribute that the chronicler could make to his power was that he had even imprisoned his own brother Odo; a king who could seize a man as mighty as Odo was surely a very impressive ruler indeed. The chronicler said that William dominated Wales and Scotland, and he thought that had William lived two years longer he would have conquered Ireland by peaceful means.

The author of the obituary also drew attention to grievous flaws: 'in his time people had much oppression and very many injuries'. Greed and avarice disfigured William's character. He took gold and hundreds of pounds of silver from his people unjustly and with little need. The collection of money became an obsession: he 'loved greediness above all'. He was addicted to hunting and imposed draconian laws to protect game. Blinding was the penalty for killing deer. 'He preserved the harts and boars, and loved the stags as much as if he were their father' – the purpose was of course not to conserve wild creatures, but to slaughter them. The author noted that there was widespread opposition to William's pursuit of the chase among both rich and poor, but that the king did not care. He lamented that one man should think himself so much above others and prayed that God would show mercy. He hoped that William's good characteristics would be an example to be imitated by those who sought the kingdom of Heaven, but that the bad would be avoided.

There is obvious exaggeration at some points in the chronicler's account. William never came, for example, to dominate Wales and Scotland as completely as suggested, and the peace described is clearly idealized. The chronicler was also a victim of the Norman Conquest and, despite his praise for William's achievements, is likely to have over-emphasized his faults. As we have seen in the last chapter, William does not appear to have cared much for England or the English and, as we will see even more clearly in the next chapter, his visits to his kingdom after 1072 were few in number and almost exclusively businesslike in purpose. The chronicler's image of his king was therefore likely to be that of an absentee ruler whose appearances in England were essentially displays of power, and which were usually associated with the taking of money to support wars in France. We need also to keep in mind that the obituary is very much a verdict on a great ruler in his last years, when age had hardened the autocratic characteristics in his personality. The vision presented is definitely one of a king and a conqueror; the pleasanter features which had helped William to mix with his warriors and build up loyalty, and which are mentioned in other sources which will be discussed below, have all become submerged in the display of majesty and power.

Much of the obituary's verdict is, however, confirmed in other sources. William's piety was consistently praised and will be examined later (see Chapter 10). We know that after his death in 1087 the royal treasury was found to contain a great mass of treasure. His cruelty was a theme taken up by several commentators, such as Guibert, Abbot of Nogent, who wrote an account of his own life and times during the late eleventh and early twelfth centuries, and commented that William treated those captured in war with a severity otherwise unknown in northern France. His opinion deserves respect because it was based on personal knowledge, his father having been one of William's prisoners after the Battle of Mortemer; apparently William did not ransom captives, as was customary, but kept them imprisoned for ever. In another source we hear of a prisoner whose limbs were being steadily crushed on William's orders. As we have already seen, William's devastation of northern England was condemned by Orderic Vitalis, who also put a list of William's supposed crimes into an imaginary speech by one of his enemies. These included his bastardy, disinheritance without just cause, murder, and the inequitable distribution of English estates. In an age when physical cruelty was common, William does seem to have been regarded as especially cruel.

William's passion for hunting was taken up by William of Malmesbury, who specifically condemned him for the creation of the New Forest in Hampshire, painting a grim picture of depopulation and the destruction of churches. He thought that the fact that two of William's sons – Richard and William – died as a result of hunting accidents in the Forest was surely a sign of God's disapproval. In his love of hunting, William was, however, no different from his aristocratic contemporaries; Edward the Confessor had been a great hunter and hawker and the Conqueror's own sons were devotees of the chase. Moreover, the task of repairing the king's deer-hedge was a well established duty of the people of England before 1066. Hunting was seen in the medieval period as an excellent training for war. Involving as it did either a chase behind the hounds or shooting at deer driven into an enclosure by the dogs, it was a means to acquire the basic skills of manoeuvring a horse at speed or shooting at moving targets. For William, a man who spent much of his life on campaign or preparing to campaign, hunting was a way to keep in condition.

Modern studies of the New Forest in Domesday Book cannot avoid the conclusion that depopulation and destruction did take place, although they show that William of Malmesbury certainly exaggerated its severity; the area had always been infertile and the population recorded there before the Normans came was a small one. William's zeal for the chase may well have been excessive and it was as a result of his love of hunting that significant areas of land were placed under the special jurisdiction of the forest law. But we need to remember that the clergy who wrote chronicles disliked this innovation of making large areas of land subject only to the king's special forest jurisdiction and in the twelfth century criticized too much hunting as a waste of time. As far as they were concerned, William was at fault on both counts.

William's cheerfulness, generosity and eloquence are referred to in a brief description of the reminiscences of his courtiers at his funeral in the late eleventh-century chronicle of the Burgundian Hugh of Flavigny. These may seem surprising qualities given William's sometimes brutal behaviour, but a general sociability and liberality appropriate to a prince is something which is either mentioned in other sources or can be deduced from them. Orderic, for example, says that William outshone contemporary northern French princes in magnificence, an indication that he knew the value of display. It is also clear that William had a code of correct behaviour for the battlefield and an appreciation of what was proper in relations between vassals and a lord, punishing, for example, one of his soldiers who hacked at Harold's corpse during the Battle of Hastings and the murderers of Earl Edwin because they had betrayed their lord. This suggests that William practised a primitive kind of chivalry. He was also capable of affection, and appears to have treated Simon, for a time Count of Amiens, Valois and the Vexin (1074-7), with kindness and even love. It is possible that he saw Simon, a great warrior with profound, if morbid, religious principles, who had been brought up in his household, as being in some ways made in his own image. William could display emotion through dramatic embraces and, according to Orderic, was much upset by the death of Earl Edwin. He could be forgiving to defeated enemies like Edgar the Ætheling, who was allowed to stay on at court after his final submission in 1074.

All this may amount to no more than saying that William knew and practised the standards of behaviour required of a king, giving, rewarding and punishing as convention required, and that he was at ease among his aristocratic companions, with whom a vigorous display of comradeship would have been essential. It is certain, however, that, if William was capable of warm and generous emotions, he could also sustain unrelenting hatred, as a succession of victims from Counts Guy of Brionne and William of Arques in the 1040s and 1050s through to his eldest son Robert and his brother Odo in the 1070s and 1080s testifies. As far as William is concerned, it is doubtful whether any emotion other than anger ever interfered more than fitfully with the exercise of power.

What passed for William's sense of humour is illustrated by an incident at the Winchester Easter council of 1069, where he demonstrated the perpetual security of a grant of property by making as if to thrust a knife into the palm of a quizzical abbot. The charter which describes the incident says that it was done as a joke, although it was one which must have required a cool nerve on both sides. Violent play-acting of this type was a feature of William's public behaviour; shortly before 1066 he had attacked a forester with an animal bone for querying another grant to a monastery. These look like masterful displays of power disguised under a cloak of camaraderie. William's sense of humour also extended to treating his children with mockery, and perhaps, malice. William of Malmesbury tells us that he nicknamed his stocky eldest son 'Curthose' (that is, 'Short Trousers') because he was so short, adding that the boy was going to be a great fighter. After Robert's first revolt, however, the king continually poured scorn on his son's failings in public.

One anecdote suggests that, at least in his youth, William possessed a sense of pathos. In the late 1040s, having exiled Lanfranc without giving him a hearing, he was moved to pity and laughter when he met him riding in poverty into exile. Lanfranc suggested that if he must be banished, it ought at least to be on a decent horse. The two were soon exchanging embraces. A more ambiguous anecdote appears in the twelfth-century *Vita Lanfranci* ('Life of Lanfranc'), which recounts that William was seated at one of the crown-wearings, which were a feature of his English kingship, wearing his crown and dressed in gold and jewels, with Archbishop Lanfranc seated beside him. A jester, seeing the king, cried out in mock adulation 'Behold, I see God! Behold, I see God!'. Lanfranc suggested that the fool be flogged, to which William agreed. Given that it was Lanfranc who suggested the punishment, it is possible that William would under normal circumstances have let the blasphemy pass. But we cannot tell whether this was because he was capable of laughing at his own pretensions or because he enjoyed the outrageous flattery.

William was a faithful husband, something which made him almost unique among eleventh-century rulers. His loyalty to his wife Mathilda was judged to be remarkable by all writers who touched on the subject. William's sexual restraint might therefore be explained simply by the success of his marriage. However, according to William of Malmesbury, rumours about possible impotence circulated during William's youth, and this may suggest that he was not in general especially interested in women. A nobleman's youth was a time when the young man was supposed to sow his wild oats and father a number of illegitimate children, and William's apparent indifference to this normal mode of behaviour suggests that it was a cause of concern. We do not know the basis of this coldness, but it is a reasonable supposition that it was at least partly based in strong and violent feelings about his illegitimacy. The circumstances of his birth were clearly a subject of universal knowledge throughout his life, since his nickname in a wide variety of late-eleventh and early twelfth-century sources is 'the Bastard'. His maiming of the defenders of Alençon, who made fun of his origins during the warfare of 1051 and 1052, points to an extreme sensitivity about the subject, and the fact that his apologists William of Jumièges and William of Poitiers do not mention his beginnings suggests that he felt shame about them. His strong support for the Church's campaign to stop priests keeping wives and mistresses appears to be another sign of a fundamental dislike of illicit sexual relationships.

Orderic thought that William kept an orderly and moral court. This, he considered was in contrast with his sons, Duke Robert and Kings William II and Henry I, whose courtiers were effeminate and dissolute, had long hair, and dressed extravagantly. In William's time men had worn sensible shoes and had had their hair cut short, a point illustrated by the Bayeux Tapestry where William is shown with a short haircut in a popular style whose pedigree went back to the Vikings. We need, however, to treat Orderic's strictures on his own time with some caution. He was a writer who frequently bemoaned the contemporary decline of moral standards and who looked back, as people often do, to a better and idealized past. William was undoubtedly in some ways puritanical, but his court was probably not that pure; it certainly contained jesters and the prevalent atmosphere was boisterous and military. The Conqueror's sons all learnt their looser moral habits somewhere, and Robert, the eldest, is known to have maintained an entourage which contained jesters, entertainers and prostitutes of both sexes during his father's lifetime. William probably had that puritanism which is common in those who have grown up in austere times, but flamboyant habits must have developed easily around him as he became successful and developed a taste for showing off the material rewards of wealth and power. A study of poetry presented to the Anglo-Norman kings has suggested that William's court was most definitely not a centre of culture.

William is said to have been a wise judge in lawsuits, but with no official judicial records to help us, we have to rely for evidence on a few accounts of cases preserved by churches which were involved in them. These are generally uninformative. William is normally said to have brought a court together and presided over it, leaving the task of finding a verdict to his assembled magnates. His personal authority was exercised only when the judges could not agree, as when, shortly before 1066 at Domfront, he had to decide on a dispute between the abbeys of St-Pierre-de-la-Couture at Le Mans and Marmoutier. More informatively, he dealt between 1068 and 1070 with a case where a boy had been substituted for a dead baby in order to provide an heir. The plot had misfired when the child's mother claimed him back after his pretended father's death and proved her right by passing unharmed through an ordeal by hot iron at Bayeux. William's verdict was to return the child to his mother and confiscate the property he was intended to inherit; the logical decision. As a whole the documents show William operating within the accepted contemporary framework whereby the assembled court acted as judges and in difficult cases the verdict was reached by ordeal. In property disputes William often preferred a negotiated settlement to an ordeal, showing simply that like everyone in authority at this date, he treated any form of ordeal as a last resort. He thereby displayed no rational distrust of ordeals, merely a conventional eleventh-century preference for a compromise between the two parties, rather than a clear-cut judgement in favour of one of them.

It is obvious from the above material that while William the Conqueror was a strong and forceful personality, there was nothing subtle about him, and his attitude to most matters was conventional. His record as Duke of Normandy and King of England shows that he brought a powerful sense of duty and responsibility to religion and kingship, protecting, and making gifts to, the Church and upholding the law with that savage ferocity which contemporary churchmen found appealing. He was passionate and capable of implacable anger, a puritan and a loyal husband, but by temperament probably most at home in the associated occupations of war and hunting. His closest companions and advisers – Lanfranc, William fitz Osbern, Roger de Montgommery and their like – show that he could select men of ability and retain their loyalty. As we shall see when we look at his relations with his family, he gives the impression of never truly understanding those who crossed him and his level of tolerance was low. The charges of cruelty and greed are impossible to dismiss. In the end it is the sheer brute power of the man which is astonishing; his dominating and direct approach frequently bulldozed all in its path and, while in politics and war he was often cautious, events like the decision to invade England, the destruction of northern England, and the making of Domesday Book in 1085-6 indicate someone possessed of the most ruthless political imagination and the most powerful inner will.

The Family

When we consider a noble family in the medieval period, we are not just thinking in terms of a group of people with whom proportionately more time was spent than with others, but in terms of a group who all had an interest in the same property and offices. In eleventh-century Normandy, as elsewhere at this time, government was an operation which involved most of the duke's close kindred and in which most of them participated. The office of duke was indivisible and passed from one occupant to the next, but the rest of his family were generally provided for with land or money and a place in the military household. The brothers of a reigning duke were usually endowed from within the ducal lands or put into the Church. Duke Richard II, for example, had made his brothers either into counts, with lands around a strategically placed castle and a unique status within Norman society, because only they and the duke bore the privileged title of count, or more rarely into bishops. As we saw in the early chapters of this book, Robert I's two half-brothers, who were therefore William's uncles, were made Count of Arques and Archbishop of Rouen early in William's minority. The daughters of the Norman rulers sometimes became nuns, but were more often used to cement political alliances with neighbours through diplomatic marriages. Like any medieval aristocratic family, however, that of the Norman dukes was not just a corporation involved in running its duchy like a family estate; it was also a potentially quarrelsome organism, likely to row over the distribution of property and power. The classic conflicts in eleventh-century society were between father and eldest son, when the father refused to give his impatient heir as much power as he thought he deserved, or between brothers over the division of the family property.

William's family group consisted of his closest circle of relatives; in charters he usually asks that prayers be said for his parents, himself and his wife, often his children, and perhaps his brothers. He used and relied on his family in the same way that previous Norman dukes had done, and as most princely families of the time did. After 1066 he extended the arrangements to reinforce the government of his cross-Channel realm by establishing his wife Mathilda, his brother Odo, and his eldest son Robert to act with the fullness of his authority in one of his territories at times when he was likely to be occupied for a lengthy period elsewhere. As the centre of his family corporation, William emerges as a domineering husband and father who expected his relatives to fit into an Anglo-Norman structure of government within which he kept the final say for himself. The scheme worked well and productively for more than a decade after 1066 during which the family was a united and successful group, but thereafter it began to fall apart as William quarrelled irrevocably with his eldest son Robert and his brother Bishop Odo in the later 1070s and 1080s. Although it is now impossible to grasp precisely the effect of Robert's waywardness and Odo's treachery, it is notable that these desertions coincided with a time when the wheel of fortune turned against William, and that the effects of the quarrels criss-crossed with the emergence of new rivals in northern France. The course and consequences of the disputes will be followed through as part of the narrative in Chapters Eleven and Twelve. In this chapter we will look mostly at the people in William's family and the roles he assigned to them.

William's wife Mathilda, whom he married in or shortly after the year 1050, came from an ancestry which was much more prestigious than her husband's and undoubtedly added lustre to his authority; her mother was Adela, the daughter of the French King Robert the Pious (996-1031) and her father's family, the Counts of Flanders, were related to both the Kings of France and Germany. She was about five years younger than her husband. It is often suggested that she was no more than 1.3 m (4 ft 3 in) tall, a theory based on an examination of the bones in her tomb in the abbey church of La Trinité of Caen. However, since the tomb was despoiled during religious riots in the sixteenth century, the bones may not be hers. It is in any case unlikely that a woman of so small a size could have borne numerous healthy children at regular intervals; seven children were living in 1066, of whom three were sons and four daughters, and a further son and daughter were born between 1066 and 1069. All these offspring were fit; four lived into their sixties and beyond, while the lives of two of the others were cut short by accidental deaths. Mathilda predeceased her husband, dying on 2 November 1083.

Orderic, perhaps copying William of Poitiers, says that Mathilda was fair of face, devout, learned, the bearer of many children, and a generous giver of alms. She witnessed charters alongside her husband throughout the entire period of their marriage and on occasion they are said to have acted together in the exercise of authority. In 1066 she provided the ship in which William crossed the Channel and after 1066 she sometimes remained behind in Normandy with the authority to act in his place; this was certainly so in 1066-7, 1067-8 and 1071 while William was struggling to subdue the English, and was probably so in 1075-6 when there was a major rebellion in England. It is possible that on all these occasions she was acting as guardian for their eldest son Robert, who had already been nominated as heir to Normandy and is actually called duke in a few charters and by William of Jumièges. His authority must, however, have been circumscribed by his mother's, since a number of charters show that it was apparently only Mathilda who could confirm grants which would normally have required William's confirmation. She was also generously endowed with lands in England and at times apparently shared William's authority there, as when she persuaded Bishop Osbern of Exeter to return a church to Bishop Giso of Wells. She made many benefactions to churches and in this area acted on William's behalf when he appeared to have been remiss. It was Mathilda, for example, who made a donation to the abbey of Le Bec when she and William had to miss the dedication ceremony in 1077, and it was again Mathilda who paid for a tomb in Rome for Simon, the former Count of Amiens, Valois and the Vexin. She encouraged her husband's religious life and was praised by Pope Gregory VII for doing so. But she also joined in the ransacking of the English Church after 1066, ordering the abbey of Abingdon to send her some precious ornaments, and when the monks sent a selection which she thought inadequate, demanding more.

Mathilda is portrayed in all the sources as an effective and devoted spouse, the very essence of the ideal medieval wife and queen. We may in fact wonder whether we can get anywhere near the woman's personality, since so many of these qualities are those of stereotyped motherly and wifely devotion and pious good works. The most obvious signs of individuality are her distress at the quarrel between her husband and their eldest son after 1077 and her pride in her royal ancestry. She tried to soften William's harshness towards Robert and, having failed, she incurred his fury by sending Robert money in exile. Even after this, she was ready to infuriate him further by sending more money, an act which placed those around her in great danger; William even ordered one of her servants to be blinded, a fate he escaped only by becoming a monk. Her pride in her connections with the French royal house is shown by the names of her children and her epitaph. Three out of five daughters were given her own name, her mother's (Adela) and her grandmother's (Constance); her first three sons were named after Norman dukes, but the fourth was called Henry, after her uncle, King Henry I of France. In the same vein, her epitaph, which can still be seen on her tombstone in the abbey of La Trinité at Caen, says she was 'sprung from royal stem; child of a Flemish duke; her mother was Adela, daughter of a King of France, sister of Henry, Robert's royal son, married to William, most illustrious king'.

William's brother Odo was prominent in William's counsels from soon after his appointment to the bishopric of Bayeux in either late 1049 or early 1050 and became as good as indispensable to William's government after 1066. The son of Herleva and Herluin de Conteville, the exact date of his birth is unknown; it is likely to have been around the year 1035. We can be certain that when he was given the bishopric of Bayeux, he was well below the minimum legal age of thirty for a bishop. The appointment was a blatantly political one, part of the process by which William extended his authority throughout his duchy during the years after Val-ès-Dunes. On reaching adulthood, he began to make his cathedral and its town a centre of grand architecture and artistic and literary patronage, a kind of churchman's equivalent of William's Caen. He first acted as his brother's deputy in England in 1067, alongside William fitz Osbern. After fitz Osbern's death in 1071 he must have become even more important and numerous chroniclers tell us that after that date it was Odo who ruled England when William was in Normandy. From Domesday Book and other sources we can see that it was Odo, and Odo alone, of the deputies used by William who could act with the fullness of royal authority, although the period of his power was probably confined to the awkward time between late 1077 and the summer of 1080 when William was preoccupied with and kept in Normandy by the quarrel with his son, Robert Curthose. Odo was also Earl of Kent from soon after 1066 and possessed immense estates scattered throughout the south and east of England. From the highest levels of power downwards in Norman England, we encounter men whose careers he had advanced. One protégé was the first Norman Archbishop of York; another, the notorious Rannulf Flambard, the chief minister of William's son and successor in England, King William II. There were also many among William's secular servants who carried out the mundane administrative tasks of organizing the Norman conquest of England who owed their positions to Odo; Adam fitz Hubert, who was a Domesday Book commissioner in the West Midlands, or Hugh de Port, sheriff of Hampshire and a royal representative in several shires, are two good examples from among many.

It is tempting to portray William's brother Odo as the evil genius of the Norman Conquest. Orderic provides us with a scathing portrait of a regent who abused his responsibilities, oppressing the poor and unjustly seizing England's wealth. His estates in Domesday Book supply numerous instances of apparently unjust acquisitions. A chronicler at the abbey of Evesham called him 'a ravening wolf' after he had carried out an enquiry into the abbey's estates, and redistributed them, taking a number for himself. On the other hand, a record from the archives of Rochester cathedral tells how the church lost an estate because an inquest jury had been intimidated by the Norman sheriff of Cambridgeshire, but recovered it because Odo persisted with the enquiry until the jury admitted perjury. At Bayeux, despite his frequent absences, he was, in a material sense, a great success as a bishop. He built a new cathedral, parts of which can still be seen. He assembled a large chapter, provided grants for young scholars to study at schools outside Normandy, patronized poets, and made his bishopric extremely wealthy. And of course it was Odo who commissioned the magnificent Bayeux Tapestry, made in England, and probably displayed at the dedication of his new cathedral on 14 July 1077.

Odo was an extravagant, larger-than-life character, who revelled in the rewards brought by Norman achievement. The final bitter quarrel between William and Odo, which occurred in 1082, should not be allowed to disguise the fact that William depended heavily on Odo and owed a lot to him and to the men whose careers he had supported. It is important to recognize that for a very long time William confirmed and presumably approved of his wayward brother's acts. In the end, it was a combination of Odo's consistently grand ambitions and the regular Norman diet of success which in 1082 involved him in an extraordinary scheme to purchase the papacy for himself (see further, Chapter 12). William treated this as a betrayal and imprisoned him, accusing Odo of taking over, for service abroad, knights who were needed in England. His bitterness was probably fuelled further by Odo's high-handedness and arrogance while acting as regent. There is also a marvellous scene on the Bayeux Tapestry where Odo, William and Count Robert of Mortain are portrayed in council before the Battle of Hastings. It is Odo who is doing the talking, with William listening attentively. It is almost as if the Tapestry was trying to show Odo as the architect of the Norman Conquest.

William's other brother, Robert, was a less colourful character. William of Malmesbury even described him as a slow and ponderous man, but despite this he made a career which was typical of that required of a brother of a Norman duke. He was given the frontier county of Mortain by William a few years before 1066, and after 1066 received vast lands in England, including most of Cornwall, a section of Yorkshire, a block of land around the landing site of Pevensey, and estates of varying sizes in many other counties. His most obvious achievements were as a soldier in many of his brother's campaigns; in the scene on the Bayeux Tapestry mentioned above, which shows the council of war before the Battle of Hastings, he is shown unsheathing his sword ready for battle. But he also instituted major religious and economic developments in the county of Mortain and his charters, on close study, demonstrate a remarkable administrative thoughtfulness. His benefactions raised his father's monastic foundation at Grestain to the level of a major abbey. If Odo was an exciting and difficult character, Robert appears to have been a competent, dogged and loyal man. It is noteworthy that he was the only member of William's close family present when he died.

William's sons were named, in order of birth, Robert, Richard, William, and Henry. Once out of early childhood, all four regularly witnessed charters and, with the exception that the eldest son Robert did not apparently cross to England until 1080, were very frequently in their father's company. This suggests that, with the partial exception of Robert, they were kept within William's military household, the core of a group of boisterous young warriors which comprised the young bloods of Norman aristocratic society, living military and very masculine lives, and enjoying a high measure of sexual licence. There are no signs of any attempt being made to marry the boys off after the early betrothal of Robert to a sister of Count Herbert II of Maine. A common kind of medieval arranged marriage, its purpose was to try to strengthen the debatable Norman hold on Maine. But it came to nothing because the girl died before the marriage could take place. It is interesting that the acquisition of England's immense wealth did nothing to change William's typically early medieval patriarchal attitudes: there was never any question of giving land to his sons, or of using them to forge political alliances.

Robert, the eldest son, is usually thought to have been born around 1053 and witnessed charters regularly for some years before 1066. Orderic, who was biased against him, portrays him as a feckless and ungrateful young man, easily influenced by those around him and unable to say no to requests for money. He was certainly dissolute and kept a lavish and immoral court during his father's lifetime. His temperament is illustrated by the story of a woman who one day turned up at court claiming that her two children were Robert's sons. He denied this, until the woman proved her case by ordeal by hot iron, carrying the hot iron rod and presumably recovering sufficiently quickly from the burns to be declared to be telling the truth. The boys were then acknowledged as Robert's sons and brought up at court. Robert was an outstanding soldier who was popular among the aristocracy. He is said to have been talkative, generous and courageous.

Robert had been acknowledged as the heir to Normandy before 1066 and subsequently on at least two further occasions before 1078, and had also done homage to the Count of Anjou for Maine. He often appears in charters as 'count' or 'duke' of the Normans, and is also frequently called Count of Maine where he confirms charters and is even described in one of 1076 as governing the county. He must have enjoyed considerable personal independence during the late 1060s and early 1070s when William was deeply occupied in England, a period when Robert passed through his late teens and built up a military household containing the younger sons of many of William's most powerful nobles. But once William was back in Normandy for lengthy periods after 1072, he kept overall control and gave Robert little true responsibility in either Normandy or Maine. This is said to have been the basic cause of their disagreements; Orderic has Robert accuse William of treating him like a hired soldier. Because Robert's life was ultimately a failure, in that he lost Normandy to his brother Henry I and died in 1134 as his prisoner, it is easy with hindsight to magnify his deficiencies. But between the 1060s and the 1080s his character must have seemed a light relief to many younger nobles in comparison with his father's greed and puritanism. The clash of father and son was surely one of temperaments as well as an example of the age-old struggle between impatient youth and an unyielding older generation.

The second son Richard, born around 1055, was taken to England after 1066 in a way that his elder brother was not, and was killed there in a hunting accident in the New Forest between 1069 and 1074. Like many who die

Plate 1. Duke Robert I of Normandy, William the Conqueror's father, from a twelfth-century manuscript. (Courtesy of Trevor Rowley)

Plate 2. The Abbey church of St-Etienne, Caen, founded by William and where he was buried. (Courtesy of Trevor Rowley)

Plate 3. Archbishop Lanfranc, William's friend and ally in the reshaping of the Church in England, from a twelfth-century document. (Courtesy of Trevor Rowley)

The following series of photographs was shot at a re-enactment of the Battle of Hastings in the October 2000. Such events, as well as providing fun for all involved, often give an accurate representation not just of the sights, sounds and spectacle of medieval combat but also of arms, armour and equipment.

Of particularly high accuracy, and worthy of special note, are:

Plate 5: Eleventh-century arms, including a round shield of a type used by some Anglo-Saxons, a helmet with nasal guard and a typical sword of the period with simple quillions and a 'brazil-nut' pommel. Such swords were light and easy to wield by trained soldiers. In the centre is an early form of crossbow, which was spanned by the bowman placing his feet against the bowstave on either side of the stock or tiller and drawing the string sharply backwards. The bow arms might be made of wood or, as here, of a composite mixture of horn and sinew. Such weapons had a slow rate of fire but Norman sources speak of their great penetrative power and their lethal impact on the well-armoured Anglo-Saxon housecarls.

Plate 7: A typical eleventh-century shield, made of laminated wood edged with an iron rim and a metal boss to protect the hand. The 'kite shape' design was particularly suited to cavalry warfare, as it protected both the chest and left side of a knight in the saddle, and was supported by a long strap around the rider's neck. Its size, however, offered equally good protection for foot combat, and shields of this type, together with round shields of an older design, were also used by the Anglo-Saxons at Hastings. The Bayeux Tapestry shows many shields painted with geometric or, as here, zoomorphic devices. True heraldry, however, was only to develop in the twelfth century, when devices became hereditary and began to conform to rules of colour and design.

Plate 9: A Norman knight, wearing a mail shirt hauberk, the principal defensive armour of the period. The integral hood, or coif, padded inside for comfort and protection, was fastened across the face by a flap or 'ventail'. the helmet is of the type known as 'Spangenhelm', made of plates rivetted to a frame, and has a nasal guard to protect the face. Only the wealthiest lords, such as Duke William himself, would have worn mail leggings (chausses).

Plate 15: A Norman archer., whose only defensive armour is his helmet with a nasal guard. Most infantry could not afford the highly expensive mail shirt, though, as here, they might carry a sword as a side-arm. His principal weapon is the longbow, usually made of yew or elm, able to achieve a range of well over 200 yards. Norman superiority in archers and crossbowmen at Hastings was one of the crucial factors in William's success.

(All photographs reproduced courtesy of Dr M.K. Lawson)

Plate 4.

Plate 5.

Plate 6.

Plate 7.

Plate 8.

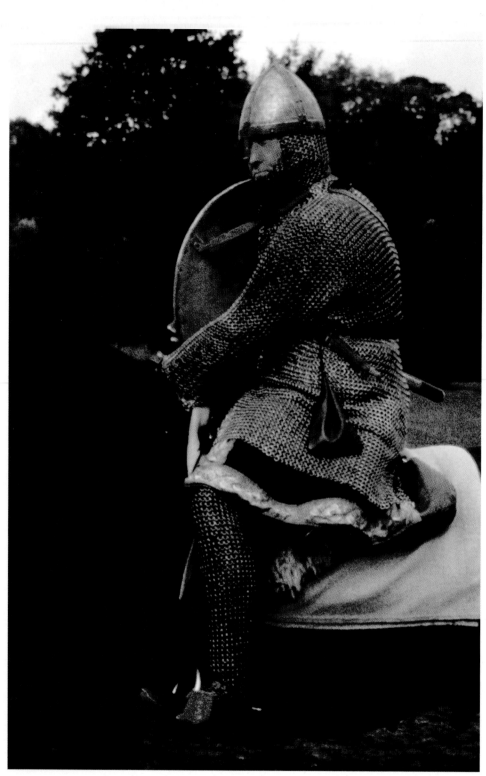

Plate 9.

Plate 10.

Plate 11.

Plate 12.

Plate 13.

Plate 14.

Plate 15.

young, he was considered to have been of exceptional promise. Versions of his death suggest either that he hit an overhanging bough or, less credibly, expired in a cloud of poisonous gas. The third son, William, his father's eventual successor in England, was born around 1060 and witnessed charters from 1074. The fourth, Henry, was born in 1069 and witnessed charters from 1080. Although William and Henry were later to be kings, neither had particularly good prospects until late in their father's reign. William is supposed to have been his father's favourite. He grew in some ways in his father's image: strong both mentally and physically, and a fine soldier. He was more humorous than his father, with a particular liking for shocking high-principled clerics. His homosexuality was notorious, and, as king, his court was dissolute and rapacious. Henry was eighteen when his father died. He may at first have been destined for the Church, but this idea was apparently speedily abandoned since he was knighted in 1086. He may have received a little more education than his brothers, although all were illiterate, like their father. In the 1080s Henry appears to have stayed in England when the rest of the family were in France. In contrast with Robert, neither William nor Henry apparently found any difficulty in remaining loyal to their father, and William was even wounded fighting against Robert at the Battle of Gerberoi in 1079.

Because we tend usually to be poorly informed about early medieval women, it is difficult to know who William's daughters were, let alone what they did. The sources not only disagree with one another about their names, but the same author (Orderic) can give different lists of the names in different parts of the same work. There were probably five girls, of whom three, Cecilia, Adela and Constance, had clearly discernible careers. Cecilia was given in 1066 as a novice at her mother's abbey of La Trinité of Caen, when she would have been around seven years old. She lived to a great age, becoming abbess in1113, and dying in 1127, a highly respected figure, the recipient, for example, of a poem from the noted intellectual Baldric of Bourgueil. She was also probably responsible for the choir of the abbey of La Trinité, with its superb capital sculpture. Adela, the youngest, was married to Stephen, Count of Blois-Chartres, in c. 1080 and bore him numerous children, including the future King Stephen. She has a reputation for being formidable, despatching her husband to rejoin the First Crusade after he had returned home from the siege of Antioch. Like Cecilia, she lived to be old, dying in 1137, having become a nun. Constance was married to Alan IV Fergant, Count of Brittany, in 1086, but died in 1090.

The other daughters are more shadowy figures. There are stories of betrothals to Harold, Earl of Wessex, Earl Edwin of Mercia, and perhaps to a Spanish king. All may have involved the same daughter; according to Orderic, the girl betrothed to Harold was also betrothed to the Spanish king, but she disliked the idea of marriage in so remote a land and died on the journey, a virgin. This possible Spanish match apart, the marriages arranged for William's daughters were matches with northern French princes in the traditional manner of the Norman dukes. Kingship did not give William any grand ideas; indeed, the marriages of the two girls who married the Counts of Brittany and Blois-Chartres must have been related to continuing worries about Normandy's security. The same conservative policy is evident in the case of William's one sister or half-sister, Adelaide, who married three northern French nobles. A sister of Bishop Odo and Count Robert, named Muriel, was considered less important and was married within the Norman aristocracy to a *vicomte* of the Cotentin.

William's treatment of his relatives followed traditional patterns and his children were brought up in a thoroughly conventional way. As the centre of a family corporation, William was for a long time highly successful – and even at its worst, William's family could not rival the Angevin Henry II's notorious brood, with their legendary squabbling and numerous acts of treachery. But William's quarrels with his son and brother were a major blot on the last decade of his life. And their significance was far more than simply domestic. Because a traditional arrangement had broken down, government was impaired, enemies were given hope, and the future after William's death, whenever it might occur, was made to look uncertain. Family life had profound implications for the history of William's Anglo-Norman dominions. Its difficulties encouraged and intertwined with the revival of the power of the King of France and the Count of Anjou which caused so many problems in the last twelve years of his life. The matter of the succession after William's death raises questions about his attitude to the territories which had been brought together by his conquests. The resumption of hostilities in northern France will be described in the last two chapters of this book; William's treatment of his cross-Channel dominions, a crucial dimension in any estimate of his achievements, is the theme of the next chapter.

Eight

William and his Anglo-Norman Dominions

After 1066 William's response to the problem of ruling lands on both sides of the English Channel was simply to expand his régime of constant travelling to cover England and Maine, as well as Normandy. His household remained the centre of government as it had been before 1066, although, as we shall see, its itinerary was a carefully arranged one which presumably reflected what William considered to be the most efficient means of exercising power. But before we start to look in detail at William's method of governing his cross-Channel dominions, it is worth pointing out that the picture we mostly obtain from the sources, of William's movements being determined by war or preparations for war and by great ceremonial occasions at major residences or churches, can be misleading. Chronicles tend to concentrate on the major events, and charters were frequently confirmed at great courts held at palaces, which means that the sources rarely mention the part of William's life which was less structured and informal. It is interesting, therefore, when a charter mentions him confirming a grant to a monastery while sitting on a carpet at a small village between the forester's house and the church. In 1069 he was hunting in the Forest of Dean when he must have known that the Danes were coming. This is not a display of sang-froid in the face of extreme danger; it is a sign that William's apparently ceaseless and purposeful travelling must have been punctuated by frequent diversions of which we usually know nothing.

William probably crossed the Channel nineteen times between 1067 and his death on 9 September 1087. Out of the 239 months of his life between the Battle of Hastings and his death, he spent around 145 in Normandy – with a small number of these being spent in Maine – and 94 in England. Since he was almost continuously in England between 1066 and 1072 completing the conquest, the preponderance of time spent in Normandy after 1072 is quite staggering; out of the 170 months between his probable crossing time in 1072 and his death, around 130 were spent in Normandy or Maine. As far as England was concerned, he was virtually an absentee ruler between 1072 and 1080, although after 1080 he did divide his time somewhat more equally between the two sides of the Channel. This great disparity is partly explained by his being kept continuously in Normandy between the middle of 1076 and the later months of 1080 by the renewed activity of his traditional northern French enemies and by the revolt of his eldest son, but the clear overall impression is that his personal preference was always for residence in Normandy. His four recorded visits to England after 1072 were all associated with a highly practical purpose: namely, in 1075-6 and 1082-3 to deal with revolts, the former of which received assistance from Denmark; in 1080-1 to restore order after his four-year absence in France; and in 1085-6 to prepare to confront another invasion from Denmark and to preside over the making of Domesday Book.

The evidence of William's travelling also indicates that his itinerary after 1072 was usually confined within fairly narrow geographical limits. He apparently visited Britain north of a line from London to Gloucester only when political crises required him to do so and all his known visits to Maine were to deal with invasions or rebellions – surprising as it may seem, there is in fact no record at all of a personal visit to the north of England after 1072. There may of course have been journeys about which nothing is known but, certainly, as the narrative in Chapters Eleven and Twelve will show, it is hard to see how William could have fitted in much more travelling than we know about on his four visits to England. The heart of William's realm therefore consisted of Normandy and the old Anglo-Saxon kingdom of Wessex. In consequence, we should not think of William as a genuinely Anglo-Norman ruler following an itinerary which covered all his lands. While Normandy was very much home-base, in England, when he was there, his itinerary resembled that of Edward the Confessor, who had usually remained south of a line from Gloucester to London. It is probable that, although he was never willing to relinquish overall control over any part of his territories, he in practice relied in large measure on delegating power around the fringes of his dominions. Several districts known as *comtés* around the Norman frontier were in the hands of counts who controlled a major castle. In Maine his power was based on a group of trusted supporters and a garrison in Le Mans, and much of northern and western England was organized around territorial castellanries.

William's Channel crossings were just an exotic aspect of his normal itineration. We have little specific information about them, but since chroniclers expressed surprise when his son William II made a hasty crossing in stormy weather in 1099, it is likely that both he and his father took great care before embarking on the sea. Later evidence shows that kings could be detained for long periods in a Channel port waiting for a favourable wind – William II was once held up for six weeks at Hastings – but no similar setbacks are known to have befallen his father, except of course in 1066. While on the sea, or waiting to cross, William would, as always, have been surrounded by his chaplains, his household knights, his servants and some of the great magnates. The size of the flotilla which would have accompanied him is never recorded, although a possible pointer is that in 1170 Henry II crossed the Channel amidst a-fleet of twenty-five ships. In Wiilliam's day, the boats must have resembled the Viking ships portrayed on the Bayeux Tapestry. These could be large; the tragic 'White Ship', for example, which sank off the Norman coast in November 1120, taking to the bottom the only son of King Henry I and numerous younger members of magnate houses, is said to have contained 300 people. Since the ships could be dragged up on to the beach at the end of their journey, there would have been no need for extensive harbour facilities. The ships would be equipped with both oars and a sail, but the oars would probably be used only to clear the coast and make land on the other side. The captain of William's ship was a man named Stephen, son of Airard, who appears in several places in Domesday Book. If he can be identified with the Stephen the steersman who had two houses in Southampton, then we have a clue to the port William may have used most regularly. Southampton of course happened to be convenient for Winchester and the hunting grounds of the New Forest.

In Normandy after 1066 William continued to frequent the same main residences that he had used before 1066. At various times the sources show him at Fécamp, Rouen, Bonneville-sur-Touque and Caen, on several occasions among a vast concourse of nobles and warriors. With regard to his itinerary in England, an entry in the Anglo-Saxon Chronicle' for 1087 announces that:

> ...three times a year he wore his crown, as often as he was in England. At Easter he wore it at Winchester, at Whitsuntide at Westminster, and at Christmas at Gloucester, and then there were with him all the powerful men from all over England, archbishops and bishops, abbots and earls, thegns and knights.

The crown-wearings referred to in this passage have been much discussed by historians. An obvious problem with the chronicler's statement is that William was not at the places he mentions all that often. Easter was spent at Winchester on five occasions in 1068, 1069, 1070, 1072 and 1086, Whitsun at Westminster only in 1068 and 1086, and Christmas at Gloucester only in 1080 and 1085. Another difficulty is that William is sometimes known to have spent the religious festivals in the 'wrong' place: in 1070 and 1072, for example, he spent Easter at Windsor and in 1081 at Winchester. There may of course have been other crown-wearings that we do not know about, but given the prolonged absences in Normandy, there cannot have been that many. The most convincing interpretation of the passage is that the chronicler was stating an ideal or a policy, a pattern which William wanted to follow in the later years of his reign – when he can be shown to have frequently been at the 'right' centre at the 'right' time – rather than an invariable practice. What is important above all is the significance of these occasions for William's kingship. The places chosen were major residences of William's immediate Old English predecessors, and in this sense he was therefore stressing continuity. But as there was no serious English precedent for these crown-wearings, they were in reality novel displays of Norman power. They must have become all the more impressive when William was such an irregular visitor to his kingdom. As he had shown from the very beginning of his reign in England, kingship for William implied a spectacular display of majesty and power.

The splendour of the greatest of such gatherings, whether they were crown-wearings in England or courts in Normandy, can in some measure be grasped from the witness lists of charters drawn up while they were in progress. For example, an original charter for the abbey of St-Denis, dating from the Winchester assembly of Easter 1069, is attested by William, Mathilda, one of their sons, both William's brothers, William fitz Osbern, the two English archbishops, five other English bishops, Bishop Geoffrey of Coutances, and many others. A similar gathering in Normandy at Caen, in the year 1080, is illustrated by the famous *pancarte* of the abbey of Lessay, a document which was sadly destroyed when the archives of the Norman *département* of Manche were bombed in 1944. It shows not only a gathering at which many Norman magnates were present, but also, because some of the names are obviously written in a different handwriting, that other attestations to a charter of this type might be added at a later date. Since no building survives from the Conqueror's time in which one of these assemblies took place, the nearest we can come in physical terms to one of them is either Westminster Hall, now part of the Houses of Parliament, built for King William II, but greatly refashioned and reroofed by King Richard II, or the *Salle de l'Echiquier* in the castle at Caen, built for Henry I.

Over the period from 1066 to 1087 cross-Channel government came to be closely integrated around the movements of William's itinerant household. A system of communications developed after 1066 which kept William in touch with what was happening throughout his lands and allowed his will to be known throughout his dominions. The best illustrations of its operation appear in the letters which Archbishop Lanfranc wrote to various correspondents during the revolt which took place in England in 1075 while William was in Normandy. He wrote, for example, to advise William that the rebellion was under control and that there was no need for him to return to England. He also mentioned that he was sending a monk with the letter who could be trusted; this was presumably a special emissary to discuss the situation with the king and report back. In a letter written to Bishop Walcher of Durham, Lanfranc supplied advance information, which must have been brought by special courier from Normandy, that the king was about to cross the Channel to England, as well as the news, which had come from William, that there was going to be an invasion from Denmark. In another of the letters, Lanfranc passed on to the rebel Earl Roger of Hereford the details of an order which William had given to his sheriffs.

Other sources show that routine administrative orders could be issued from one part of William's lands to take effect in another; in one case, a writ dealing with the lands of the abbey of St Augustine at Canterbury was despatched to England during the time of the dedication of Bayeux cathedral in July 1077. During long absences from either Normandy or England, deputies were usually appointed. When the absences were likely to be unusually lengthy, a member of William's family would be endowed with full authority to act in his name; thus, Bishop Odo filled this role in England between 1077 and 1080 and Mathilda did the same in Normandy at intervals between 1066 and 1071. Specific individuals could be deputed to hear important land disputes and Bishop Geoffrey of Coutances was especially prominent in this role. But William could always be personally approached wherever he was and he could always communicate directly with local officials on both sides of the Channel, even when there was a formally constituted regent or deputy.

William's military household can also be shown to have made a major contribution to cross-Channel integration. The evidence for its activities is fragmentary, but nonetheless persuasive; after all, if earlier English kings and later Norman ones possessed such a force, then William surely did so too. It served as a kind of standing army. In the last years of the reign – the period for which the evidence is best – it is said by Orderic to have been left by William to conduct a war in Maine in 1084-86. Its leaders were drawn from the topmost ranks of the Anglo-Norman aristocracy; in this particular case, Count Alan the Red of Brittany, William de Warenne and Count William of Evreux. The *familia*, or part of it, was also at Lincoln during the great campaign of 1069. William's military household appears to have divided its time and manpower between permanent attendance on the king and garrison duty at strategic fortifications. We can reasonably infer that garrisons placed in William's castles throughout Normandy, England and Maine would often be drawn from it, as well as from knights performing obligatory military service. The *familia*'s presence at strategic castles would explain the constant readiness of Norman frontier castles when attacked, or the ability of Roger d'Ivry to beat off the surprise attack made by William's rebellious son Robert on the castle of Rouen in late 1077 or 1078.

The Relationship of Normandy, England and Maine

The institution known as the *Laudes Regiae* and William's use of a seal to authenticate charters are important developments which illuminate his kingship and provide the best evidence for his conception of the relationship between the various lands he ruled. The *Laudes* were ritual chants sung during Mass at great religious festivals, and in England were therefore an aspect of the great crown-wearings. They honoured the powers wielding authority in Heaven and on Earth and, from William's point of view, were a dramatic and very public assertion of his place within that hierarchy. The *Laudes* sung in Normandy, for example, began with the choir singing in Latin 'Christ conquers, Christ reigns, Christ rules' (*Christus vincit, Christus regnat, Christus imperat*), which was repeated by the congregation. The choir then called on Christ's support for the pope, the King of the Franks, Duke William of the Normans, all bishops, and so on, with the congregation interposing the *Christus vincit* after each appeal. *Laudes* may have been sung for William as Duke of Normandy before 1066, but it is more likely that they were instituted after the triumph at Hastings and that they were first sung at Easter 1067. No *Laudes* are known in England before 1066; like the crown-wearings, they were an innovation which followed the Norman Conquest, borrowed from the French and German monarchies, and presumably devised by clergy who wished to flatter the new king. It is probable that special *Laudes* were written for Mathilda's coronation in 1068, a sign of the importance of that occasion.

Six genuine specimens of William's seal survive for the period from 1066 to 1087. There is no fully convincing evidence that he had a seal as Duke of Normandy before 1066, while Edward the Confessor certainly did have a seal as King of England; like the *Laudes* therefore, the seal was a development which drew attention to William's new and imposing dignity. On the seal's obverse is shown a knight on horseback with the inscription + *HOC NORMANNORUM WILLELMUM NOSCE PATRONUM SI* (With this seal recognize here William, patron of the Normans, or) and on the reverse, a

43 and 44 (above). The obverse and reverse of William's seal, marking respectively his authority as Duke of Normandy and King of England.

45 (right). Edward the Confessor's royal seal, clearly the model for William's.

king seated in majesty and the inscription + *HOC ANGLIS REGEM SIGNO FATEARIS EUNDEM* (with this acknowledge him as King of the English). This seal was a display of authority to all who received a royal writ or charter and had great symbolic significance. The side showing a king in majesty demonstrated the sacred character of kingship, a responsibility exercised by God's gift, and was obviously copied from Edward the Confessor's seal, which had a king in majesty and the inscription + *SIGILLUM EDUUARDI ANGLORUM BASILEI* (the seal of Edward, King of the English) on both sides. The knight on William's seal is the earliest surviving specimen of an equestrian seal; it appears to emphasize William's powers of lordship and may be derived from French princely models. William's seal appears to have been used in the same way as Edward the Confessor's, being attached to documents known as writs, and to the occasional diploma.

Both the *Laudes* and the seal demonstrate that William saw himself as the ruler of separate territories, rather than of a single unified cross-Channel realm. The essential differences, for example, between the English and the Norman *Laudes* are that in Normandy William was acclaimed as a duke, not as a king, and that prayers for his safety were preceded by prayers for the French king's, which can only reflect the fact that Normandy was within the kingdom of the Franks and that the Norman duke was traditionally his vassal. In the same way, the seal was fundamentally a personal seal which drew attention to William's two titles, and made no attempt to present him as the ruler of a single unified realm.

The titles given to William in contemporary charters also emphasize the conceptual separateness of Normandy and England. The fact that William is often described in them only as a king, with no reference to his being either Duke of Normandy or Count of Maine, on first glance suggests an integration of the two lands. This is, however, misleading. In England it is to be expected that he would usually be called simply 'king' (*rex*), since he was only a king there. Although William is on some occasions described as exercising 'royal' authority in Normandy, as, for example, when Bishop Geoffrey of Coutances acted 'on royal authority' in a judicial suit in 1076, this only means that William's personal authority was kingly because 'king' was his most prestigious title. As several literary sources say, William had been personally transformed from a duke into a king by the result of the Battle of Hastings. Normandy, however, remained a duchy whose ruler was entitled either a duke or a count, even though after 1066 William happened to be a king. Norman charters describe William in a bewildering variety of ways, but titles such as 'lord of Normandy and, having been so created by hereditary right, King (*basileus*) of the English' or 'the Duke of the Normans, who acquired the kingdom of England by war' or 'King William, conqueror of England, and Duke of the Normans' leave no doubt that their writers still thought of William as 'Duke of the Normans' in Normandy. On occasions, there are definite signs that ducal authority in Normandy acquired a new and more majestic aura as a result of William's kingship; a number of Norman charters, for example, were prepared for sealing, and two Norman documents refer to a tax called geld, meaning presumably an arbitrary kingly exaction, rather than a new tax resembling Danegeld. But the essential separateness of the territories William ruled is made emphatically clear in a contemporary original charter which announced that the penalty for infringing its terms was to pay a fine to King William or to whichever count should in future rule Normandy.

It is fully in accord with the idea of Normandy, England and Maine as three distinct territories that there are few signs of governmental assimilation between them. William's policy was to sustain the essentially different characteristics of the governments of the territories under his rule.

Administrative organization in Normandy and England after 1066 continued along the distinctive patterns which had existed before that date. The charters written in William's name in England were essentially a continuation of the writ and diploma forms of Anglo-Saxon England, while in Normandy the diplomas from 1066 to 1087 are in the same style as their equivalents from before 1066. Similarly, William's administration in England continued what was basically the same system of minting coin which had existed before 1066, whereby numerous mints throughout the kingdom produced good-quality silver pennies, which were replaced on a three-year cycle, and were the only coins accepted as legal tender in the kingdom. In Normandy, both before and after 1066, coins were of poor standard and low silver content, were rarely reminted, and were not the only coins to circulate; coins minted at Le Mans, for example, were freely used in southern Normandy. Discoveries in coin hoards have shown that some English coins did reach Normandy, but not, on present evidence, in anywhere near sufficient numbers to suggest an attempt to integrate the two coinages. Major differences in the organization of local government or the importance of the Truce of God in Normandy, but not in England, are other illustrations of a distinctiveness in organization and institutions which continued throughout William's reign and beyond. Finally, and on the same point, the legal basis of William's rule in England was the law of King Edward's day, whereas such Norman legislation and customs as exist stress legal continuity from the time before William became duke; Norman law and English law were, and remained, two different sets of customs.

William's ideas on what was going to happen to Normandy and England after his death are far from clear. For us, the logical assumption is that he would pass his dominions on to one son in order to preserve a union created with such immense difficulty. It is not certain, however, that William saw things in this way, and in recent years scholars have discussed his intentions without reaching a clear consensus. At the heart of the problem is the inadequacy of the sources and disagreement between those that do exist.

One fact is indisputable; William had promised the succession to Normandy to his son Robert. Before 1066 Robert had probably done fealty to the French king and become his vassal in the traditional manner of the Norman dukes. The great nobles of Normandy had also clone fealty to Robert and accepted that he was William's heir in the duchy. He was also acknowledged as the successor to Maine. England's future is, however, hard to unravel. Orderic Vitalis assumed throughout his *Ecclesiastical History* that William had made no provision for succession to the kingdom. In a deathbed speech which he attributed to William, he makes him say:

> I dare not transmit the government of this kingdom, won with so many sins, to any man, but entrust it to God alone, for fear that after my death my evil deeds should become the cause of even worse things. I hope that my son William, who has always been loyal to me from his earliest years, may . . . bring lustre to the kingdom if such is the divine will.

The speech was Orderic's opportunity to present his own view of the Norman Conquest, which he believed to have been an act of violence for which William must atone before God's stern judgement. We need not believe that William actually said what Orderic makes him say, but we cannot disregard Orderic's underlying assumption that William had made no arrangements for the English succession. In another place in his *History*, when discussing the outbreak of the quarrel between William and Robert Curthose, he says that Robert's brothers thought it shameful that he should aim for the whole inheritance. On the other hand, seemingly contradictory evidence comes from William of Malmesbury who commented in two places that Robert had been deprived of the inheritance of England, and from the twelfth-century historian Robert of Torigny who, in interpolations made after 1139 into the *Gesta Normannorum Ducum* of William of Jumièges, said that the kingdom of England had been taken from Robert by his brother.

It is difficult to know where the truth lies, although the balance of probability favours Orderic. The statements by Malmesbury and Torigny are vague and contain no reference to an actual promise having been made; it is difficult to believe that if there had been one, that Orderic or a contemporary source like the Anglo-Saxon Chronicle would not have mentioned it. The fact that there is no clear evidence that Robert visited England before 1080 is also against his having been designated heir to the kingdom, and although the visit which he did make in 1080-81 might have created the expectation that he would succeed, his final break with his father in 1084 scuppered this. It is also notable that writers such as Malmesbury, Torigny and Orderic, when dealing with Robert's wars against his brother King Henry I between 1101 and 1106 and with Robert's son William Clito's conflicts with Henry, never mention any promise to Robert of the English succession as the justification of their cause; William Clito did not indeed claim England until after Henry's son's drowning in 1120, an event which made him the direct heir.

After 1066 there was no traditional pattern for William to follow to decide the succession. Kingdoms and duchies were usually regarded as indivisible units by contemporaries, but the combination of the two posed problems. In 1071 William had allowed the elder son of William fitz Osbern to succeed to his father's Norman lands and the second to the English. This looks like a division made on the basis of a distinction between inherited family lands and acquisitions, a procedure which was ultimately enshrined in the law of Normandy. It could have created a precedent which William ultimately chose to follow, although in the end there is just no evidence to show what specific influences were brought to bear on his thinking. There was no predetermined assumption that Normandy and England should go to one son, and William never at any stage indicated that this is what he wanted to happen. It seems most likely that the rivalries which developed within his family cut across whatever plans he may have intended to make, and caused him to leave the decision until the moment of death. One certainty in this obscure problem is that William always took the line that his lands and offices were his to dispose of as he personally saw fit. This means that he eventually assigned his various lands in exactly the same way as previous Norman dukes had done, that is, by appointing the eldest son as heir to the duchy, and then making provision for the other sons. It also means that William acted according to the practices which were well-nigh universal among the northern French aristocracy of his day, passing the inherited patrimony on to the first son, and dealing with the acquisitions as he saw fit.

William tackled the task of ruling his cross-Channel dominions by energetic, calculated, and, for their time, exceptionally well-organized methods. His lands were held together essentially by vigorous travelling, an organized system of communications, and an extravagant exhibition of authority. The long periods spent in Normandy and the dramatic nature of his visits to England are in many ways suggestive more of domination over his kingdom rather than of government in the genuine sense of the word; his abandonment of the attempt to learn English and the rapacity of his taxation are indicative of a man who may have felt little sympathy or empathy with his acquired kingdom. He did not try to bring about an institutional assimilation of Normandy and England and, in essence, took up and maintained systems which already worked. This was partly because his fundamental concern was with the immediate practical problems of the exercise of power, but also because he consciously ruled his lands within an ideological structure which stressed legitimacy; he claimed to rule England as King Edward's heir and he respected the fact that Normandy and Maine should be held as a vassal of the King of France and the Count of Anjou respectively.

It is probable that before 1072 the uncertainties involved in subjugating England, and afterwards the drift towards the breach with his eldest son, created a succession problem which William decided not to face until the imminence of death forced him to do so. For us, the uncertain future of his lands, which had been won with such toil, appears as a gaping hole in the heart of a magnificent political achievement. But William's perception of the situation would not have been the same as ours – he would have thought of himself as having the power to dispose of his territories in total conformity with contemporary practice. In England it was his wish to present himself as the epitome of powerful Anglo-Saxon kingship. But when it came to the succession, it was the mentality of the Norman duke and the Frankish territorial prince which prevailed; it is rarely more evident than in this matter that William was essentially a northern French territorial prince who became a king.

Nine

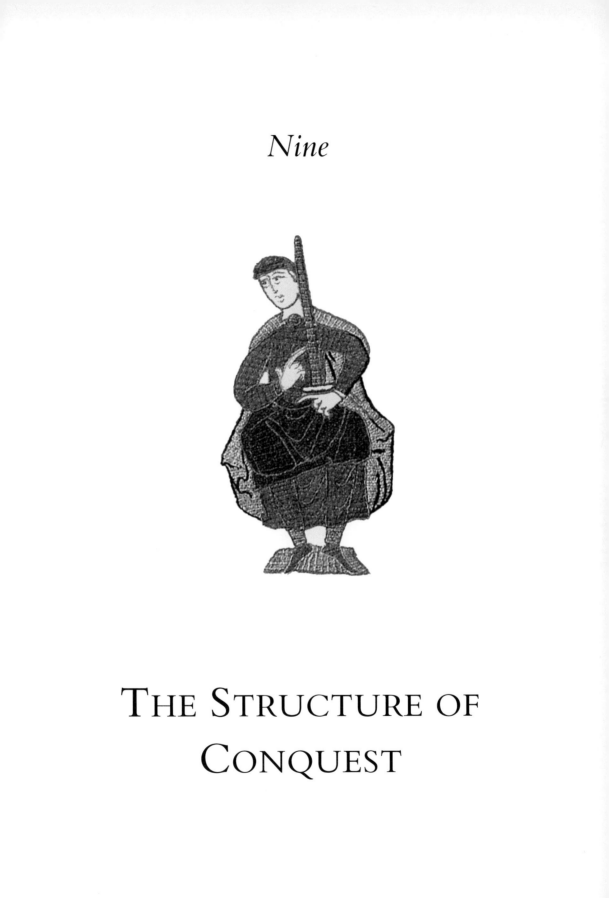

THE STRUCTURE OF
CONQUEST

By the end of William's reign in 1087, all the significant sources of wealth and power in England had been as good as completely taken over by Normans and men from other parts of northern France. Almost the entire English upper aristocracy had been replaced, and nearly all land and almost all the offices in central and local government had been transferred to newcomers. However, despite the initial impression of overwhelming domination which these facts convey, the Normans' situation in England after 1066 resembled that of a modern colonial power. William and his followers were no more than a tiny minority of the total population – it is reasonable to guess that they were considerably fewer than 25,000 in a total population of around 2,000,000. Security was therefore very much their initial preoccupation, especially since rebellion in England was usually likely to be associated with invasion from Scandinavia. As a result, the maintenance of the Norman Conquest depended at first on extensive castle building and permanent garrisons.

From the earliest days of the Conquest William's policy was to erect a castle as soon as a place had been subdued; the Bayeux Tapestry shows this being done at Hastings, and the chronicles tell of their construction on William's orders at London, York, Warwick, Nottingham and elsewhere during subsequent campaigns. Both in the years immediately after 1066 and later, compact blocks of territory were sometimes specially created around a single strategic castle to control a particularly sensitive region; this happened, for example, around the Sussex castles of Arundel, Bramber, Hastings, Lewes and Pevensey, on the Welsh border at Shrewsbury and Chester, and in the north of England. The fortifications built were usually, although not invariably, of the motte-and-bailey type, a mound surmounted by a wooden tower and looking down on an area surrounded by a ditch and palisade. Such mounds can still be seen in a number of English towns, such as Oxford, Lincoln and Cambridge. Great towers or halls built in stone, an even starker reminder of Norman power, were begun subsequently at places of outstanding importance; the great

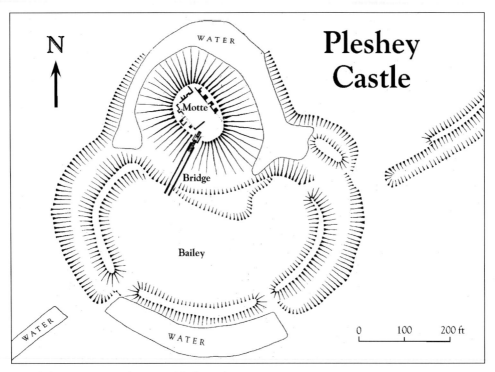

N

WATER

Pleshey Castle

Motte

Bridge

Bailey

WATER

WATER

0   100   200 ft

46. Pleshey, Essex: a typical motte-and-bailey castle.

keep of the Tower of London, for example, was begun on William's orders and finished in the reign of his son William II. Orderic considered that this castle building was the fundamental reason for the success of the Norman Conquest: 'for the fortifications called castles built by the Normans were scarcely known in the English provinces, and so the English, in spite of their courage and love of fighting, could put up only a weak resistance to their enemies'. We would now express this slightly differently and say that the castles gave William and his followers a monopoly of strategic power. They were refuges into which a threatened group of Normans could retreat, and their garrisons were for a long time effectively an army of occupation.

The replacement of the English aristocracy by a Norman and French one was up to a point simply the extension of Normandy's pre-1066 power structure into the new kingdom. A list of the wealthiest landholders in Domesday Book comprises a top ten consisting of Bishop Odo of Bayeux, Roger de Montgommery, Count Robert of Mortain, William fitz Osbern (although he died in 1071, a good proportion of his estates can be traced), William de Warenne, Count Alan of Brittany, Count Eustace of Boulogne, Earl Hugh of Chester, Richard fitz Gilbert, and Bishop Geoffrey of Coutances. Two of these, Counts Alan and Eustace, were non-Normans from eminent northern French princely families, whose lands bordered Normandy, and whose co-operation was undoubtedly useful for William to have – William was even willing to forgive Count Eustace an attempted invasion in 1067 to maintain the connection. But the remainder of the ten were members of the chosen group of magnates who had gathered around William before 1066. They and others, such as Count Robert of Eu, constituted a cross-Channel super-aristocracy, a group who moved between northern France and England, much in the manner of William himself. They made arrangements to organize their vast cross-Channel landholdings and to follow William's court. We know, for example, that Bishop Odo of Bayeux, much in the same manner as his brother, had castles in England at Dover, Rochester, Deddington (Oxfordshire) and Snettisham (Norfok) and houses in Caen, Rouen and London. In a sense, then, William's rule in Normandy and England after 1066 was simply an extension of his rule in Normandy before 1066. He continued to dominate through the same group who had been his supporters and closest companions in the years of struggle before the Conquest; their long-lasting loyalty was rewarded with massive estates scattered throughout many English counties.

There were, however, members of Normandy's aristocracy who acquired surprisingly little land in England. Roger de Beaumont, one of William's chief associates before 1066 and a major figure in the government of Normandy throughout the 1060s and 1070s, was the most important of these. They also included Count William of Evreux, who had made a contribution of ships in 1066 and was prominent in the Norman campaigns in Maine in the last years of William's reign. This reluctance of some great Norman magnates to acquire English lands cannot be explained entirely convincingly; the fact that Normandy was the homeland and England an inhospitable, barely subdued, kingdom probably influenced the choices individuals made. But the consequences are obvious enough; many among those who obtained land and office in England came from relatively lowly, sometimes untraceable, backgrounds. This even applies to the eleventh wealthiest Norman or French magnate in England, Geoffrey de Mandeville, and is also true of many of the Normans who were appointed as sheriffs in England, such as Picot of Cambridgeshire, Urse d'Abetôt of Worcestershire, Roger Bigot of Norfolk, and to a lesser extent of Hugh de Port of Hampshire. The folios of Domesday Book readily reveal that many of these Norman *parvenus* used their new-found status to seize lands to which they were not entitled. William therefore faced the dual problem in England of dominating a large kingdom with a relatively small number of followers and of controlling a collection of greedy social climbers who were likely to behave unscrupulously towards the natives.

During the wars of the six years after Hastings, William had to deal with a host of problems which we would include under the heading of 'man-

management'. Some of his followers found the going in England much too tough for their liking – desertions appear to have been quite common. The strain placed by the incessant campaigns on the domestic lives of some of the newcomers is apparent in a story told by Orderic of how in 1068 certain Norman wives begged their husbands to return to Normandy, threatening to commit adultery if they did not. With the common medieval churchman's prejudice against women – which was based on Eve's betrayal in the Garden of Eden – Orderic condemned the women for lust. We would probably explain the situation in terms of the effects of lengthy separations and anxiety. William's response to the wives' pleadings was to promise lands, revenues and great authority to their husbands, but to punish those who actually left by confiscating the lands they had received. This combination of the stick and the carrot may reflect his calculated response to the possibility of desertions during this difficult period; it also shows the pressure on him to sustain manpower at a sufficient level by making promises of rewards.

William's control over the potentially disruptive and anarchic land settlement which followed the Conquest was founded first of all on his own immense prestige and on his dominating personality. These assets were reinforced by the vast wealth and lands he acquired when he became King of the English. As Edward the Confessor's self-proclaimed heir, he logically regarded himself as entitled to all the lands which that king had held, and to all the rights and revenues which he had exercised and received. He also took over a substantial portion of the forfeited lands of Harold and his family. This meant that William's royal estates lay in a total of twenty-nine counties and, with towns included, produced an aggregate value in Domesday Book of almost £14,000. This figure is meaningless in modern terms, but just how powerful these lands made him becomes clearer when we appreciate that they were over four times as valuable as those of the leading magnate, his brother, Bishop Odo, and around seven times more valuable than those of the second best endowed, Roger de Montgommery. It is possible that the Anglo-Saxon Chronicler was indicating that William had a policy of assigning the administration of the royal lands to those willing to exploit them ruthlessly when he wrote that 'The king sold his land on very hard terms – as hard as he could. Then somebody else came and offered more than the other had given, and the king let it go to the man who had offered him more. Then came a third, and offered still more, and the king gave it into the hands of the man who offered him most of all, and did not care how sinfully the reeves had got it from poor men, nor how many unlawful things they did.' On many royal manors Domesday Book certainly shows that the estate was paying a rent

47 and 48. Coins of William I.

considerably greater than its recognized value, suggesting a harsh and vigorous exploitation.

A second element in William's power in England was taxation. In his kingdom he enjoyed the benefit of the Danegeld, the only universal tax available at this time to a western European ruler. Originally a special tax first taken in the reign of King Æthelred the Unready to pay off the Danish invaders, Danegeld became under William an annual tax levied throughout the kingdom on an organized system of land assessment – the hide was the normal unit in most English counties, with the carucate as its equivalent in the more Scandinavian eastern counties. William's administration normally collected Danegeld at a rate of two shillings on the hide, but in the crisis year of 1084, when a Danish invasion was pending, and perhaps again in 1086, in preparation for William's attack on King Philip I, it was taken at the very high rate of six shillings. Taxation at this level had not been a feature of Edward the Confessor's reign, and the Anglo-Saxon Chronicler was therefore right to highlight the relentless exaction of money as one of the central features of William's rule in England. Another aspect of Norman taxation in operation was the maintenance of every major aspect of the system of minting coin which had existed under Edward the Confessor, with coins being reminted every two or three years and the king drawing revenue from the recoinages. In the mid-1070s steps were taken to extract increased profits from this traditional system. The weight of the coins issued in William's name was increased, a device which indirectly contributed to royal revenue because it meant that the silver content of the coins was greater. Also, at about the same time those who minted coins were made to make higher payments for the right to do so.

William's rule was based not only on financial power, but on the application of a set of ideas which originated in his claim to be King Edward the Confessor's designated heir. Like his immediate English predecessors, he was obliged by his coronation oath to uphold the customary law of the English kingdom and to protect the legal rights of his loyal subjects. His writs and charters therefore frequently announced that he was doing this by maintaining all rights and lands as they had existed in King Edward's day. But, given that a great deal of land in fact passed from English to French landholders after 1066, it was necessary to develop the idea of a tenurial continuity from before 1066 to after 1066. In consequence, the legal fiction was developed that the new Norman and French landholders, who had taken over Englishmen's and Englishwomen's estates, derived their lands, powers and rights from an English predecessor (*antecessor*), who might of course have died in the warfare in or after 1066, or who might have had their property confiscated. In fact, individual newcomers often received the lands of one or more specific Englishmen, which conveniently demonstrated the notion that they were the heirs to their landholdings and rights.

The idea that William presided over a society in England which was a continuation of that which had existed before 1066 produced some of the great showpieces of Norman government, the great land pleas. In what was probably the first of these, an enquiry held on Penenden Heath near Maidstone in 1072, Archbishop Lanfranc of Canterbury claimed certain rights against the king and certain estates against the Earl of Kent, William's brother, Bishop Odo, on the grounds that Odo had come to hold lands which had been wrongfully held by the English lords who had held them before him. Here we see Norman government at work in almost idealized form. The court which heard the case was the shire court of Kent at its traditional meeting place on Penenden Heath. One of William's greatest magnates,

Bishop Geoffrey of Coutances, presided at the hearing, which lasted for three days, with all the Frenchmen of the county present and also those English acquainted with the traditional laws and customs of the shire. The deposed English bishop of Selsey, Æthelric, a very old man, was brought along in a cart to expound English law. The verdict in general favoured Lanfranc where he could convincingly demonstrate an English precedent.

Similar principles were applied in other inquests such as the elaborate series of inquiries into the lands of the abbey of Ely, which began in earnest in 1080, as well as in the countless other tenurial disputes which are recorded in Domesday Book. These land pleas were one of many measures which William's government had to take to stop the takeover of English land degenerating into anarchy. Another is the famous writ ordering sheriffs who had received or taken lands which rightfully belonged to the English Church to return them; this text shows more graphically than any other how hard William had to work in order to control the excesses of his wilder followers.

The arbitrary power inherent in early medieval kingship was another important element in the Norman Conquest. William's kingly authority gave him the power to override the straightforward continuity in landholding from a given Englishman to a given newcomer if he so wished. Domesday Book supplies numerous examples of an original continuity of landholding over 1066 being changed by a gift, purchase or exchange made on royal authority or with royal consent. It also mentions many such transactions which had taken place without William's permission, pinpointing the obvious facts that many changes were too small to require his acknowledgement and that many took place without his knowing about them.

Dramatic breaches of the principle of the direct transfer of land and rights from an English predecessor to a Norman successor took place when blocks of land were consolidated around a castle or allocated to a specific individual. In the same way, there was often considerable destruction of urban property when castles were built in towns. At Norwich, for example, eighty-one houses were demolished to create the necessary space. William of Malmesbury tells a good story of a clash between the English Archbishop of York, Ealdred, and the new Norman sheriff of Worcestershire, Urse d'Abetôt, when Urse's new castle within Worcester enclosed part of the cemetery of the monks who served the cathedral church. Urse's refusal to move it drew a poetic Old English curse from the archbishop, which began 'Thou art called Urse. May you have God's curse.' All these major changes certainly took place on William's authority. The general impression is that, for all the emphasis on continuity and its decisive role in supporting a relatively orderly transfer of land, a massive quantity of English land was redistributed on William's direct authority. It looks as if William and his companions made few compromises with local opinion or established property rights when it came to consolidating their grip on England or to providing for the favoured beneficiaries of royal patronage. William's rule in England was just as arbitrary, just as ruthless, and just as generous to the power and pockets of his closest associates as his rule in Normandy before 1066 had been (see Chapter Four).

Although this is not a book about Norman government or the Norman Conquest, it needs to be emphasized that the basic structure which supported William's rule in England was almost identical with that of a pre-1066 English king. At the centre, in the household, was a chamber (*camera*) to store and disburse money and a chancery which supervised the production of writs in a form which was a development on those issued in King Edward's name. There was a permanent treasury at Winchester. The chief institutions of local government remained the courts of the shire and its subdivision, the hundred, with the control of a particular shire entrusted to a sheriff. The Norman and French newcomers, as the Penenden plea shows, were encouraged by William to settle their disputes in the shire and hundred courts, and administratively, both assemblies were crucial to the making of Domesday Book. The territorial earldoms, comprising several shires, which had been a familiar feature of late Anglo-Saxon England, did, however, disappear.

The one other major governmental change sponsored by William came in the vital area of military organization. The process of development is an obscure topic, but the essential point to bear in mind is that it is inextricably associated with the installation of the new aristocracy. A twelfth-century source, the chronicle of the abbey of Abingdon paints a plausible scenario of a nervy conquering aristocracy keeping permanent troops of warriors around them. In time, however, as more peaceful conditions appeared and as the Norman lords received estates, their warriors were granted land by their lords as a reward for their services and in return for an agreement to provide further service in the future. The Normans and the other newcomers thereby structured relationships among themselves according to the patterns of lordship and vassalage with which they were familiar in northern France, and created an organized system of military service which underpinned their conquest, and enabled them to raise armies and garrison castles.

William's personal role in these changes appears to have been simply to supervise the preliminary distribution of estates to the lords, who were thereafter responsible for organizing their lands themselves. He did, however, make it obligatory for every major tenant-in-chief (that is, lord who held his lands as a direct vassal of William himself) to render a quota of military service in return for his landholding, a requirement which was extended to the English bishoprics and monasteries, and which involved not only service in the king's army, but often also a contribution to the defence of a particular castle. These quotas, which were often multiples of five knights, should be thought of as a rough-and-ready device to meet an immediate problem of control. They were an innovation in England where military service had been customarily based on territorial units defined in terms of hides and carucates, rather than on arbitrary quotas agreed between king and tenant-in-chief.

The English

The corollary of William's belief that he was Edward the Confessor's legitimate heir was that Harold was a usurper, who had not been a true king, and whose short reign was an illegal interlude. This theory was fully developed by the time that Domesday Book was made, since Harold, though often mentioned in the survey, is never once called king. There are, however, signs that this dismissal of Harold's reign had not been fully formulated during the brief Anglo-Norman phase from 1066 to 1068. One writ issued in William's name makes the mistake – from the Norman point of view – of calling Harold 'king', while the Bayeux Tapestry, a work of Norman propaganda made in England in the 1070s, still calls Harold 'king'. However, it looks as if the Norman version of the Conquest was beginning to fall securely into place by the later 1060s, for when the abbot of Bury St Edmunds raised the question of who rightly held lands which had been held by the tenants of the abbey who had died fighting against William, they were adjudged to belong to the king. The abbey was confirmed only as holding its other lands and rights as in King Edward's day.

The consigning of Harold's reign to legal oblivion had the sinister implication, which is set out clearly by William of Poitiers, that anyone who had fought against William at Hastings was a rebel. The fact that this theory can be shown to have evolved suggests that, although rooted in William's claim to succeed Edward, it was in reality an expedient device developed to justify the transfer of lands from Normans to English. In this context, it is obvious that once William was securely installed as king, and as his followers' appetite for English wealth grew, few English landholders can have felt secure when the Normans' definition of treachery was set so widely as to include defending one's kingdom against an invader.

In spite of what finally happened, William appears to have tried to incorporate his English subjects in his régime at the start of his reign. But any pretence that anyone beyond a small selected band whom he chose to trust had any actual power disappeared with the upheavals of 1068-70. Archbishop Ealdred of York, who died in 1069, Bishop Wulfstan of Worcester, the one significant native-born bishop to survive the purge of the episcopate in 1070, and Abbot Æthelwig of Evesham, who died in 1077 after having exercised some sort of general responsibility for the west Midlands, head a very short list of English trustees. Attempts to integrate the English at the highest levels of power did not, however, entirely cease. At the end of the reign, for example, a small number of English sheriffs and abbots were still in office, and the case of Æthelsige, an Abbot of St Augustine's, Canterbury, who fled, but later returned to be appointed Abbot of Ramsey in 1080, shows that a disgraced Englishman could retrieve his fortunes. But, in general, the English were mostly used to service and sustain Norman power. For example, William took English troops on his campaign in the West Country in 1068, and in 1073 and 1079 took some of them to fight in his wars in France – at the Battle of Gerberoi (1079), an English thegn, Toki, son of Wigot of Wallingford, is said to have saved William's life. Englishmen also served on the juries which supplied the basic information to William's commissioners for the making of Domesday Book, while the great majority of the moneyers who minted William's English coinage bore English names and were presumably therefore of English birth. William's rule therefore created and relied on an entire English 'underclass' whose efforts supported his and his followers' domination over the kingdom.

It appears to have been William's policy to encourage mixed marriages between the conquerors and the conquered. His own niece, for example, was married to Waltheof, Earl of Northumbria, and he also gave permission for a daughter of William fitz Osbern to marry Ralph, Earl of Norfolk and Suffolk, the son of a Breton protégé of Edward the Confessor and an English mother. Marriages between French men and English women were apparently quite common, and presumably had the blessing not only of William, but of his chief followers as well. It was one such mixed marriage between a French priest in the entourage of Roger de Montgommery and an English woman which produced the historian Orderic Vitalis, who was born near Shrewsbury in 1075. Another attempt at reconciliation appears in a letter written by Archbishop Lanfranc to the Bishop of Rochester giving the sympathetic opinion, with William's approval, that terrified Englishwomen, who had become nuns to escape the sexual and marital advances of the Norman conquerors, should be allowed to renounce the veil if they had no true vocation. Orderic's childhood memories – he left England in 1085 – may have gone into a romanticized portrait of William's England, although the passage could equally have been one he copied from the lost concluding sections of William of Poitiers:

> English and Normans lived peacefully together in settlements, walled towns and cities, and intermarried with each other. You could see many villages or town markets filled with displays of French wares and merchandise, and observe the English, who had previously seemed contemptible to the French in their native dress, completely transformed by foreign fashions.

The small quantity of legislation attributable to William dealt with two aspects of relations between French and English. One development was the institution of the so-called *murdrum* fine, about which the relevant clause in the text known as 'the Articles of William' (*Articuli Willelmi*) states:

> I desire that all the men whom I have brought with me or who have come after me shall enjoy the benefit of my protection. And if any one of them is slain, his lord shall arrest the slayer within five days if he can. If not, however, he shall begin to pay me forty-six marks of silver from the property of that lord as long as it lasts out. When, however, the property of the lord fails, the whole hundred in which the murder is committed shall pay in common what remains.

A century later, the treatise known as the 'Dialogue of the Exchequer', in the midst of a fanciful account of the Norman Conquest, said that the *murdrum* fine had been introduced to stop terrorist assassinations by placing a heavy financial burden on the community (i.e. the hundred) in which a murder had taken place. The amount of space taken up with refinements to this basic procedure in later treatises, such as the early twelfth-century *Laws of King Henry I*, suggests that such murders were relatively frequent. William, or whoever drafted the legislation, was using the time-honoured, and morally unpleasant, method whereby the law-abiding members of an oppressed community were made responsible for curtailing the activities of its wilder spirits. However, in the event of a Frenchman summoning an Englishman to defend himself on a serious criminal charge, such as perjury, murder or theft, a concession was made to English legal procedure; the Englishman was allowed to choose between ordeal by hot iron, which was used in England before 1066, or trial by combat, which was not. These two pieces of legislation admirably sum up William's attitude to the English; on the one hand, the ferocious crushing of all acts of violent resistance in the name of law and order, and on the other, the creation of mechanisms to resolve areas of social difference for those willing to live at peace.

For all the apparent efforts to achieve integration and reconciliation, the historian cannot overlook the fact that the Norman Conquest was an unmitigated catastrophe as far as the English aristocracy was concerned. Many lost their lands and many more chose to emigrate in preference to living under Norman rule. Whatever William's actual role in the great transfer of land from English to French, there is no doubt that the arrival in England of large bands of land-hungry warriors imposed a pressure on the natives which caused rebellion, led to the despoliation of church lands, and must have resulted in many English losing their lands for varying acts of defiance. Domesday Book and the charters, the crucial sources on the matter, are in fact notably silent on the reasons why the estates of a particular English landholder were transferred to a particular newcomer. And on balance the evidence suggests that the apparent respect for legality and continuity which characterizes William's settlement of conquered England was in reality an imposed structure which was developed as circumstances required and came in considerable degree to satisfy the needs of the conquerors. The writing out from history of Harold's reign made the punishment of disloyalty, real or imagined, easy. It also fitted neatly into a setting where William, whatever his own instincts may have been, was obliged to redistribute lands to defend the security of the Norman settlement and to reward the followers on whose co-operation that settlement depended.

In the hands of William the Conqueror and that warrior aristocracy with which he had collaborated since adolescence, the whole apparatus of arbitrary kingship and proclaimed continuity from King Edward's reign became a magnificent means of distributing power from one ruling class to another. It demonstrates superbly how, within the structures of early medieval kingship, the law could be turned into the servant of what was, in practice, revolutionary change. The true nature of events after 1066 is put into perspective by the fact that when yet another Danish invasion was threatened in 1085, it is known to have received widespread encouragement from England, just as those of 1068-70 had done. Although many of the English undoubtedly came positively to support William's rule, and although considerable efforts were made to woo them, those who served William were usually from sections of society which had no real choice. By William's death, the march of time was certainly changing English hostility into a resigned acceptance of defeat. His rule did eventually bring peace to England, but it is a measure of the bitterness caused by the imposition of Norman rule under his authority that the kingdom's loss of liberty continued to be lamented by English writers well on into the twelfth century.

William the Conqueror

The effects and consequences of the Norman Conquest of England are a complex historical topic which is far beyond what this book is supposed to be about. In any case, it can be argued that the Conquest was not a process of change which was confined to William's reign, since Normans continued to arrive in England until well into the twelfth century and major changes continued to take place. And even when the subject of the Norman Conquest is limited to William's reign, the answers which can be given to the question: 'What were the results of the Norman Conquest?' are extraordinarily diverse. There is, for example, massive variation from one region to another. To cite extremes, ports in southern England benefited from increased commercial and maritime contacts with the Continent, whereas areas of northern England suffered an economic and social catastrophe. However, the one question to which some answer must be given is: 'What was William's personal role in the Norman Conquest and settlement?'

The first point to make is that William appears to have been directly involved in all major decisions of policy. This is well illustrated by Lanfranc's letter concerning the Englishwomen who had become nuns in order to escape from the marauding Normans; it includes the blunt statement that what was described was the king's policy as well as Lanfranc's own. William's purpose was to be, and appear to be, an English king, albeit a more powerful and majestic one than his predecessors had been; the institution of the *Laudes* and the crown-wearings as well as the unprecedented double coronation with Mathilda in 1068 and the further crowning by papal legates in 1070 are all indications of this striving for greater magnificence. His policy of continuity meant that he had no ambitions to extend his authority into Wales or Scotland; as will be seen in Chapter Eleven, he sought no more than stable co-existence and an acknowledgement of his rights as King Edward's heir. In practice, however, as has been stressed throughout this chapter, William in England was not just another Anglo-Saxon king; he was both Duke of Normandy with debts to discharge to a large number of followers who had supported him through enormous hardships, and he was a ruler trying to maintain order in an exceptionally turbulent society. The fulfillment of these utterly incompatible objectives led to continuity in the institutions through which England was governed and a massive redistribution of property to Normans and other Frenchmen.

Given William's apparent early endeavours to produce a truly Anglo-Norman aristocracy in England, we can reasonably doubt whether the society which had emerged by the time of his death was anything at all like the one he anticipated ruling over when he became king in 1066. During the period from 1066 to 1087, we are looking at a man who took decisions in an atmosphere of recurrent crisis and who could rarely have perceived where his actions were leading him. In the end, the quest for power and security in England, Maine and Normandy led to him adopting the course of giving wealth, lands and power to those on whom he could rely, of crushing the English except where they demonstrated positive support, and of exploiting England to fight wars in France.

The details of William's cross-Channel itinerary, which were described in Chapter Eight, suggest that he scarcely governed England at all in the true meaning of the word. His visits were so brief and so connected with crises that they must have resembled triumphal tours of inspection rather than genuine acts of government. William's immense personal prestige, which derived from a lifetime of success, made his authority as king secure against all opposition. But, in practice, he depended to a considerable extent on his brother Odo, (especially during the long period of absence from 1076 to 1080), on Archbishop Lanfranc, and on numerous local officials, of whom the sheriffs were the most important. The only one of these whom William appears to have found entirely satisfactory was Lanfranc, whose duties consisted mainly of passing on royal orders from France, and of organizing the Norman settlement of the English Church. The records which survive of Odo's rule as regent show him initiating land pleas and resolving disputes, but William clearly believed that he had been both oppressive and negligent. The greed and over-zealousness of some of William's sheriffs were notorious.

Considerable blame for all the disturbances and the maladministration must, however, be placed at the door of William's absenteeism, since government inevitably lacked the stability which an active and present king would have provided. In this context, the Domesday survey of 1085-7, which was a comprehensive record of William's new kingdom designed to meet his government's needs, would appear to have been his solution to the legal and tenurial confusion and an attempt to bring to an end the acts of local tyranny which abound in the evidence for the first twenty years of Norman rule in England. This great enterprise will be examined more closely in Chapter Twelve. Suffice to say here that the making of

Domesday Book was an act of tremendous political vision. It consolidated the Norman grip on England, and it established standards of tenurial holding and tax assessment to which all could refer. But neither it nor anything else could ensure the continuation of William's cross-Channel realm if, as we saw in Chapter Eight, he was set on dividing it. Militarily and politically, William the Conqueror was wonderfully effective as a conqueror. Yet he was also very much a man of his own day and age, with all the limitations imposed by that fact.

William's financial administration resembles more the efficient and unremitting exaction of established sources of revenue than simple extortion. The chance survival of the document known as the Northamptonshire Geld Roll, for example, shows that in that county Danegeld was reassessed downwards to a more economically realistic level. Domesday Book suggests a similar pattern of change in other over-assessed counties. But it is also clear that wars in Normandy, which were related exclusively to the duchy's interests, were financed from English taxation; the Anglo-Saxon Chronicler, again in 1086, noted that:

> All the same he first acted according to his custom, that is to say
> he obtained a very great amount of money from his men where
> he had any pretext for it either justly or otherwise. He
> afterwards went into Normandy.

In addition, architectural historians have been impressed by the increased lavishness in the later stages of construction in the abbey church of St-Etienne at Caen; William surely also used English resources to foster his pet building project. Finally, when the evidence in Domesday Book of exemptions from Danegeld (what is technically termed 'beneficial hidation') is analysed, it shows that a significant proportion of taxation was being creamed off to increase still further the fortunes of William's most favoured followers. The Norman Conquest of England was a process in which William, many of his Norman followers and the duchy of Normandy in general were massively and deliberately enriched.

Finally, something must be said about William's first conquest, the county of Maine. There, his rule was from the start based mainly on the presence of a Norman garrison at Le Mans and on local supporters. Even after having effectively to reinvade the county in 1073, he returned to ruling it by the same methods used between 1063, when he first acquired it, and 1069, when control was lost. The churchmen of Maine – especially Bishop Arnold of Le Mans – were particularly staunch supporters of Norman rule. Their role as a bastion of William's power was further strengthened by the removal of the unreliable Abbot Rainaid of St-Pierre-de-la-Couture in either 1074 or 1075 and his replacement by the pro-Norman Juhel. The aristocracy of the county remained less pliant, however. In particular, Geoffrey de Mayenne, whom William apparently never attempted to dispossess, was permanently ready to hinder the Normans. His charter attestations show that his sympathies were always with the Angevins, and even after the defeat of 1073, he was once more back in Count Fulk Rechin's company at Angers in 1076. William's charters for Maine are mainly confirmations of earlier grants by others, suggesting a remarkably non-interventionist method of government.

In spite of the massive contrasts between William's methods of rule in Maine and England, there are also some fundamental similarities. In both, he sought a legal basis for his rule in existing custom, accepting in Maine that he and his son Robert held the county as a vassal of the Count of Anjou, and of course announcing that he held England as King Edward's heir. The contrasts between William's treatment of Maine and England can perhaps be explained by the fact that he ruled one as a king subject to no outside authority, and the other as a count who was a vassal of another count who was a vassal of the King of France. Alternatively, he may have decided that the problems involved in subduing England were so massive that they could only be solved by the most ruthless methods, or decided that England's relative isolation as an island gave him more freedom to act decisively than in Maine, which was surrounded by northern French enemies. In Maine the pattern of regular revolts and invasions from Anjou was to be maintained throughout William's life, so that in the 1080s his rule there was little more secure than it had been after the conquest of 1063-4. In contrast, England was, by this stage, becoming thoroughly subjugated to his will.

Ten

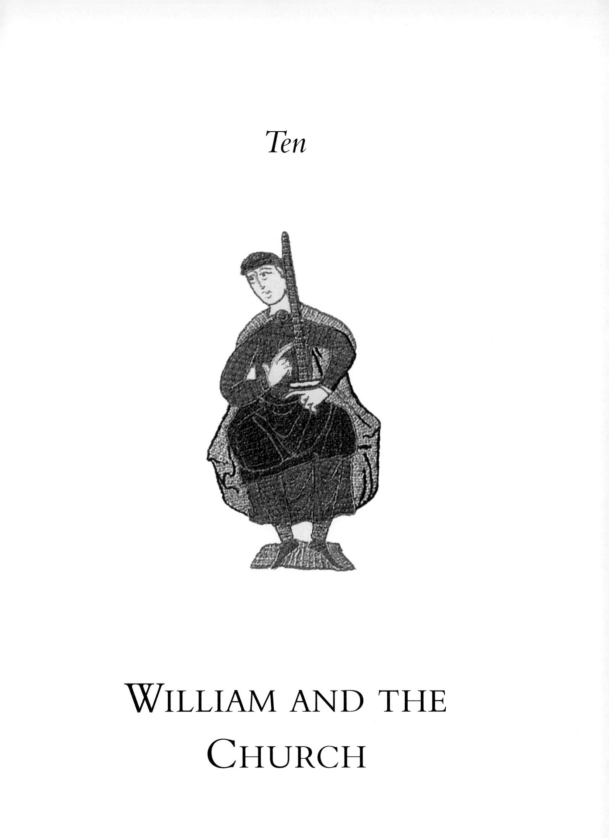

WILLIAM AND THE
CHURCH

The importance of the Church in medieval society was discussed briefly in Chapter One. The ramifications of its role have been apparent at many moments in William's life, as, for example, when he had to atone for his marriage to Mathilda by building the abbey of St-Etienne at Caen or when papal sanction was sought for the campaign of 1066. For the secular, post-Freudian late twentieth century it is vital to an understanding of William's relations with the Church to appreciate that people in the eleventh century had little sense of a morality other than a Christian morality and accepted that the course of events around them was directed entirely by God's will. The Christian Church had a central place in society and exercised a dominating power over people's thoughts. It created a structure of authority and morality from which few escaped, and they, the heretics, usually came to an unhappy end. The Church's role in the conquest of England might seem surprising to us, accustomed as we are to a Christian faith which can put a heavy emphasis on peace and reconciliation and a Church of England which refuses a service of celebration for the British victory in the Falklands. But in its eleventh-century context, the Norman Church's performance is a tribute to William's political success in his duchy. He had been its protector and ruler ever since he had been able to exercise effective political power and he had appointed its bishops. Its loyalties were to him as territorial prince, rather than to any abstract notion of justice, love or fairness.

William's personal relationship with the Church has to be seen as operating on two levels. Firstly, there was by the eleventh century a long-established tradition that a ruler possessed responsibilities for the protection and organization of the Church within his area of authority. Great Frankish kings like Charlemagne (768-814) epitomized the ideal; they fought wars on behalf of Christianity, they oversaw the appointment of bishops and abbots, and they presided at ecclesiastical synods which organized and reformed the Church. This theocratic system had been taken up by William's immediate predecessors as Dukes of Normandy and by English kings from Alfred the Great in the ninth century and Edgar in the tenth onwards, so that the roles which William filled in Normandy from 1035 and England from 1066 were essentially identical. As far as the universal Christian Church and the unity of Christendom were concerned, there was papal authority to be taken account of. But in the middle of the eleventh century, the pope's authority was usually exerted through kings and princes and in practice the papacy accepted their domination over the churches within their lands, even if, from around 1050, the first stirrings of a more censorious and ultimately more authoritarian papacy can be perceived. A second dimension is that a duke or king was responsible, like any other individual Christian, for the salvation of his own soul. Among those who took their ultimate fate seriously, this normally resulted in generous gifts of land or money to churches as a means to compensate for the many sins which such a man inevitably committed during a lifetime of warfare.

The Church and the Conquest

William's domination over the Church in Normandy, his personal commitment to the welfare of the Church in his lands, and the good relations which he had built up with the papacy before 1066, were all crucial elements in the campaign of 1066. As we saw in Chapter Four, there is outstandingly good evidence for his involvement in ecclesiastical councils and for his being a ruler who took a serious and positive interest in the welfare of the Church in his lands; William of Poitiers indeed presents his efforts in idealized terms, portraying him as the scourge of bishops and clergy who did not punish moral slackness with sufficient vigour. It is fully in conformity with this earnestly religious approach that the conquest of England was surrounded by a religious paraphernalia designed to secure God's blessing for the expedition, and, after it, to obtain his forgiveness for those who had taken part in the inevitable bloodshed. The procurement of a banner from Pope Alexander II, the consecration of Mathilda's abbey of La Trinité of Caen on 18 June 1066, and the parading of the relics at St-Valéry while William and his men waited for a favourable wind to take their invasion fleet to England were all intended to propitiate the Deity. Bishops Odo of Bayeux and Geoffrey of Coutances were present at Hastings, along with several monks. According to William of Poitiers, they were there to help with their prayers, although the Bayeux Tapestry also shows Odo in a more active role, driving hesitant trainee knights back into the fray.

Acts of propitiation continued to be made after the victory at Hastings. Penances were imposed on those of William's Norman vassals who had taken part in the campaigns of 1066, according to which soldiers would have to perform some pious work for a set period of time. These were drawn up by the bishops of Normandy and confirmed by the papal legate, Bishop Ermenfrid of

Sion, either on a visit to Normandy in 1067 or to England in 1070, and must have had William's approval. The ordinances, which amounted to a symbolic cleansing of the Norman Conquest in the eyes of God, tackled various circumstances in which injuries and death might have been inflicted, such as during the Battle of Hastings, between the battle and William's coronation, and after the coronation. Thus, among the many regulations, anyone who had killed in the Battle of Hastings was required to do a year's penance for each victim slain, and everyone who injured and killed, but did not know the number of the victims, was to do penance for one day a week for the rest of his life or build a church. One aspect of William's personal contribution to this process of atonement was the despatch of a multitude of gifts to churches in Normandy and France. Another was the foundation of an abbey on the battlefield of Hastings, of which more will be said later in this chapter. The final phase was the visit of the papal legates in 1070, which was the logical conclusion of Pope Alexander's gift of the banner in 1066, and which set the papacy's stamp of approval on the major changes which William wanted to make within the English Church. Its climax was William's special coronation by the legates at Winchester at Easter 1070.

The scale of this religious apparatus is an indication that William's policy was to do everything possible to bring the Conquest within the existing contemporary framework of legitimate Christian warfare. There were precedents for all that he did. Papal banners, although a recent development, had been given to other war leaders before 1066. Penances imposed on whole armies were also known, and a previous English king, Cnut, had founded a religious community on a battlefield. The general impression is of a conservatively religious man taking every pious precaution known to contemporaries to protect an enterprise fraught with moral and spiritual perils, as well as physical danger. The continuation of the process of atonement long after 1066 suggests that the fate of his conquest and of his own soul was an enduring source of anxiety to William. We see again the thoroughness evident in so many other aspects of William's career and his typical concern to give legitimacy to his acts. It is obvious that, from the moment the papal banner was sought, William intended to do all he could to justify and validate his violent seizure of the English kingdom, just as he also took enormous pains to structure his government of England within a framework of legality and continuity.

The Government of the Anglo-Norman Church

William permitted no arguments about who had the final say in the government of the Church within his dominions, even though he always recognized that the Church in a general way possessed a superior moral and spiritual authority over all laymen, himself included. A good illustration of his attitude is provided by Orderic's account of the early history of his own monastery of St-Evroult, which had been founded in c. 1050, and whose second abbot, Robert de Grandmesnil, was appointed in 1059. When Robert's brother Hugh, along with other lords who had been benefactors of St-Evroult, was accused of rebellion against William in 1059 and driven into exile, Abbot Robert was summoned before the ducal court on the accusation of his own prior that he had made jokes about William. Rather than appear, he fled and William proceeded to appoint a new abbot. Robert meanwhile put his case before Pope Nicholas II (1059-61) and, having obtained the pope's support, set off for Normandy in the company of two papal legates to reclaim his abbacy. On learning of this development, William flew into a violent rage, declared that he was prepared to receive legates from the pope on matters concerning the Christian faith, but that if any monk from his duchy dared to bring a plea against him, he would ignore his sacred cloth and hang him by his cowl from the top of the highest nearby oak tree. Robert decided that discretion was the better party of valour and retreated to Paris and afterwards southern Italy. The pope made no further effort to intervene, deciding presumably that, although the replacement of an abbot was undoubtedly a matter over which the pope ought to have jurisdiction, there was nothing that could be done in this case.

William's treatment of the English churchmen inherited from before 1066 roughly parallels his treatment of the English aristocracy. There was a period of co-existence until the revolts of 1068-9, followed by the deposition of a considerable number of bishops and abbots. William's earliest English charters show the two English archbishops, Stigand of Canterbury and Ealdred of York, in his company, apparently enjoying their traditional positions at the court of an English king. Ealdred, who crowned William in 1066 and who threw in his lot with the Normans, died in 1069. Stigand, whose position was regarded as irregular by the papacy, was deposed in 1070 by the papal legates at the Easter council at Winchester; he was afterwards treated as a political prisoner and kept in chains for the rest of his life. Four other English bishops lost their sees in 1070, leaving only two English prelates in office from before 1066, along with several foreigners appointed by Edward the Confessor. English abbots were by and large less ruthlessly treated, unless they had participated in rebellion, and most of them kept their positions until their deaths. Entire religious communities which had offended were also punished; the abbey of Abingdon, for example, had its estates and treasures plundered, while the abbey of Ely suffered appallingly for its support of the English rebel Hereward the Wake. The whole exercise of replacing English churchmen was conducted, like that of the English aristocracy, with a respect for proper legal form, notably in the use made of papal legates. It was, however, a procedure whose ruthlessness provoked anxieties about its legality at Rome and bitterness in its victims; Pope Alexander unavailingly asked for further enquiries into the case of Bishop Æthelric of Selsey and, according to William of Malmesbury, Archbishop Stigand believed that his treatment at William's hands amounted to a betrayal.

Stigand was replaced as Archbishop of Canterbury by Lanfranc. Lanfranc was William's choice for the archbishopric, even though he was already around fifty-five years of age. Because a collection of his letters written while he was archbishop has been preserved and because he had been a monk at Le Bec, an abbey which produced an extensive literature devoted to its own early history, we know more about Lanfranc than about most characters in this period. The letter collection, an interesting read, shows a man confident in his own knowledge and authority, but with considerable patience and understanding. He often tried to restrain the more hot-headed among the new Norman bishops in England. It shows clearly that this great churchman had both the personality and the status to heal the wounds of the battered English Church. An episode which is revealing for William's relations with his archbishop, and for his general attitude to the Norman Conquest, occurred in 1070 when Lanfranc proposed that the new Archbishop of York, Thomas of Bayeux, should make a profession of obedience to him. When Thomas refused, William's first instinct was to favour him, on the grounds that Lanfranc's argument was probably founded more on guile than on reason and truth – possible evidence that William, the crude soldier, often distrusted the schemes of his intellectual archbishop. But his suspicions were allayed when Lanfranc demonstrated that what he proposed was English custom. William also responded to the strategic point about the usefulness of a single source of authority in the English Church, especially when York was a potential focus for a Danish attack.

William's decision did not in fact end this particular argument. Thomas raised the matter again with Pope Alexander II during the visit to Rome which he and Lanfranc made to collect their symbolic *pallia* (the vestments of office appropriate to an archbishop) in 1071. The pope referred the dispute back to William's court which – unsurprisingly – found in Lanfranc's favour at a hearing at Winchester at Easter 1072 (around 8 April). Two original documents describing this settlement have survived in the archives of Canterbury cathedral. Both are exceptionally interesting; one especially so because it has on it the handwriting of several bishops, including Lanfranc. The procedure and the settlement in this affair show superbly the nature of the understanding between William and the papacy; the verdict was the one William wanted, but the authority for its enforcement was portrayed as being the pope's, which satisfied the honour and pretensions of both authorities. However, although the papacy accepted that Lanfranc should have primatial status, it made its general unease about a settlement which conflicted with normal papal policy evident by refusing to allow Lanfranc to pass his authority on to his successors. A favour to William was not necessarily going to set an undesirable precedent for the future.

After 1066 William maintained for himself the role in both England and Normandy which he had established in the Norman Church before the Conquest. As we have seen, his attitudes were in no major way alien to the traditions of an English Church already accustomed to domination by a succession of masterful kings. In Normandy, there were major councils at Rouen in 1070, 1072 and 1074 and at Lillebonne in 1080. The legislation of the Council of Lillebonne was especially important and demonstrated m a number of ways how ducal authority could be used to support the Church's mission. Following this Norman model, William revived the practice of holding councils of the entire English Church, with major synods being held at Winchester and Windsor in 1070, Winchester in 1072, London in 1075, Winchester in 1076, London in 1077 or 1078, and Gloucester in 1080 and 1085. William was present at most of them, and the near-contemporary, albeit prejudiced, Eadmer of Canterbury, believed that no legislation could be initiated by them without William's prior consent. The evidence for the history of the English Church during William's reign also shows that, as in Normandy, William was prepared to strengthen the Church's authority with his own where he thought it necessary; thus, a famous writ on the relationship of lay and ecclesiastical jurisdiction stated that anyone in England who refused to submit to the jurisdiction of a bishop was to be coerced by the king's sheriff.

William's support for the Church in England was reciprocated as the new Norman bishops and abbots lent their weight to the enforcement of the Norman Conquest. The mutual self-interest of king and Church is especially well illustrated by the requirements of the synod held at Winchester at Easter 1072 that every priest m England say three Masses for the king's health, and that anyone who spoke treason against William or his rule should be excommunicated. If the Norman soldiers did not catch the English rebels, then the clergy would! One story told by Orderic suggests that not all Normans were entirely happy with the ethics of the Norman takeover. Guitmund, a monk of the Norman abbey of La-Croix-Saint-Leuffroy, is said to have been summoned to England by William and offered an English bishopric. After careful Guitmund refused, telling the king to his face that the Conquest represented the spoils of robbery and that he could find no authority in the Scriptures for the imposition on Christians of a pastor chosen from among their enemies. He pointed out that Edgar the Ætheling had a better hereditary right to rule England than William and instructed him to watch out for the salvation of his soul. Since Orderic wrote over fifty years after events, we cannot be sure this incident ever took place. What may give it some credibility is that Guitmund, a noted theologian, took the unusual step between 1073 and 1077 of leaving Normandy and joining the entourage of Pope Gregory VII. He was exactly the type of man whom William would have wanted to become a bishop in England, and his departure suggests that the story may have a basis in truth. But the Winchester legislation shows how William's power encompassed all, and that the reorganization of the English Church was proceeding with the same ruthlessness which distinguished the Conquest and the land settlement. Guitmund's was a very lonely voice crying in a very large wilderness.

After Gregory VII became pope in 1073 relations between Rome and William and his Anglo-Norman clergy became more strained. The zealous Gregory represented a radical wing of the eleventh-century papal reform movement, and under him papal authority became much demanding and much less sympathetic to a king whose rule over the Church within his lands Gregory and his followers found objectionable in principle. Gregory differed from his immediate predecessors in believing that kings were not partners with whom the papacy should co-operate, but officials who should be obedient. He quarrelled bitterly with King Henry IV of Germany, and also with Philip I of France, excommunicating both. He sought to centralize the church as a means of instituting moral reform, and to this end he made the major innovation of appointing permanent legates to act on his behalf in France, men who were temperamentally and ideologically very different from the pliable likes of Bishop Ermenfrid of Sion, with whom William had usually dealt up to this point. Gregory also tried to insist that bishops make regular visits to Rome to attend papal synods.

In the decade after 1073 numerous embassies must have passed between William and Gregory and between the Anglo-Norman Church and Gregory's legates. Several aspects of William's rule over the Church in Normandy and England were challenged. The aged Lanfranc, for example, was rather unreasonably censured for his reluctance to travel to Rome, while the credentials for appointment of William '*Bona Anima*' ('Good Soul'), who was nominated to the archbishopric of Rouen in 1079, were closely examined because he was thought to be the son of a priest. Yet, in general, Gregory treated William with respect and never proceeded to extremes against him. Not only did he consistently praise William's kingship in his surviving letters, but he was also willing to favour his political interests, more than once overruling his permanent legates when they tried to attack him. For example, he upheld William's power in Maine by squashing efforts in 1079-80 to reinstate the abbot of the monastery of St-Pierre-de-la-Couture whom William had deposed, and in 1082 by favouring William's candidate for the bishopric of Le Mans against a rival supported by Count Fulk of Anjou. Gregory's opinion of William is revealed in a remarkably candid letter sent to his permanent legates in France in 1081: William should be handled gently and encouraged to improve because, although he did not show scrupulous obedience to the papacy, he did strive to provide peace and righteousness for his subjects, he did cause priests to leave their wives and mistresses, he had not supported Gregory's enemies, and he neither destroyed nor sold churches.

William appears to have dealt with Gregory on the basis that nothing should change from the way relations between the papacy and the Anglo-Norman dominions had been conducted before 1073. He was fully supported in this policy by Archbishop Lanfranc. The most remarkable illustration of William's belief that existing custom should determine relations with the papacy is the letter written in his name in 1080 in response to Gregory's demand that the annual payment from England to the papacy, known as Peter's Pence, be sent and that William become his vassal for the English kingdom. William's letter recognized that since Peter's Pence was a customary payment, it would be sent, and even apologized that its collection had fallen behind while he was in Normandy. However, he utterly rejected the request that he should become a papal vassal because it had no precedent and therefore was not customary. With regard to Anglo-Norman relations with the papacy in general, the monk Eadmer said that William enforced the rule that no one in his lands could receive a letter from a pope unless it had first been submitted to him. He also believed that no papal legate could enter William's lands without having first obtained permission. These rules have to be interpreted not as a barrier against papal authority, but as a statement that the Church in William's Anglo-Norman dominions was governed by king and pope in collaboration, as it had been up until 1073; William always remained willing to consult Gregory on matters which he thought to be legitimately his concern. To the end of his life, William governed the Church in his lands in the traditional manner of his predecessors. He clearly thought that Gregory VII represented a novel breed of pope who would soon disappear. When a papal schism developed in the 1080s, because the German King Henry IV had launched armies against Gregory and had nominated an anti-pope, William and Lanfranc must have believed, with considerable justification, that it was their protectiveness which secured the welfare of the Anglo-Norman Church against such chaos.

William and Religion

We are assured by William of Poitiers that William heard Mass daily and had done so from his early years. It may be that, like Edward the Confessor, he heard Mass before setting out on the morning's hunting. This would probably often have been in the chapel of one of his residences; St John's chapel in the Tower of London, which was begun in William's reign, but finished under William Rufus, is probably an example of a building designed for this purpose.

Like any ruler of his time, William would have had clergy in regular attendance as his court travelled around his lands. These clerics, his chaplains, would have conducted services in his chapel, as well as perform administrative functions. According to Orderic, William was humble and respectful in the company of especially religious men, listening carefully to what they said. He was certainly able to put on a display of appropriate religious humility, for when he was admitted into the confraternity of the abbey of Cluny in either 1074 or 1075, his demeanour was apparently so humble that it appeared as if he was being invested with the gift of God's grace by an angel. He informed the barons who were with him that joining the community of Cluny was a pledge of eternal salvation, something far greater than the crown he had gained, which was merely an ephemeral, worldly possession.

One insight into William's religious attitudes is given by the character of the clergy who were his most frequent companions and of the men he chose to appoint to bishoprics. One of the chaplains always served after 1066 as William's chancellor, supervising the drafting and writing of charters. The first chancellor, the Englishman Regenbald, represents the survival of English personnel in high office in the first part of the reign. Of later chancellors, one, Herfast, who became Bishop of Thetford, was censured by Lanfranc for his ignorance of the law, while another, Maurice, the later Bishop of London, was certainly not sexually chaste. The presence at one stage of the historian William of Poitiers as one of the chaplains shows that high literary abilities were valued in William's clerical household. Thomas, who became Archbishop of York in 1070, was notable for both his spiritual and moral qualities and his competence as a bishop. But, taken as a whole, the chaplains were a mixed bunch, and in general, administrative ability and worldliness appear to have been preferred to any display of religion. At the end of the reign, William's clerical servants included the lecherous Rannulf Flambard, the formidably intelligent chief adviser of King William Rufus, a man who made himself notorious for his financial exactions from the Church, but who later made a successful Bishop of Durham.

A high proportion of William's appointments to bishoprics were made from among his chaplains, suggesting that he regarded administrative ability and worldly wisdom as the most desirable qualifications for appointment to the office of bishop. The majority of appointees were Normans, although their number also included the Italian Michael, who became Bishop of Avranches in 1068, and the chancellor Maurice, who came from Maine and became Bishop of London in 1085. The occasional appointment could be exceptionally distinguished, such as the Lotharingian Robert, a very religious man and a notable astronomer and mathematician, who was made Bishop of Hereford. But some of the men chosen for bishoprics in William's reign were deficient in terms of education, or dealt tactlessly with the English, or were not sexually chaste. It is probable that the need to find suitable bishops and abbots for the English Church stretched the resources of the Norman Church to breaking point; Normandy was after all a relatively small province. That William was sensitive to this problem is suggested by his approach in the late 1070s to Abbot Hugh of Cluny to purchase six (or possibly twelve) of his monks to fill ecclesiastical offices in England. Given Cluny's great reputation, William's wish to obtain the best is notable. But his methods were amazingly crude. Abbot Hugh's reply is barely courteous; he pointed out that his monks were not for sale and that he did not wish to hazard their lives in a distant and barbarous kingdom. Crushingly, in the context of the Norman Conquest, he quoted at William the text from Matthew's Gospel: 'For what has a man profited, if he shall gain the whole world, but lose his own soul?'

Another explanation of this approach to Cluny and indeed of the worldliness of some of William's chaplains and bishops is that, like most of his contemporaries, he believed that all truly religious men and women were monks and nuns. A bishop was in practice an administrator and courtier, as well as a pastor, and a degree of worldly wisdom was therefore highly desirable. Monks and nuns, however, were thought to live their lives in intimate contact with God and, for this reason, William would have thought his soul best safeguarded by the numerous. gifts which he can be shown to have made to monasteries throughout his life. He was personally responsible for two major foundations, St-Etienne of Caen and Battle abbey. The well-preserved charters of St-Etienne show that William made an initial generous provision of land and thereafter kept a close watch over the community's welfare. He also exerted himself on the new abbey's behalf to acquire a suitable set of relics, purchasing a portion of St Stephen's arm and a phial of his blood from Besançon in eastern central France. The late twelfth-century chronicle of Battle abbey, a rather untrustworthy source, says that the abbey's foundation was the result of a vow which William made before the beginning of the Battle of Hastings. However, given the considerable lapse of time before the start of building at Battle, the abbey is more likely to have been an act of atonement after the battle was over. The chronicler's story that William insisted that the abbey be built on the site where Harold had fallen is probably true. It suggests that in Battle abbey we are dealing with something more like a modern war memorial than a pure act of penance. It drew attention to the fact of William's victory, while at the same time acting as a reminder that many men had died around this place.

These major foundations were merely part of a much more wide-ranging religious patronage. In various ways William acted as a patron to a large number of churches. Four examples from very many are his procurement of an arm bone of its patron saint for the abbey of Cerisy, which had been founded by his

49. The seal of Battle Abbey, founded by William the Conqueror after his victory there. It was said that the altar of the Abbey Church was located exactly on the spot where Harold was killed.

father; his patronage of Westminster abbey, which had been greatly enriched by Edward the Confessor; a gift to the cathedral church of Le Mans when it had been damaged in war; and one of property to support the establishment of a cathedral church at Lincoln. In his later years he developed into a patron on an international scale, for example, obtaining monks from the abbey of Marmoutier near Tours for Battle abbey and also giving Marmoutier the funds with which to construct a new dormitory. He also gave money to the abbey of St-Denis near Paris to build a new tower which, however, fell down before it was completed. The underlying motive was always the salvation of his soul, but the specific motives would vary from one gift to another; some would be grants to a famous church or saint, whereas others would be to support churches over which he had authority or for which he had special responsibilities. On occasion, it is likely that William went out of his way for specific personal reasons, as when he attended the dedication of a small priory founded by two courtiers who had become hermits. But it was also possible for patronage and protection to be withdrawn. The Norman abbeys of Fécamp and Mont St-Michel both offended at some stage and had estates taken away, while the resources of some English communities took a bad beating after 1066. After arresting his brother Odo, he actually dissolved the abbey which he had founded just outside Bayeux. In short, his charity, like his government and his wars, was determined by policy, not indiscriminate generosity.

To modern eyes the Conqueror's practice of Christianity appears deeply superstitious. To his contemporaries, however, he was the opposite of superstitious. There were several unpromising omens during the Hastings campaign, such as his hauberk being the wrong way round, but he dismissed them saying that these trifles would be overcome by God's favour. It is noticeable that William's religious patronage became especially generous at difficult times. He founded a college of canons at Cherbourg during a serious illness, founded the two Caen abbeys with Mathilda as a penance, had one of them dedicated before the invasion of 1066 and the other in 1077 within a year of his first military defeat, and established Battle abbey on the site of his bloodiest battle. These are the actions of a man trying to propitiate a demanding deity, aware that his violent way of life placed him in danger of being despatched to hell by sudden death and that his brutal actions imposed a heavy burden of sin. There can be no doubt that William spent his whole life in fear of eternal damnation. He was more than conventionally pious for a layman of his time – we should note, above all, that few contemporary rulers took as much trouble as he did to reform the Church and that many of them quarrelled with the reforming popes of the second half of the eleventh century. But his Christianity was essentially the unimaginative compliance of a worldly man in the forms and fashions set out by the eleventh-century Church. The clergy who surrounded him would have encouraged his sense of guilt, and he, perhaps beneath the warrior's exterior, a rather pessimistic spirit, responded.

William's government of the Church was a task well and sincerely performed, although it is likely that the duty to uphold the existing traditions of royal and ducal authority, which always weighed so heavily with him, was a major determinant of many of his actions. In the end, we have to see him as cut off from all notions of a reconciling and loving God, rarely able to forget that he would one day be judged. The epitaph written by the Anglo-Saxon Chronicler noted that the Church in England had prospered under William's rule, but that he did good and bad things during his life. He preferred to leave the judgement about the fate of this fearsome man's soul to God.

Eleven

DIFFICULT TIMES

Orderic Vitalis noticed that in the last years of his life William did not enjoy the same success as previously. In the normal medieval manner he tried to explain this in terms of the removal of divine favour. He identified the decisive turning point as the beheading of Earl Waltheof of Northumbria on 31 May 1076, remarking that many men criticized William for Waltheof's death and that by the just judgement of God he suffered great adversity for the rest of his life. Henceforth, Orderic said, the king never drove an army from the field of battle and did not succeed in storming any fortress which he besieged; it was only his great personal fortitude which enabled him to struggle on. Nowadays we naturally seek earthly causes for William's difficulties. The revival of his traditional enemies in France was obviously one; his rivals in the 1050s, the French monarchy and the county of Anjou, were once again under the control of effective rulers. Another was the emergence of a younger and impatient generation who were anxious to share in the rewards of success with a king who showed no wish to relinquish any of the reins of power, and whose ambitions found a focus in the dissatisfaction of William's eldest son. A third was the continuing instability around the northern and western fringes of the English kingdom, which erupted into life again once it became clear that William was tied down by events in Normandy.

Although William was fifty in 1077-78 and became extremely fat in his last years, there does not appear to have been much of a decline in health and vigour; like many medieval men, he remained active right up to the moment that a final fatal illness struck him down. The fundamental point is that the challenges to his domination multiplied and sharpened from the mid-1070s and that he was at the same time harnessed to his own achievement. William himself seems to have decided that the great days of expansion and conquest were over and that it was now necessary to consolidate in England and hold on to the gains. The last three chapters have shown how efficiently much of this was done. As a result, there were many triumphant moments in the years from 1074 until William's death in 1087 and there is nothing which resembles a serious failure. But a man who had shown himself more capable of controlling events around him than most mortals, was more obviously confronted in these later years than previously by the limitations on action and achievement which all have to accept.

The Onset of Troubles

After spending 1074 in Normandy, William remained there for much of 1075 as well, staying at Fécamp for Easter, where he forbad private vengeance in cases of murder to everyone except the father or a son of the victim. This was part of a policy in Normandy, which had begun with the proclamation of the Truce of God in 1047, of bringing the punishment of serious crimes of violence under the authority of the duke and his courts, and reducing the long-established right of the kindred to exact revenge. Also at Easter his daughter Cecilia, who had been received as a child in 1066 to be a novice in the abbey of La Trinité of Caen, was ordained as a nun by Archbishop John of Rouen. Although we have very little evidence for this year, it is a fair presumption that William spent most of it scrutinizing the projects of his enemies around the Norman frontier. In the meantime, however, a major revolt had broken out in England. Two letters written by Archbishop Lanfranc show that the king was in close touch with events and that he was ready to return as soon as needed. Lanfranc dissuaded him from doing so while the warfare involved only the subjugation of rebels within England:

> we should welcome seeing you as we would God's angel, yet we do not want you to cross the sea at this moment; for you would be offering us a grave insult were you to come to our assistance in subduing such perjured brigands.

The central figures in the revolt were Ralph, Earl of Norfolk and Suffolk, and Roger, Earl of Hereford, the son of William fitz Osbern. Their conspiracy was hatched at the wedding feast celebrating Earl Ralph's marriage to Roger's sister Emma, a union which, so the earliest sources tell us, had been arranged with the king's permission, and which joined together the son of one of Edward the Confessor's protégés and one of the greatest Norman families. The causes of the rebellion are obscure. Ralph had no obvious motive that we can see. Roger, whom Orderic thought a proud man, had inherited his father's lands in England, but clearly disliked not succeeding automatically to the privileges and prominent political position which his father had enjoyed. Another of Lanfranc's letters from the year reveals that one aspect of Roger's demotion was that the king's sheriffs had been holding courts on his lands and that this was resented. William sought a basis for compromise by ordering that the sheriffs desist until he returned to England to hold an enquiry. This evidently was not enough for Roger, who wanted an immediate end to the intrusions.

Earls Ralph and Roger hoped to lead a large-scale revolt. The half-Breton Ralph, who had estates in Brittany, was able to involve many of the Bretons who had settled in England since 1066. A request for assistance was also sent to the King of Denmark, thereby stirring up the possibility of a rerun of the events of 1069-70. However, the prompt action of William's deputies in England ensured that the revolt was crushed before the Danes arrived. Ralph's forces were beaten near Cambridge and he was compelled to retreat to his castle at Norwich. An army commanded by the Englishmen, Bishop Wulfstan of Worcester and Abbot Æthelwig of Evesham, kept Earl Roger confined in the west. Ralph left Norwich in his wife's custody while he tried to hasten the Danes' arrival, but the castle was forced to surrender. He then returned to Brittany where he established himself in the castle at Dol from which he could launch raids across Normandy's eastern frontier. Roger surrendered and was ultimately condemned by William's court to loss of lands and perpetual imprisonment.

The imminent arrival of the rebels' Danish allies brought William across the Channel in the autumn of 1075. Normandy was left in Mathilda's custody, supported by Archbishop John of Rouen and Roger de Beaumont, with Robert Curthose possibly as a figurehead titular ruler. A remarkable original charter from this period shows Mathilda and her colleagues present in Rouen cathedral when Simon, Count of Amiens, Valois and the Vexin, restored an estate on the frontier between Normandy and his county into the possession of the cathedral. The Danes, however, did not dare to fight with William, preferring to return home with a lot of treasure after sacking York – or rather what was left of it after the events of 1069-70.

With most of the troubles in England over, William spent Christmas 1075 at Westminster. The feast was probably celebrated with a major court and crown-wearing, following the traditional pattern when William was in England. Many of the Bretons who had supported Earl Ralph were either exiled or blinded and William also organized the burial of King Edward the Confessor's widow Edith in Westminster abbey, near to her husband. She had lived at Winchester since 1066, and had died in the week prior to Christmas 1075. As far as we know, she had kept out of great affairs since the Conquest, although as King Harold's sister, she must have felt the course of events profoundly. Her emotional experiences may be reflected in the 'Life of King Edward' (*Vita Ædwardi Regis*), written for her in the period either side of 1066. The period of its composition is reflected in its change of tone from a celebration of the triumphs of Harold and his brothers, through gloom and despair, to a description of King Edward's religious life. It is typical of William to have given an honourable and especially ostentatious burial to the widow of the man who had given him his title to rule England; he was once more emphasizing his belief in the continuity of his rule from that of the Old English kings.

The part played in the revolt of 1075 by the last Englishman still holding the position of earl, Waltheof of Northumbria and Huntingdon, was a subject of differing opinions among eleventh and twelfth-century historians. Waltheof was certainly present at the wedding feast where treason was plotted. According to Orderic Vitalis, who had access to the traditions of Crowland abbey where Waltheof was buried, the earl refused to take part when sounded out by the conspirators, but was then bound by an oath not to reveal their plans. William of Malmesbury also knew these traditions and remarked that the Normans and the English disagreed on the extent to which Waltheof was culpable. He came to prefer the English view, and thought that Waltheof became involved in the oath only because of the conviviality of the feasting. At some stage in the summer or autumn, he crossed to Normandy to seek William's mercy. He was brought back to England and tried, and when the court could not agree on a verdict, he was kept in prison at Winchester. He was subsequently condemned and on 31 May 1076 beheaded outside the city on St Giles Hill, the punishment being that required by English law. It is not entirely clear that William was present when sentence was passed.

Different, and passionate, opinions were held on Waltheof's fate. A great influence on both Orderic and William of Malmesbury, as on others, was the miracles which took place at his tomb at Crowland. They and other writers therefore thought the punishment excessively severe. One early twelfth-century source, the chronicle known as 'Florence of Worcester', even offered the opinion that no less a person than Archbishop Lanfranc had thought Waltheof innocent. On the other hand, another early twelfth-century writer, who was clearly less influenced by the miracles, thought him a traitor and called him a 'second Absalom'. Orderic believed that the earl had been condemned 'by a powerful group of enemies' who coveted his lands. A clear judgement on William's treatment of Waltheof needs to take account of the fact that the earl had rebelled before in the 1060s, had been forgiven and reinstated, and had been given the king's niece in marriage. In support of his relative innocence is the fact that there is no record of his playing any discernible part in the fighting in 1075. On the other hand, his willingness to become at all involved in the conspiracy shows that he was at the least susceptible to talk of sedition; he thereby became an accomplice, if not a participant. William must have approved of his execution, even if he was not actually present when it was agreed. He may be open to criticism for killing someone who may only have flirted with treachery on this occasion, as indeed he may also be criticized for imprisoning for ever the young and relatively inexperienced Earl Roger. But, as we have seen, William was never notable for his tolerance of those who were persistently disloyal, and both Waltheof and Roger had been given their chances to draw back.

William may have stayed in England until Easter (1 April) 1076, when an important ecclesiastical council was held under Lanfranc's presidency at Winchester, and he may even have remained until Waltheof's execution on 31 May; there is no specific reference in the sources to his presence on either occasion. One decision that was certainly taken while he was still in England was to fill the gap in the far north left by Waltheof's defection by giving responsibility there to Bishop Walcher of Durham, who was willing to purchase the office of Earl of Northumbria. On his return to Normandy William's immediate preoccupation was the threat posed to western Normandy by the presence of the unrepentant Earl Ralph in the castle of Dol, especially as Ralph had allied himself with rebels against the rule of Count Hoel in Brittany and had received a detachment of troops from Count Fulk Rechin of Anjou. William led an army to Dol in September and set about reducing the castle by his usual tactic of terrorizing the surrounding countryside. Some time later, probably in November, the King of France, Philip I, arrived and caught William's army by surprise, gaining a decisive victory. The sources do not tell us how the normally resourceful William was so badly out-generalled. It is at least clear, however, that King Philip had prepared his lightning stroke very thoroughly; in October, for example, he had been at Poitiers seeking the support of the Duke of Aquitaine. William is said to have sustained great losses of men, horses and treasure. He retreated back to Normandy, having suffered the first major military setback of his life.

The defeat at Dol, although a dramatic event, was one without major consequences. William had simply been shown to be vulnerable on the battlefield, where he had previously appeared unbeatable. There was even some good news either in late 1076, or perhaps in early 1077, when an attack on the castle of La Flèche in southern Maine by Count Fulk Rechin was beaten off, and Count Fulk wounded during the unsuccessful siege. The garrison of La Flèche, commanded by its pro-Norman castellan, John de La Flèche, had been helped by reinforcements from Normandy. There was a considerable setback, however, before May 1077 when Simon, Count of Amiens, Valois and the Vexin, became a monk and handed the territory known as the French Vexin over to King Philip I. Simon's action was legally correct since he was Philip's vassal for most of his lands and counties, even though he was actually the vassal of the important abbey of St-Denis for the county of the

French Vexin. But since he had been educated at William's court and was so close to him that William is said to have thought of him as a foster son, his retirement was a serious blow; his lands had created a barrier between Normandy and one of its encircling enemies. Given that Simon had been the vassal of the abbey of St-Denis, William probably took the view that he had no legitimate basis on which to act against this unfavourable turn of events. A peace was agreed between him and Philip at some time in 1077. Late in 1077, or perhaps early in 1078, William also made a truce with Count Fulk Rechin. Political relations in northern France had apparently been stabilized again, but the *cordon sanitaire* which had existed around Normandy's frontiers from around 1060 had been irretrievably breached.

Family Quarrels

A notable feature of the year 1077 was the dedication of several important churches in Normandy. Bishop Odo's new cathedral at Bayeux was consecrated on 14 July and William's abbey of St-Etienne of Caen on 13 September. Also consecrated in the same year were the cathedral church of Evreux at an unknown date, and the church of the abbey of Le Bec, where Lanfranc had first become a monk, on 23 October. William attended the ceremonies at Bayeux and Caen, but was not at Le Bec; it is not known whether he was at Evreux.

The assemblies at Bayeux and Caen were magnificent occasions, attended by great gatherings of the Anglo-Norman aristocracy. An original charter which dates from the time of the dedication of St-Etienne was attested by a galaxy of Anglo-Norman notables: William, Mathilda, their sons Robert and William, Bishop Odo, Roger de Montgommery, Roger de Beaumont, Earl Hugh of Chester, Count Robert of Eu, and others. The two English archbishops, Lanfranc of Canterbury and Thomas of York, both crossed the Channel specially – in addition to the social pressure to attend, both had a personal interest in the churches since Lanfranc was a former abbot of St-Etienne and Thomas was a former canon and treasurer of Bayeux. Bayeux cathedral was a suitably splendid building for a prelate with Odo's extravagant tastes; the monumental carvings which survive from the crossing of the cathedral, for example, were extremely ambitious pieces of sculpture for eleventh-century Normandy. In the case of St-Etienne, the church which was consecrated was the one of which the nave and west front can still be seen (see Chapter 4). The year was clearly one of major religious and ceremonial importance for William and his family, as well as supplying an opportunity to show off their achievements. No source suggests that the dedications were timed to propitiate God's anger after a military defeat, but the possibility cannot be ruled out.

William's continuing anxieties about events around Normandy's frontiers may account for his surprising absence from the consecration of the abbey church at Le Bec, a ceremony which under normal circumstances he would surely have attended. His preoccupations are shown by the fact that in late 1077 or early 1078 he was at Laigle, prowling around the southern regions of Normandy. It was there that the quarrel with his son Robert came into the open, a rift which destroyed the unity of William's family and of the Anglo-Norman ruling group for several years to come.

The breach between William and Robert is described by Orderic Vitalis in a passage which gets us as near as we ever get to daily life in William's court. He tells us that the family was at Laigle and that Robert was staying in the house of one Roger Cauchois. His younger brothers William and Henry went to visit him, taking along the group of young warriors who must have been their constant companions. They went into the upper storey and began to play dice and to behave in a rowdy way; their antics included throwing water down on to Robert and his party below. Robert, egged on by his companions, took exception to this disturbance. He was told that he should not tolerate such insubordination and, in any case, was not his brothers' occupation of the upper floor symbolic? He went upstairs in a fury and a row ensued. Their father arrived and patched up the quarrel, but during the following night Robert and his followers deserted from the army and tried to take the castle at Rouen by surprise. The motive was obviously to take control of the duchy of Normandy. Foiled by the vigilant castellan, they left Normandy and began to make war on its frontiers.

This story may not be true in every detail; the participation of the youngest brother Henry is unlikely, since he was at most nine years old in 1078. Otherwise it seems acceptable, especially since Laigle is situated less than ten miles from the monastery at which Orderic was later to be a monk. At a personal level the ages of the sons look to be an important factor in the quarrel. Robert in his mid-twenties had had some experience and was now chafing at the bit under his father's tutelage. William, in his late teens, was prominent in charter attestations from 1074; his emergence may have been resented. Robert's basic grievance, however, was one felt by many sons in this age when succession to property was the only way to power. According to Orderic he had already argued violently with his father about his lack of lands and resources, and had gone as far as to demand possession of the duchy of Normandy and of the county of Maine. As we saw in Chapter Seven, William saw his family as sharing in and supporting his own power. He was, however, implacably opposed to relinquishing any of it on more than a temporary basis.

50. Effigy of Robert of Normandy, son of William the Conqueror, Gloucester Cathedral.

Robert left Normandy with a group of similarly discontented young men, some of them the sons of William's own companions, such as Robert de Bellême, the son of Roger de Montgommery, William de Breteuil, the son and successor in Normandy of William fitz Oshern, and Roger, the son of Richard fitz Gilbert. They were welcomed by William's enemies around the duchy's frontiers. Hugh de Châteauneuf, who was Robert de Bellême's brother-in-law, gave them the use of his castles, and they installed themselves at Rémalard, twenty-five miles due south of Laigle and the same distance due east of Alençon, in the hope of making raids into Normandy and attracting allies. William retaliated by confiscating the rebels' lands and buying the support of Hugh de Châteauneuf's lord, Count Rotrou of Mortagne. He then invested Rémalard with four fortifications of his own. Robert, who was already negotiating with King Philip of France, apparently decided to try to obtain further allies and to widen the front on which he could attack. He visited his uncle, Count Robert of Flanders, who, since seizing the county in 1070-1 and winning the battle in which William fitz Osbern had been killed, had been William's enemy. As a result, by the winter of 1078-9 Robert had occupied the castle of Gerberoi to the south-east of Normandy, which he had been given by King Philip, and from where he began to make raids across the Norman frontier and to offer lavish promises to anyone who would support him.

William reacted by fortifying the Norman castles near Gerberoi and by making a settlement with King Philip, a man who, as he grew older, was usually willing to take money rather than fight. In January 1079 William invested Gerberoi and maintained a siege for three weeks until the garrison sallied forth and engaged his besieging army in battle. In the mêlée Robert fought against his own father and wounded him in the hand. William, as personally involved in the conflict as ever, also had a horse shot from under him. The early twelfth-century chronicle known as 'Florence of Worcester' suggests that Robert did not recognize his father until he heard him speak. This is possible, since heraldic devices were not yet in use, but intrinsically unlikely. William, a large man who was becoming increasingly corpulent, was surely too striking a figure not to be spotted, especially by his own son. It is hard to avoid the conclusion that Robert had come to hate his father. Robert's brother William, who had continued to support his father, was also wounded. The king withdrew to Rouen; his son Robert to Flanders. William of Malmesbury thought this defeat William's one misfortune in a dazzling career.

The effects of this quarrel were profoundly damaging to William and to his power. A family which had previously carried all before it was now divided; as we saw in Chapter Seven, Mathilda was torn between loyalty and affection for husband and son. The king was detained permanently in Normandy and could not cross to England when he wished to do so, a problem which was apparently resolved by giving his brother Odo a commission to act as regent, a position he probably retained until the late summer of 1080 when William was at last able to sail over the Channel. The Norman aristocracy was divided by the quarrel, since members of the younger generation of a number of families supported Robert. This was civil war at its bitterest and most desolating which also gave William's northern French enemies a chance to attack him.

The older members of the Norman aristocracy appear to have grasped the need for peace. Roger de Montgommery, Roger de Beaumont and Earl Hugh of Chester were among those who tried to effect a reconciliation and to persuade William to forgive his son. The former Count Simon of the Vexin, whose resignation from his county had caused such a stir in 1077, and who was now a hermit, also visited the Norman court in 1079 to try to mediate. He had a strong personal interest since he was a contemporary of Robert and, having been brought up by William, must have known all the combatants intimately. The quarrel even attracted diplomatic representations from as far afield as the papal court, from where Gregory VII appears to have tried to exert his influence. William remained stubborn, however, and a peace was not finally sealed until a little before Easter (12 April) 1080, when William and Robert were together at a great assembly held at Rouen, along with many of the major Norman magnates and some distinguished non-Norman ones, including representatives of the pope. Pope Gregory subsequently wrote Robert a letter about filial duty.

The Anglo-Norman Frontiers

The peace terms confirmed Robert's status as the heir to Normandy. If William had wished to be vindictive, he was not allowed to be. The two remained in Normandy until at least 14 July 1080, when both were at Caen. In the intervening period William had spent Whitsun at Lillebonne, which is near the River Seine, to the north-east of Rouen, where a major council of the Norman Church was held. This synod's legislation was of great importance, mainly as a definition of bishops' rights to fines, and was sufficiently fundamental to the development of the Church in Normandy to merit a later confirmation by King Henry II. After July William crossed to England, taking Mathilda, Robert, and his younger son William with him. This visit to the kingdom was something of a triumphal return after an absence of around four years. There were great ceremonial crown-wearings at Gloucester at Christmas 1080 and at Winchester at Whitsun 1081. It was during this visit that William would have received the famous embassy from Pope Gregory VII requesting that he do fealty to the papacy for the English kingdom, and which he dismissed so imperiously.

The visit enabled William to tackle problems which had arisen in northern England and in Wales. In the North the framework for peaceful co-existence finally established in 1072 by the Peace of Abernethy with King Malcolm of Scotland had collapsed. The Scottish king had raided northern England in August and September 1079, departing with much plunder and many slaves, and encountering no effective resistance from the Normans. On 14 May 1080 William's representative in Northumbria since the execution of Earl Waltheof, Bishop Walcher of Durham, was murdered at Gateshead, apparently as a consequence of feuds among the native aristocracy. This event triggered an expedition in the summer of 1080 by William's regent, Bishop Odo, which avenged Walcher's death by carrying out a policy of devastation in Northumbria similar to William's in Yorkshire in 1069-70. In the autumn William sent his son Robert north with a large army to deal with the King of the Scots, but Robert found King Malcolm as elusive as his father had done in 1072. There was no pitched battle because Malcolm retreated before Robert's advance. They eventually confronted one another at Falkirk where terms similar to those of the Peace of Abernethy were agreed, Malcolm doing homage to Robert and giving hostages for future good behaviour. An early twelfth-century Durham writer thought the expedition ineffective but, in truth, it is hard to see how Robert could have achieved more; Scotland's remoteness and its geography made it an impregnable fortress.

William made his only known visit to Wales in 1081. It is possible that his journey took place in the spring, using the Christmas court at Gloucester as a stepping-off point, but more likely that it occurred in the summer. He moved through south Wales as far as St Davids in the far west. The Anglo-Saxon Chronicle presents this as a military campaign on which many prisoners (presumably Welsh ones) were released. The Welsh sources see it as a pilgrimage to honour St David. The former is more likely, if only because William appears to have reacted to a recent disturbance in the balance of power in south Wales. Up until 1081 Chepstow and the River Wye had been the effective limit of Norman power. There had been no significant attempt at an advance and peace had been kept by an alliance with the dominant power in Glamorgan, King Caradog ap Gruffydd, which had been made by the Earls of Hereford, William fitz Osbern and his son Roger. When some of the Welsh supported Earl Roger's rebellion in 1075, William may have sent troops into Glamorgan to chastise them, but this was no more than a punitive expedition. The general stability of relations was not threatened until King Caradog's defeat and death in 1081 at the hands of the most powerful of the Welsh princes, the King of Deheubarth, Rhys ap Tewdwr. The evidence of Domesday Book shows that a consequence of William's expedition was that Rhys agreed to pay a tribute of forty pounds a year. A secondary result was the establishment of a mint at what was later to become the town of Cardiff.

In the latter part of 1081 William recrossed the Channel and took an army to the southern region of Maine. Count Fulk of Anjou had again attacked the castle of La Flèche, from which he had previously been repulsed either in late 1076 or in 1077. This time he had both a large army and an alliance with Count Hoel of Brittany. His strategy was obviously to profit from William's absence in Britain and he was able to take and burn the castle. According to Orderic, William's advance to La Flèche seemed likely to cause a major battle but, instead, a papal legate arrived and started negotiations for peace. Among the Normans, Roger de Montgommery and Count William of Evreux, both lords with major possessions in the south of Normandy, encouraged a settlement. The result was an affirmation of the status quo. Fulk accepted that the Normans held Maine and William's son Robert did homage to him for it, as he had previously done to Count Geoffrey the Bearded in *c.*1064. There was an amnesty for the supporters of both sides, a reflection of that perennial and unresolved division of political loyalties within the aristocracy of the county of Maine which always weakened William's authority there.

The five years from 1076 until the end of 1081 were full of alarms for William. Mostly he had held his lands together and had capably survived some serious and, as far as he was concerned, unaccustomed setbacks. Events had shown that neither King Philip nor Count Fulk, nor any Norman or English rebels, nor the King of Scots could inflict any deep hurt on him. A useful perspective on the troubles of these years is that William's campaigns all took place beyond Normandy's frontiers; the contrast with the period before 1060 is a striking one. William in fact emerged from six difficult years with his power only slightly weakened. He had merely learnt – if he needed to do so – that the Achilles heel of many powerful men is their own family and that his capacity to dominate events beyond his lands' frontiers was limited.

William's objectives throughout this awkward period had been to consolidate, rather than to make further gains, and this, by and large, is what he accomplished. He had clearly come to the conclusion that the years of conquest were over and that it was time to hold on to what he had. Norman territorial power was moved a little further northwards by Bishop Odo and this had been given symbolic expression when, on his return journey from Scotland, Robert Curthose built a castle, called the 'New Castle', at what is now Newcastle-upon-Tyne. To secure the advance a new French earl was sent north to Northumbria; he resigned within a year, but his successor, Robert de Mowbray, described by Orderic as a strong and dark man with a hairy body who rarely smiled, made a success of the job for the rest of William's reign. Wales was always a threat to the security of the Norman settlement in the neighbouring regions of England. But the campaign of 1081 established a stable relationship through expedient means with its numerous small kingdoms, which lasted for the rest of William's life. As with Scotland, William had no aspirations to conquest, but aimed merely to construct *a modus vivendi*. In Maine William was also content to produce a diplomatic confirmation of existing relations through a show of force. The marriage of his youngest daughter Adela to Stephen, Count of Blois and Chartres, which took place at about this time, is a sign that in the early 1080s, he was attempting to gain allies to neutralize his northern French enemies. Again he achieved a degree of success; according to Orderic, the settlement with Count Fulk ended hostilities with Anjou for the rest of William's life.

Twelve

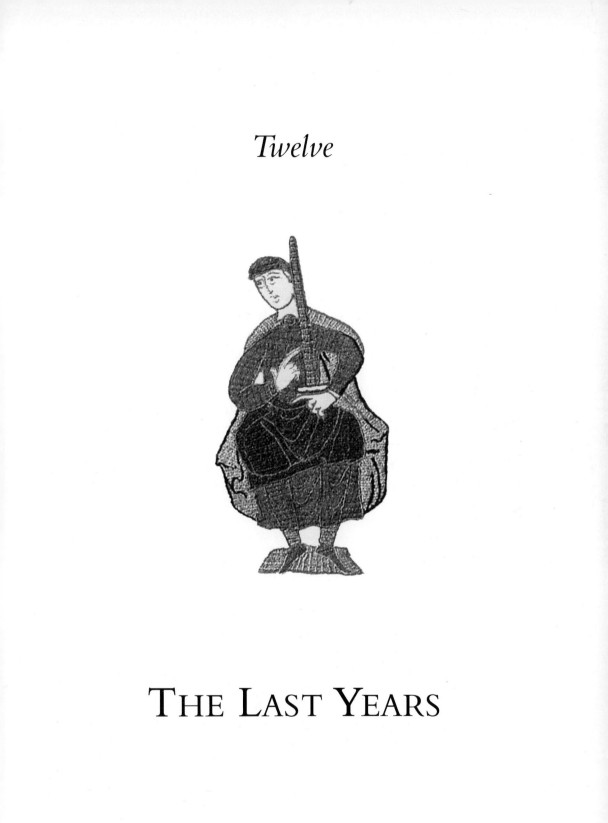

THE LAST YEARS

The years between 1082 and 1084 are the most obscure of William s reign as king. The chronicles almost dry up and even Orderic can give specific information only about a small number of subjects. The probable explanation is that these were mostly years of relative peace in Normandy and England, with only a few crises. In addition, since William spent most of this period in France, there was nothing for the Anglo-Saxon Chronicler to record in England. The outstanding events were further family quarrels, more revolts in Maine, and Mathilda's death.

The evidence of charters suggests that after concluding the treaty with Count Fulk Rechin of Anjou in late 1081, William returned to Normandy by way of Le Mans. There, in a charter dated to 'the year of the death of Bishop Arnold' (Bishop Arnold of Le Mans died on 29 November 1081), he confirmed the grant of a fief by the collegiate church of St-Pierre-de-la-Cour of Le Mans to a vassal who was to serve the Church in England, Normandy or anywhere else for one month every year. As St-Pierre was the private chapel of the Counts of Maine, and therefore William's personal chapel in Le Mans, its need to have a vassal who could serve throughout the king's far-flung dominions may reflect its special relationship with William. Nonetheless, the fact that a church in Maine, where there had been no significant Norman colonization, should expect such a service is remarkable testimony to how strong William's personal power throughout his lands must have appeared by the 1080s.

After departing from Maine, William spent most of 1082 moving around Normandy. The main charters from this year are confirmations of grants to various churches by William's less flamboyant half-brother, Count Robert of Mortain. One among them must have been of special interest to William, since it confirmed the possessions of the abbey of Grestain, which Count Robert's father Herluin de Conteville had founded, and where William's and Robert's mother was buried. The charter shows that Robert had taken over Herluin's religious foundation and endowed it richly with lands in Normandy and England, but that William himself had not made any large gifts of land. He had, however, demonstrated his special regard for the monastery by agreeing that the gifts he had made should be held on the same terms as those he had made to the abbey of St-Etienne of Caen. The document is undated, but can probably be assigned to the autumn of 1082. It was witnessed not only by William and Count Robert of Mortain, but also by their other brother, Bishop Odo of Bayeux, and must therefore represent one of the last occasions on which William and Odo were together on amicable terms.

The story of Odo's fall is bizarre. However, since it is told in essentially the same details by three independent early twelfth-century writers, it has to be believed. Orderic, William of Malmesbury and the incorrectly named 'Hyde Chronicle' all say that Odo was involved in a scheme to purchase the papacy for himself. He had bribed Romans and purchased a palace in Rome, perhaps by using pilgrims as his agents. He had also recruited large numbers of knights to support his cause, including no less a figure than Earl Hugh of Chester. This fantastic scheme is just credible if we accept that Odo knew of Gregory VII's mounting difficulties as his cardinals deserted him and as the armies of the German King Henry IV threatened Rome. It is possible that Odo hoped to present himself as an acceptable compromise between Gregory and Henry's anti-pope Clement III, and that he expected assistance from the Normans who had settled in southern Italy. William, however, disapproved strongly of the project and, having crossed to England, captured Odo just as he was about to leave the Isle of Wight for Normandy, either in late 1082 or early 1083. His great complaint against his brother was apparently that he was taking knights away from England at a time when they were needed for its defence, and he appears also to have objected to Odo's arrogance and to his maladministration during his period as regent. He brought him before a council, whose location is unknown, at which Odo pronounced that he could not be tried because he was a bishop and that he should be given the benefit of his clerical status which made him subject only to the pope's jurisdiction. It must be assumed that Odo did not actually wish to be tried by the pope, but that he was seeking only to escape from William's court. William's reply to this device was that he was not trying a bishop, but rather a layman who was Earl of Kent and who had been given the position of regent in England, a piece of legal subtlety which William of Malmesbury attributed to Archbishop Lanfranc. The court may still have been reluctant to convict. Hence, according to Orderic, William seized his brother himself and had him taken to Rouen where he was shut up in prison.

The only other major business known to have been transacted in England during William's visit of 1082-83 was the establishment of an enquiry into the landholdings of the abbey of Ely, which was to be conducted by Bishop Geoffrey of Coutances and Count Robert of Mortain, with the purpose of restoring to the abbey estates which had been taken from it since 1066. It is a clear sign of returning 'normality' in England that Ely, which had given such committed support to Hereward the Wake's rebellion, was back in favour. By Easter 1083 William and Mathilda were back in Normandy, spending the festival at Fécamp. On 18 July they were at Caen, but Mathilda's health must have begun to deteriorate shortly afterwards, since she died on 2 November. William of Malmesbury tells a story that William had taken a mistress, who had been killed on Mathilda's orders, and that William had beaten his wife to death in revenge; he added, however, that he thought the story incredible, and it is a rumour which receives no support from any other source. Mathilda was buried in the abbey of La Trinité at Caen, to which she had bequeathed her crown and sceptre and many other precious objects, and a monument in gold and precious stones was built over her tomb. This has disappeared, but her tombstone with her epitaph can still be seen in the church. Her funeral is said to have been attended by many monks and bishops. William was apparently much distressed by her death, weeping profusely for several days afterwards. Malmesbury says that he abstained from sexual relations until his own death four years later.

William and his son Robert quarrelled again soon after Mathilda's death. The last time at which the evidence confidently allows us to put the two in each other's company is on 9 January 1084. Although Robert had travelled regularly with his father around the Anglo-Norman dominions since their reconciliation in 1080, close proximity had evidently not bred understanding between them. If Orderic is to be believed, William had taken to frequently drawing attention in public to what he considered to be Robert's deficiencies. In return Robert treated his father with contempt. A further contributory factor to the breakdown may be that there is no sign in the evidence of William giving any clear guidance about the English succession. It is also obvious that Mathilda's death and Odo's imprisonment removed Robert's closest friends in the royal family; Mathilda had tried to mediate between him and his father during their first quarrel and evidence from after William's death indicates Odo's preference for Robert over the other sons. We do not know if any specific incident was the immediate cause of Robert being banished from Normandy for a second time. The exile was not, however, as politically disruptive as the first. None of the Normans who had been his allies during his first revolt took up his cause, and the friendless exile was therefore of little use to his father's northern French enemies. Robert made his way around the courts of Europe, visiting, so we are told, the Rhineland, Germany, Aquitaine and Gascony, and even trying to secure the hand of a great heiress, Countess Mathilda of Tuscany. According to Orderic he dissipated the financial help he received on loose living.

William reacted to the family crisis by advancing the younger members. The next eldest surviving son, William Rufus, replaced Robert and appears regularly alongside his father in the witness lists of charters on both sides of the Channel from 1084 onwards. The youngest boy, Henry, was in England at Easter 1084 when his father and brother were in Normandy, and may well have been left as a representative in England. The Ely land pleas mentioned above show that Count Robert of Mortain took his brother Odo's place at least once in hearing major land pleas. As far as the strength of William's rule in England was concerned, a boy in his teens and the unimaginative Count Robert were surely poor substitutes for Odo and Mathilda. In addition, Robert Curthose's absence put Normandy's and Maine's futures in doubt. With his family decimated, William had to spend the last three years of his life grappling with the same problems which had been his major preoccupations during the previous two decades. His actions sometimes have a drastic quality which could be explained by loneliness, by an awareness of advancing age, or by desperation in the face of apparently insoluble difficulties.

The Final Crises

Maine remained the grumbling appendix of William's dominions in the last years of his life. A dispute developed about the succession to the bishopric of Le Mans after Bishop Arnold's death on 29 November 1081. Given the importance of a loyal bishop at Le Mans to the maintenance of Norman rule in Maine, William nominated a clerk from his own chapel, named Hoel, who was also one of Arnold's protégés. However, this simple plan fell foul of the difficulty that a bishop normally could not take up his office until he had been consecrated by the archbishop who had jurisdiction over his diocese. In the case of Le Mans, the archbishop concerned was the Archbishop of Tours, whose archiepiscopal city lay within the lands of the Count of Anjou. Count Fulk, with the active assistance of King Philip, put such pressure on the archbishop that he refused to consecrate Hoel. When the Archbishop of Tours still would not consecrate, despite being ordered to do so by Pope Gregory VII, William cut through the problem by taking the irregular step in 1085 of having Hoel consecrated in Normandy by the Archbishop of Rouen.

A second crisis in Maine was the revolt of Hubert de Sainte-Suzanne, *vicomte* of Le Mans. Hubert had fought against the original Norman occupation of Maine and may well have been among the rebels of 1069-73. But he had become sufficiently reconciled with William to hold the important position of *vicomte* and to keep possession of several important castles. He was renowned as a great warrior and was exceptionally well connected, with relatives among the leading families of the Nivernais in central France and of Anjou. At an unknown date, which was probably in 1084, he rebelled, shut himself up in his castle at Sainte-Suzanne, which was situated within easy reach of Anjou, and used it as a base to harass William's supporters in Le Mans and throughout Maine. Probably in the summer of 1084, William advanced against the castle with an army, but could not isolate it sufficiently effectively to restrict the garrison's capacity to resist. Warriors came from as far afield as Burgundy and Aquitaine to reinforce Hubert's forces, and supplies were always able to penetrate William's attempted blockade, with the result that William eventually left the siege to a section of his military household under the command of the Breton Count Alan the Red. This besieging army probably remained at Sainte-Suzanne for around two years, although Orderic exaggeratedly says that the siege went on for four years. They attacked the castle and skirmished with the garrison, but with little tangible result. Ultimately, demoralized, they made a truce with Hubert, who crossed to England and made his peace with William, probably in 1085. He was restored to favour. William once more could do no more than maintain the status quo in Maine.

Apart from his journey to Sainte-Suzanne, William's movements are unclear for most of 1084 and early 1085. He may have crossed to England between 9 January 1084 and Easter to order the collection of a Danegeld at the extremely high rate of six shillings on the hide, although alternatively, and more probably, he could have organized this by a message sent to deputies. He was certainly in Normandy at Easter 1084 and at some moment in the year was at Rouen. The demand for the enormous Danegeld might be connected with the rebellion in Maine and with fears about the possible consequences of Robert Curthose's second defection. But it is more likely to be associated with preparations to counter another invasion from Denmark which William must have known was looming. Whatever the explanation for this huge tax, the money undoubtedly allowed William in 1085 to bring to England from France and Brittany what the Anglo-Saxon Chronicler called a larger force of mounted men and infantry than had ever previously come into the country (excluding presumably the army of 1066). They must have been hired mercenaries.

The anticipated invasion was led by King Cnut IV of Denmark and his uncle Count Robert of Flanders. Cnut's intention was presumably to revive the long-standing Danish claim to the English kingdom which his father had pressed somewhat ineffectually in 1069-70, and to try to distract his aristocracy from difficulties in Denmark. Count Robert had been William's enemy since 1071, when William had tried to prevent his usurpation of the county of Flanders in the campaign in which William fitz Osbern had been killed.

William billeted his large army throughout his kingdom on his vassals and had the coastline ravaged so as to make a landing unattractive because provisions could not be gathered; the consequences of this can be seen in Domesday Book for Essex and Suffolk. William and his forces remained on the alert throughout the latter part of 1085 and the first half of 1086, until King Cnut was murdered in July while at prayer in the church of Odensee. The Anglo-Saxon Chronicler noted that the English kingdom suffered much hardship and oppression during this period.

In the midst of this crisis, news would have reached William of the death of his old friend and sparring partner, Pope Gregory VII, on 25 May 1085. It is interesting to reflect that the two men, whose lives were entangled in so many ways, and who were certainly the greatest rulers of their age, never met. Relations between them remained cordial to the end, despite the evident tensions described in Chapter Ten. Gregory, for example, did no more than remonstrate politely about Bishop Odo's imprisonment; he reminded William that a number of biblical and canonical texts could be cited to show that a bishop's person was sacrosanct but, for a ferocious defender of clerical liberty, the letter he sent was remarkably mild. His end was a sad one, being driven from Rome by the armies of King Henry IV and becoming a virtual prisoner of the Normans of southern Italy who were supposed to be his protectors. From 1080 he had had to combat the anti-pope Clement III, who was sponsored by King Henry, and in 1085 one of his remaining supporters went to the desperate lengths of asking William to undertake a military intervention in Italy. The king's response is unknown. The only piece of evidence for the Anglo-Norman attitude to this papal schism is a letter written by Lanfranc to one of Clement's main supporters. Lanfranc rebuked his correspondent for slandering Gregory, admitted that King Henry could not have achieved as much as he had without God's favour, informed him that he should not come to England unless he could obtain William's permission, and said finally that the English kingdom had not decided between the claims of the two popes. The stress laid on William's ultimate authority to decide between the two popes is important and typical. With the papacy's leadership of the Church no longer certain, William and Lanfranc maintained their traditional control over the English Church to the end and waited to see what happened.

Domesday Book

The original manuscripts of the record known since the twelfth century as Domesday Book can still be seen at the Public Record Office in London. In reality, what we usually call Domesday Book consists of two volumes, so-called 'Great Domesday' and 'Little Domesday'. 'Great Domesday' is a survey of all the counties of England, south of a line from the River Tees to the River Ribble, above which Norman power was apparently too weak to allow a survey to be made, but excluding Essex, Suffolk and Norfolk. These three counties are in 'Little Domesday'. 'Great Domesday' is obviously the intended final version of the survey, written by a single scribe, and embellished with an elaborate system of rubrication. 'Little Domesday' is a less polished production, written by several scribes, and probably represents a draft immediately prior to the production of a final text like 'Great Domesday'. The whole undertaking was an enormous, indeed unique, enterprise for the eleventh century. The Anglo-Saxon Chronicler described its making in awestruck and exaggerated terms:

> So very narrowly did he have it (i.e., the kingdom) investigated, that there was no single hide nor a yard of land, nor indeed (it is a shame to relate, but it seemed no shame to him to do) one ox nor one cow nor one pig was there left out, and not put down in his record.

The decision to have the great survey made was taken during a crown-wearing at Gloucester at Christmas 1085. Afterwards, while the material was being collected, William and his household were on the move around southern England. There were crown-wearings at Winchester at Easter and Westminster at Whitsun, at the second of which his youngest son Henry was dubbed a knight. On an unspecified Sunday during this time, William was at Laycock in Wiltshire to hear a property dispute between the abbey of Fécamp and William de Briouze. The settlement was reached in the midst of an extremely prestigious gathering of magnates, suggesting that William's court was an especially magnificent one during the period of the survey's compilation. Since we know that the results of the enquiry were actually presented to William, we can be certain that it was completed at the very latest by the autumn of 1086 when he left England for Normandy for the final time. In fact, it is highly probable that the records were presented to him on 1 August 1086 at Old Sarum, the great earthwork where a new town was growing up around the Norman cathedral, when, in the words once more of the Anglo-Saxon Chronicle:

> And there his counsellors came to him, and all the people occupying land who were of any account over all England, whosoever's vassals they might be. And they all submitted to him

and became his vassals, and swore oaths of allegiance to him, that they would be loyal to him against all other men.

This event, known as the Salisbury Oath, was probably the planned climax of the Domesday survey, when William would at the same time have received the records of the survey and the oaths of allegiance of the chief men of his English kingdom. This speculative chronology of the year when Domesday Book was made does not of course necessarily mean that William actually saw the final manuscripts which we know as Domesday Book; more probably, he would have been presented with earlier unbound drafts of texts like 'Little Domesday' or the record known as 'Exeter (or Exon) Domesday', which can now be seen in the archives of Exeter cathedral.

Domesday Book is essentially a collection of county surveys; the counties concerned being roughly the units which survived until 1974. Within each county, the survey contained a description of the holdings of each individual landholder, with each landholder's entry consisting of a list of estates or manors in which each entry normally included the name of the landholder and of his predecessor in 1066, the tax assessment, the value (usually in 1066 and 1086), the number of peasants and ploughs, as well as a variety of information about resources such as mills and animals. The chief town or towns of a county usually received a separate entry.

The reasons for collecting so much information and the way in which it was done have been discussed and debated at great length by the specialists. No answer to these questions which will be fully acceptable to everyone is ever likely to emerge, because there is no conclusive statement available in the contemporary sources, and because both the method and the motive have mostly to be deduced from the Domesday text itself and from a number of related surveys which are usually referred to as 'satellites'. It is at least, however, a reasonable presumption that Domesday Book was made by dividing the kingdom into several circuits, each of which had a single group of commissioners allocated to it, who visited each individual county within their circuit in turn. In order to carry out their task so quickly, the commissioners must have had a considerable number of pre-existing administrative records at their disposal, such as taxation assessment lists, and they must have ordered the preparation of many other records. Within every county the landholders, or their representatives, would have supplied information about their estates to the commissioners, who would then have had the material checked against the local knowledge of jurors from each hundred into which a county was subdivided. We do not know whether this vast enterprise was actually William's own idea, or whether it was the brainchild of one or more of his clerical administrative servants. The latter is intrinsically the more likely probability since only a cleric would have been aware that the administrative resources existed to make the survey feasible. It is, however immensely to William's credit that he should have grasped what could be done, and that he supplied the dominant political will to persuade his Norman and French followers to take part.

One fact which has emerged very strongly from all modern discussion of the making of Domesday Book is the extent to which the whole, operation relied upon the governmental structure which William had inherited from his English predecessors. It made fundamental use of English institutions such as the shire and hundred courts and of tax lists of English origin, as well as drawing on the testimony of Englishmen and members of juries representing each hundred court. Domesday Book was therefore the culmination of the twenty years of deliberate fostering and conservation of English administration and local government which was described in Chapter Nine. The Norman contribution is not, however, one which should be under-estimated. At least one inquest resembling the Domesday enquiry, albeit on a much smaller scale, had been carried out in Normandy in the 1070s. And the whole operation was, of course, pulled together by Norman and French administrators. One of William's most gifted bishops, William de St Calais, who had been appointed to Durham in 1080, may well have overseen everything and, in general, the work would have drawn very heavily on the skills of William's most capable lay and clerical administrative servants.

A major factor in William's and his advisers' decision to have Domesday Book made appears to have been the constant Norman preoccupation with the exploitation of England's wealth, a need which had been given even greater urgency by the invasion scare of 1085-6. One objective of the survey may indeed have been a reassessment of Danegeld and, certainly, the collection of data was carried out against the background of another massive levy of that tax; a contemporary account of the year by Bishop Robert of Hereford noted that there were many disturbances in the country as a result of the king's taxation. It is obvious at a glance that Domesday Book was exceptionally useful for the efficient exploitation of the royal lands and revenues, and that the records of the holdings of other men could help his officials levy taxes, charge succession dues, and so on. For this reason, after the returns had been brought to William, and after he had left for Normandy, the manuscripts were deposited in the royal treasury. A remarkable original writ from the archives of Westminster abbey, which is dated 'after the survey of all England' (*'post descriptionem totius Anglie'*), shows that, even before William left the kingdom, business was being transacted which changed the information recorded in the survey because the scribe of Domesday Book actually made a marginal note on his manuscript to take account of the contents of the writ.

Another consideration which must have weighed heavily with William and his colleagues was the need to compile some sort of record of the tenure of land after nineteen years, during which there had been a massive transfer of property. Indeed, Domesday's value as a record of tenure probably explains England's new Norman and French aristocracy's willingness to have their lands so closely surveyed. Most tax-payers are after all usually very reluctant to divulge their resources to their masters! Great land pleas such as the one held on Penenden Heath in 1072 and the series of inquests into the estates of the abbey of Ely had unleashed a plethora of inquiries into the landholdings of the churches and lords concerned, and Domesday itself reveals the large number of other less dramatic disputes which the Conquest had created. It looks therefore as if the making of Domesday Book was associated with a desire to record, with a view perhaps eventually to resolving conflicting claims to property; two writs from the earliest weeks of William II's reign show that work on sorting out such disputes was going on well over a year after William I had received the results of the survey.

These conflicting claims form the legal context for the making of Domesday Book. And at a more general level, the long-standing collaboration between William and his aristocracy, coupled with nineteen years of insecurity in an inhospitable kingdom, supplies the political context. The Domesday survey, which recorded what every major landholder held, and the Salisbury Oath, by which William took the homage of them all, and by which they in turn must have secured a reciprocal acknowledgement of their landholdings from the king, appear to have been deliberately intended to set the seal on the Norman Conquest of England. They were also the culmination of almost twenty years of deliberate and fairly ruthless exploitation of England's wealth.

The End of the Reign

William left England in the autumn of 1086 in what the Anglo-Saxon Chronicler thought to be his usual manner, taking as much money as he could, by fair means or foul. He travelled to Normandy by way of the Isle of Wight. Back in France, he married his daughter Constance to Alan Fergant, Count of Brittany, in a continuation of the policy of marrying his daughters to northern French territorial princes, which had been initiated when his youngest daughter Adela had married Count Stephen of Blois and Chartres in c.1080. It was a policy which reflected a continuing search for allies and his anxieties about the power of Normandy's neighbours. William's preoccupation with the Danish menace in 1085-6 had been utilized by King Philip to allow his men to make raids across the Norman border into the region of Evreux from bases in the French Vexin, the county over which Philip had acquired lordship in 1077. At some stage also in 1086-7, Robert Curthose returned to northern France; the details of his activities are unknown, but it is a fair presumption that he would have incited the French king to make war. William evidently deemed the general situation to be so serious that he launched an aggressive campaign into enemy territory.

According to Orderic, William justified his attack on the French Vexin by a claim that it had been granted to his father in 1033 by King Philip's father, King Henry I. Historians' general reluctance to accept the truth of this claim gives pause for reflection on some of the other famous 'legitimate' enterprises that William had undertaken during his life; there is surely some inconsistency, for example, in historians' readiness to believe William of Poitiers's version of William's claim to the English kingdom, even though Poitiers was certainly writing to justify William's cause, while being sceptical about this story in Orderic's history. William's claim to the French Vexin, if indeed it was made, was undoubtedly a dishonest one. Although William's father had been helpful to Henry I in 1033, there is no contemporary evidence for his granting lordship over the French Vexin, or for Duke Robert exercising it. Furthermore, throughout his life, William had never acted as if he had any rights there. In particular, he had not tried to intervene in 1077 when King Philip annexed the Vexin after Count Simon's death (see pp.183-4) and he had even been prepared to allow the French king to confirm the possessions of the Norman abbey of Le Bec in the Vexin in a charter.

William's army advanced into the Vexin in the last week of July 1087 and headed directly for the town of Mantes, which had been the base for the raids across the Norman frontier. As usual his troops devastated the countryside as they advanced. Finding the town relatively unguarded, Willium's army forced an entry and set it on fire. But during the sack, William was taken ill, either because of the heat, or because of an internal injury caused when his horse tried to leap a ditch and the pommel of its saddle ripped into his stomach. He ordered his troops to retreat, and he himself was carried back to Rouen where he took to his bed. He was subsequently moved outside the city to the priory of St-Gervais for peace and quiet. He was in great pain from internal injuries, and it must have been obvious to everyone that he was dying.

There are two accounts of the scene at William the Conqueror's deathbed, but neither of them is fully trustworthy. Far and away the best is Orderic's, even though the lengthy speeches he gives are more an indication of what he thought should happen when a great prince died, than of what actually took place. The second, the so-called *'De Obitu Willelmi'* ('On the Death of William') is a tract, written in the early twelfth century, which has been shown to have been copied almost word for word from two ninth-century sources, with the names being changed where necessary. It is of little value. We have to rely on Orderic for most of the basic facts, with some extra evidence supplied by William of Malmesbury and in a charter.

William was surrounded throughout his last illness by clergy, some of whom were also doctors. At various times great magnates were also present, although the sources actually name only Archbishop William of Rouen, William's two sons William and Henry, his brother Count Robert of Mortain, the two sons of Roger de Beaumont, Count Robert of Meulan and Henry, and Ivo Taillebois. The king's condition deteriorated in early September but, according to Orderic, he remained lucid to the end. Malmesbury suggests that he panicked at the approach of death, before calming himself and ending his life as the eleventh-century Church required, by making gifts to churches for the good of his soul and to propitiate God's final judgement. He is said to have given money to rebuild the churches at Mantes, to have restored an estate to the abbey of Fécamp and to have decreed that each English minster should receive either ten or six marks of gold, that every country church in the kingdom should be given sixty pence, and that in every English county one hundred pounds should be distributed among the poor. He bequeathed his regalia to the abbey of St-Etienne at Caen, and agreed to the release of all his prisoners, trying only to make an exception of his brother Odo, an act of revenge from which he was eventually dissuaded by Odo's other brother, Count Robert of Mortain.

With regard to the succession, William permitted his son Robert to succeed him in Normandy, as he had frequently promised he would. Although he may have wished to disinherit Robert entirely, he was persuaded not to by the magnates who were present, on the grounds that they had already done homage to Robert and were therefore bound by oaths of loyalty. Aubrey de Couci, once Earl of Northumbria, was sent to tell Robert the news. No direct provision was made for England, but the second son William was given its custody and it was assumed that he would be the next king. The third son Henry was given a sum of money. This done, William ordered William Rufus to cross without delay to England to receive the crown, sending a sealed letter to Archbishop Lanfranc ordering him to receive him. All this happened on either 7 or 8 September.

William died soon after dawn on Thursday 9 September. His death, when it came, took his attendants by surprise. His last weeks echo so much in his life, and the problems which had preoccupied him so much during his last years were with him to the end. At Mantes he had behaved with typical brutality; contemporaries were shocked by the deaths of two especially religious hermits during the devastation of the town. The campaign itself was a response to threats by the same northern French enemies who had caused him problems for forty years. At the moment of death he took the Christian duties of a duke and king as seriously as he had done throughout his life. His problems with his family went unresolved; he could forgive neither his eldest son nor his brother and his final arrangements for the succession were the cause of a civil war which almost destroyed the cross-Channel realm he had created. However, given William's indecisiveness about the succession, and the irreconcilable divisions within his family, by 1087 anything he might have proposed would probably have caused war. The more durable aspects of his achievement only became obvious as time passed.

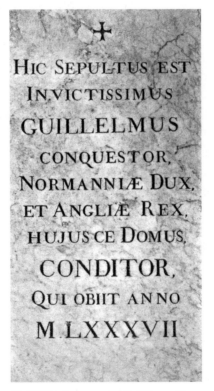

51. William's tomstone at St-Etienne, Caen.
(Courtesy of Trevor Rowley)

Epilogue

General panic followed William's death. His attendants either immediately rode off to protect their own property or looted the chamber in which their king had died. According to Orderic, the citizens of Rouen were totally disorientated by the news, reeling around as if drunk and taking measures to guard their possessions. Major Norman magnates expelled the garrisons which William had installed in their castles and fortified themselves on their estates. Robert de Belllême, the son of Roger de Montgommery, was the first to do this; William, Count of Evreux, William de Breteuil and Ralph de Tosny soon did the same. It was as if the lynch pin had been taken out of everyone's lives. All prepared for the troubled times which they expected to follow with their new duke's prestige and power so greatly compromised, and some savoured the prospect of a weakening of the iron control which William had exercised within the duchy of Normandy.

William's body remained abandoned between the early morning monastic services of prime and terce. It was the clergy of Rouen who finally took matters in hand and prepared the corpse for burial. The costs of embalming were born by an insignificant knight named Herluin, and the body was then transported by ship to Caen to be buried as William had wished in the abbey church of St-Etienne. The abbot and his monks came out in procession to meet the ship, which had presumably sailed down the River Orne into the town and, together with a great crowd of townspeople, they set out to bear the corpse the relatively short distance to the church. However, even this stage of the proceedings did not pass without incident, for one of the houses in the town suddenly caught fire, burning down many of the neighbouring properties which, like it, were presumably wooden buildings. Amidst panic, the monks alone stuck to the task of carrying the dead ruler to his last resting place.

William's funeral in the abbey church of St-Etienne was attended by all the bishops and abbots of Normandy, including his brother Odo, already released from prison. Of his sons, only Henry was present; Robert had not yet returned to Normandy, while William was in England securing his new kingdom, having heard news of his father's death as he prepared to cross the Channel. The Bishop of Evreux preached the sermon, with William's body still resting on the bier, on view to all. Then, before the body could be placed into the tomb, a citizen of Caen named Ascelin, son of Arthur, stood up and announced that the ground on which they were all standing had been taken illegally from his father by William before 1066. Hurried and embarrassed consultations took place. It was discovered that the man was speaking the truth and he was quickly recompensed with money. William's corpse was then lowered into the tomb, but it burst open because the space which had been prepared was too small. A terrible smell spread through the church – presumably from the putrefying innards – which could not be dissipated by the frankincense and other spices. The priests concluded the rites very quickly and fled. This gruesome and humiliating end provoked Orderic, who is the main source for these events, to some of that moralizing which came easily to a medieval cleric, on the insignificance of all human endeavour. A great king, once all-powerful, was reduced to nothing by these indignities.

Contemporary poets celebrated William's achievements. A piece of Latin doggerel, composed by Archbishop Thomas of York, was inscribed on his tomb in gold:

> He ruled the savage Normans; Britain's men
> He courageously conquered, and kept them in his
>   power;
> And bravely thrust back swords from Maine
> And made them subject to his rule's laws;
> William the great king lies in this little urn,
> So small a house serves for a mighty lord.
> He died when Phoebus had lain in Virgo's bosom
> For three weeks and an additional two days.

This verse surely equals any obituary before or since for its platitudes.

William's death was followed by a period of turmoil in Normandy and a struggle between his three surviving sons for control of his lands. In 1088 there was a revolt in England against King William II, led by what can almost be described as the 'old guard' of the Norman Conquest – Bishop Odo of Bayeux, Count Robert of Mortain, Bishop Geoffrey of Coutances, and Roger de Montgommery. The rebels' aim was to overthrow William and make

51. William II, as depicted on a coin of his reign.

Robert Curthose king, but they were defeated before their protégé could even manage to embark for England. This war was merely the first of a series of conflicts in Normandy and England which continued until the Conqueror's third son Henry defeated his brother Robert at the Battle of Tinchebrai and in 1106 added control over Normandy to the kingdom of England, which he had seized in 1100. During this same period, the great authority which William the Conqueror had built up over the duchy of Normandy disintegrated, as the weak and unfortunate Duke Robert had to try to cope with the loss of control which his father had exercised over the magnates' castles, the disloyalty of vassals who were the recipients of bribes from William II and, after him, Henry I, and ultimately with military interventions by his two brothers. Maine revolted against his rule in 1089, and thereafter Norman authority in the county was severely compromised.

This collapse must be seen as a commentary on the Conqueror's achievements. It is quite wrong to blame the turmoil exclusively on the machinations of his sons or on the turbulence of the aristocracy; it was William after all who had divided up his lands in the first place, had pressed his authority harshly on to his Norman vassals, and had failed to subdue Maine. The disturbed scene proves, if nothing else does, how William's policies and attitudes had been geared to his own lifetime, and not beyond, and how similar his career was to that of other builders of ephemeral eleventh-century 'empires', like Counts Fulk Nerra and Geoffrey Martel of Anjou. Yet in the midst of this chaotic situation, we can see what William's true achievements were. His son William succeeded to the English kingdom without opposition, and appears indeed to have been welcomed by the majority of the natives of the kingdom who supported him in preference to Robert Curthose. There is indeed a telling scene after the fall of the rebel castle of Rochester in 1088, when the defeated and disgraced Bishop Odo came out, to be greeted by English chants demanding the hangman's noose. A subsidiary consequence of William's achievement was the probable eventual continuation of the union of Normandy and England, because under his authority so many men had acquired estates and interests on both sides of the Channel. Between 1087 and 1106 the great magnates made their allegiances to Robert, William or Henry for a variety of reasons. There is, however, a discernible pattern in that the majority gravitated towards the son who seemed most likely to recreate William's cross-Channel realm. William the Conqueror's efforts in England between 1066 and 1087 had been so thorough that in 1087-8 there was no question that the next King of England was not going to be a Norman. His great achievement, and the true basis of his greatness, was to give Norman rule in England and the union of Normandy and England such stability that his successors should want both to continue.

William's importance as a Duke of Normandy is obvious; his personality channelled a Norman and a northern French drive towards expansion into successful conquests. His formidable achievements are at the heart of the great years of Normandy's history. When, however, we ask questions about his importance as a King of the English, then the answers are much more complex, and are likely to be controversial. All depends on the significance which is attached to the Norman Conquest, and since many books have been written to try to expound the importance of that difficult subject, it is impossible to come up with reasoned answers in one or two paragraphs at the end of this book. I shall simply say then that it is my opinion that the Conquest represents a dramatic and revolutionary transformation in England's, and Britain's, history. It seems to me undeniable that William's success brought England into closer cultural and political contact with France and that this development had profound consequences for the aristocracy, people and Church as the kingdom passed through the periods of the so-called Angevin Empire, the Twelfth-Century Renaissance, and the Hundred Years War. William's conquest also ended the long-standing relationship between England and Scandinavia and ensured that England would never again be vulnerable to invasion from across the North Sea. In addition, William's control over the settlement of Normans and others in England provided a base from which their descendants were to put ever-increasing pressure on Wales, Scotland and Ireland.

As to changes within England itself, it is impossible to be so certain; there is still fierce controversy. My own view is that the initial impact of the Normans was a shattering one, but that in the midst of the slaughter and oppression, William's rule took over and preserved, for reasons which were both ideological and practical, a well-developed English system of central and local government. By the middle of the twelfth century we are looking at a structure whose foundations are undeniably English, but which has been adapted to take account of the social customs and the 'feudalism' of the Normans, as well as of their rulers' constant demands for money. There is a school of thought which thinks that the Normans immediately brought more drive and efficiency to English government, but I cannot agree. The idea makes William sound more like a civil servant than a conqueror. He exploited ruthlessly and he used existing arrangements most capably to control and organize a conquest, but he changed little of the basic structure. Whether developments similar to all these would have taken place if Harold had won on 14 October 1066 is an unanswerable question; I personally doubt whether they would.

I began this book with a protest against insularity. I hope that I have persuaded you that William's life, personality and achievements can only be understood in a European and French, as well as an English and a British, context. When I think about William's personality, I still find words that I wrote almost ten years ago very appealing: William 'seems to have had none of the frailties which make a personality sympathetic'. I would still agree with this, and I think I was already aware what a conventional and conservative man William was when I wrote them. What I did not anticipate when I set out on this journey through William's life was the sheer brute force of the man's determination and inner will.

I think that the last words can be given to the compassionate Orderic Vitalis. Ultimately he saw William as an extremely successful man, whose success had been gained at enormous cost in terms of innocent human blood. He had gained the English kingdom 'by divine grace, not hereditary right'. God had seemed to be on William's side. Yet He would remember, as we always should, the countless, usually silent, victims of a savage and pitiless career.

Bibliographical Notes

General

Many books have been written about William the Conqueror. Of these the three which stand out are E.A. Freeman, *The History of the Norman Conquest of England, Its Causes and Its Results*, 6 vols. (1867-79), F.M. Stenton, *William the Conqueror and the rule of the Normans* (1908), and D.C. Douglas, *William the Conqueror* (1964). Freeman's massive work is anachronistic in approach and wrong on countless matters. It is, however, a mine of information and posed so many of the crucial questions that it is still worth consulting. Stenton's book summed up splendidly the state of knowledge when he wrote. Douglas was the first British historian for many years to immerse himself in the Norman sources for William's reign. The book is in many ways a classic, yet it has become dated and is patchy on several major topics.

A mass of books and articles which contribute to our knowledge of William the Conqueror's life have appeared over the past twenty years. The most notable books are F. Barlow, *Edward the Confessor* (2nd ed., 1979); F. Barlow, *William Rufus* (1983); D. Bates, *Normandy before 1066* (1982); M. Gibson, *Lanfranc of Bec* (1978); W.E. Kapelle, *The Norman Conquest of the North* (1979); and J. Le Patourel, *The Norman Empire* (1976). The novocentenary of Domesday Book stimulated publications on the survey's compilation. The two major collections of essays are P. Sawyer (ed.), *Domesday Book: a Reassessment* (1985) and J.C. Holt (ed.), *Domesday Studies* (1987). Several of the contributions in these two volumes are of fundamental importance. There is also a most useful collection of translated excerpts from the sources in R.A. Brown, *The Norman Conquest* (1984). Articles in learned journals have changed thinking on particular topics. These are too numerous for me to list more than the most important here. The reader will locate the vast majority of them through looking at journals like *English Historical Review (EHR)*, *Anglo-Norman Studies: the Proceedings of the Battle Conprence (Battle)*, *Annales de Normandie*, *Bulletin of the Institute of Historical Research (BIHR)*, *Speculum*, and *Transactions of the Royal Historical Sodety (TRHS)*.

The Chief Sources for William's Career

The best editions of the major narrative sources are *The Anglo-Saxon Chronicle: A Revised Translalation*, ed. D. Whitelock, D.C. Douglas and S.I. Tucker (1961); *Guillaume de Jumièges, Gesta Normannorum Ducum*, ed. J. Marx (1914), but the reader should note that a new, vastly improved edition and translation by Dr Elisabeth van Houts is to be published by OUP in 1990; *The Bayeux Tapestry*, ed. F.M. Stenton *et al* (1957); *The Bayeux Tapestry*, ed. D.M. Wilson (1984); *The Carmen de Hastingae Proelio of Guy, Bishop of Amiens*, ed. C. Morton and H. Muntz (1972); *The Life of King Edward who Rests at Westminster*, ed. F. Barlow (1962); Eadmer, *Historia Novorum*, ed. M. Rule (1884); *The Ecclesiastical History of Orderic Vitalis*, ed. and trans. M. Chibnall, 6 vols. (1969-80); William of Malmeshury, *De Gestis Regum Anglorum*, ed. W. Stubbs, 2 vols. (1887-9); Florence of Worcester, *Chronicon ex Chronicis*, ed. B. Thorpe, 2 vols. (1848-9). Many of these editions contain valuable introductions and critical commentaries.

In addition, the reader should consult, R.H.C. Davis, 'William of Poitiers and His History', in R.H.C. Davis and J.M. Wallace-Hadrill (eds.), *The Writing of History in the Middle Ages* (1981); E.M.C. van Houts, 'The Gesta Normannorum Ducum: A History without an End', *Battle*, 3 (1981); R.H.C. Davis, 'William of Jumièges, Robert Curthose and the Norman Succession', *EHR*, 95 (1980); N.P. Brooks and the late H.E. Walker, 'The Authority and Interpretation of the Bayeux Tapestry', *Battle*, 1 (1979); H.E.J. Cowdrey, 'Towards an Interpretation of the Bayeux Tapestry', *Battle*, 10 (1988); E Barlow, 'The *Carmen de Hastingae Proelio*', in K. Bourne and D.C. Watt (eds.), *Studies in International History presented to W. Norton Medlicott* (1967); R.H.C. Davis, 'The *Carmen de Hastingae Proelio*', *EHR*, 93 (1978); L.J. Engels, 'Once More: the *Carmen de Hastingae Proelio*', *Battle*, 2 (1980).

Domesday Book was edited by A. Farley in 1783. There are accessible translations of individual counties in unconvincingly 'modern' language in J. Morris (general ed.), *Domesday Book*, 34 vols. (1975-86), although some of the volumes have exceptionally good critical commentaries. The *Victoria County Histories of England* usually have a translation of each Domesday county with an introduction. A facsimile of Domesday Book was published by Alecto Historical Editions to commemorate the novocentenary of 1986, and this will soon be supplemented by facsimiles for each individual county which will have a critical introduction. For general bibliographical information on Domesday Book, see D. Bates, *A Bibliography of Domesday Book* (1986).

William the Conqueror's Norman charters for the period up until 1066 have been edited by M. Fauroux, *Recueil des Actes des Ducs de Normandie de 911 à 1066* (1961), and a small number of the Norman charters from after 1066 by L. Musset, *Les Actes de Guillaume le Conquérant et de la Reine Mathilde pour les Abbayes Caennaises* (1967). In general, there is only the inadequate calendar of William's charters by H.W.C. Davis, *Regesta Regum Anglo-Normannorum, 1066-1100* (1913), which is eventually to be replaced by an edition giving full texts, which is being prepared by D. Bates for Oxford University Press. For writs, see T.A.M. Bishop and P. Chaplais, *Facsimiles of English Royal Writs to AD 1100* (1957). For ecclesiastical records, it is essential to consult H.M. Clover and M.T. Gibson, *The Letters of Lanfranc, Archbishop of Canterbury* (1979) and D. Whitelock, M. Brett and C.N.L. Brooke, *Councils and Synods with Other Documents relating to the English Church, 1066-1204* (1981).

Normandy Before 1066

The approach taken to the history of Normandy before 1066 is that of D. Bates, *Normandy before 1066*, which can also be used as a bibliographical source, both for the extensive literature in French on the history of the duchy and for northern French society. For an older approach to Norman society, D.C. Douglas, *William the Conqueror*, should be consulted, along with his fundamental article 'The Earliest Norman Counts', *EHR*, 61 (1946).

For French history in general in this period, there is now the excellent general survey by J. Dunbabin, *France in the Making, 843-1180* (1985), as well as a valuable article by E.M. Hallam, 'The King and the Princes in Eleventh Century France', *BIHR*, 53 (1980).

For the history of Normandy itself, particular attention should be paid to O. Guillot, *Le Comte d'Anjou et Son Entourage au XIe siècle* (1972); the two articles by Kathleen Thompson, 'Family and Influence to the South of Normandy in the Eleventh Century: The Lordship of Bellême', *Journal of Medieval History*, 11 (1985), and 'The Norman Aristocracy before 1066: the Example of the Montgomerys', *Historical Research, 60* (1987); L. Musset, 'Autour des Modalités Juridiques de l'Expansion Normande au XIe Siècle' and J.-M. Maillefer, 'Une Famille Aristocratique aux Confins de la Normandie: les Géré au XIe Siècle', in L. Musset *et al*, *Autour du Pouvoir Ducal Normand (Xe-XIIe Siècles)* (1985). Also important is C.W. Hollister, 'The Greater Domesday Tenants-in-chief', in J.C. Holt (ed.), *Domesday Studies* (1987).

For new material on William's family, E.M.C. van Houts, 'The Origins of Herleva, mother of William the Conqueror', *EHR*, 101 (1986); D. Bates and Véronique Gazeau, 'L'Abbaye de Grestain et la Famille d'Herluin de Conteville', *Annales de Normandie*, 40 (1990).

For William's building at Caen, the reader should consult M. de Bouard, *Le Château de Caen* (1979); L. Musset, *Normandie Romane: La Basse Normandie* (2nd ed., 1975); and the numerous writings by Maylis Baylé such as *La Trinité de Caen* (1979) and 'Les Ateliers de Sculpture de Saint-Etienne de Caen', *Battle*, 10 (1988).

William and the English Succession

This has always been a controversial subject. Barlow, *Edward the Confessor* (see General Section) is the main modern account, but its conclusions are not universally accepted. See especially, E. John, 'Edward the Confessor and the Norman Succession', *EHR*, 94 (1979); A. Williams, 'Land and Power in the Eleventh Century: the Estates of Harold Godwineson', *Battle*, 3 (1980); A. Williams, 'Some Notes and Considerations on Problems connected with the English Royal Succession, 860-1066', *Battle*, 1 (1978); R. Fleming, 'Domesday Estates of the King and the Godwines: a Study in Late Saxon Politics', *Speculum*, 58 (1983); D. Bates, 'Lord Sudeley's Ancestors: The Family of the Counts of Amiens, Valois and the Vexin in France and England during the Eleventh Century', in *The Sudeleys – Lords of Toddington* (1987).

The Hastings Campaign

In addition to the books cited in the General Section, it is important to consult the article by F. Barlow in the Sources section, the studies of the Bayeux Tapestry mentioned in the Sources section, and R.A. Brown, 'The Battle of Hastings', *Battle*, 3 (1981); C.H. Lemmon, 'The Campaign of 1066', in D. Whitelock *et al*, *The Norman Conquest: its Setting and Impact* (1966); R. Glover, 'English Warfare in 1066', *EHR*, 67 (1952); C.W. Hollister, *Anglo-Saxon Military Institutions* (1962); N. Hooper, 'Anglo-Saxon Warfare on the Eve of the Conquest', *Battle*, 1 (1978); R. Abels, 'Bookland and Fyrd Service', *Battle*, 7 (1985); C. Gillmore, 'Naval Logistics of the Cross-Channel Operation, 1066', *Battle*, 7 (1985); N. Hooper, 'The Housecarls in England in the Eleventh Century', *Battle*, 7 (1985); B. Bachrach, 'Some Observations on the Military Administration of the Norman Conquest', *Battle*, 8 (1986); R.H.C. Davis, 'The Warhorses of the Normans', *Battle*, 10 (1988); E.M.C. van Houts, 'The Ship List of William the Conqueror', *Battle*, 10 (1988); I. Peirce, 'Arms, Armour and Warfare in the Eleventh Century', *Battle*, 10 (1988).

The Main Events 1066-1087

The main literature on these is provided in the books included in the General section above, notably those by Douglas, Barlow (*William Rufus*) and Kapelle. The account given in this book draws on new dating for charters. It is still worth consulting C.W. David, *Robert Curthose, Duke of Normandy* (1920), and on William's court and family, there are also D. Bates, 'The Character and Career of Odo, Bishop of Bayeux, 1049/50-1097', *Speculum*, 50 (1975) and E.M.C. van Houts, 'Poetry and the Anglo-Norman Court', *Journal of Medieval History*, 15 (1989). On an English 'survivor', the reader can now consult, N. Hooper, 'Edgar the Ætheling: Anglo-Saxon Prince, Rebel and Crusader', *Anglo-Saxon England*, 14 (1985). The article by R.H.C. Davis, 'William of Jumièges, Robert Curthose and the Norman Succession', *EHR* 95 (1980), which was also cited in the Sources section, is also important for the quarrel between William and his eldest son.

There is a vast literature connected with the making of Domesday Book. The most important items are V.H. Galbraith, *The Making of Domesday Book* (1961); S.P.J. Harvey, 'Domesday Book and its Predecessors', *EHR*, 86 (1971); S.P.J. Harvey, 'Recent Domesday Studies', *EHR*, 95 (1980); H.B. Clarke, 'The Domesday Satellites', in P. Sawyer (ed.), *Domesday Book: A Reassessment* (1985); J.C. Holt, '1086', in J.C. Holt (ed.), *Domesday Studies* (1987); P. Chaplais, 'William of Saint-Calais and the Domesday Survey', in J.C. Holt (ed.), *Domesday Studies* (1987).

William's Cross-Channel Dominions

The basic account is the book by J. Le Patourel cited in the General Section. This is supplemented by C.W. Hollister, 'Normandy, France and the Anglo-Norman *regnum*', *Speculum*, 51 (1976). Critical of both, as well as being a fully documented exposition of the argument given in this book is

D. Bates, 'Normandy and England after 1066', *EHR*, 104 (1989). On Norman government in general, J.O. Prestwich, 'The Military Household of the Norman Kings', *EHR* 95 (1980), is very important. Also on cross-Channel government, see D. Bates, 'The Origins of the Justiciarship', *Battle*, 4 (1982); M. Biddle, 'Seasonal Festivals and Residence: Winchester, Westminster and Gloucester in the Tenth to Twelfth Centuries', *Battle*, 8 (1986), although its comments on William's itinerary reflect the errors of earlier scholars. William's intentions for the succession are controversial. The basic literature is J. Le Patourel, 'The Norman Succession, 996-1135', *EHR*, 86 (1971); J.C. Holt, 'Politics and Property in Early Medieval England', *Past and Present*, no. 57 (1972), Appendix IIA; also Barlow, *William Rufus* (see General Section); J.m. Bouvris, 'Aux origines du prieuré de Vains: une version inédite de la confirmation par le Duc Robert Courte-Heuse d'une donation faite en 1087 par Guillaume le Conquérant à l'abbaye de Saint-Etienne de Caen; *Revue de L'Avranchin et du Pays de Granville*, 105 (1987).

The Government of Conquered England

Inevitably this is a topic more studied than any other. To the general books listed in the General Section should be added, F. Barlow, *William I and the Norman Conquest* (1965); H.R. Loyn, *The Norman Conquest* (1966); R.A. Brown, *The Normans and the Norman Conquest* (1969). All three are now somewhat dated. From the mass of articles and books, the following are especially useful: J. Le Patourel, 'The Norman Colonization of Britain', *Settimane di Studio sull'alto medioevo*, 16 (1969); C.W. Hollister, 'The Greater Domesday Tenants-in-Chief', in J.C. Holt (ed.), *Domesday Studies* (1987); P. Sawyer, '1066-1086: A Tenurial Revolution?', in P. Sawyer (ed.), *Domesday Book: A Reassessment* (1985); R. Fleming, 'Domesday Book and the Tenurial Revolution', *Battle*, 9 (1987); P.R. Hyams, ' "No Register of Title": The Domesday Inquest and Land Adjudication', *Battle*, 9 (1987); F.M. Stenton, 'English Families and the Norman Conquest', *TRHS*, 4th series, 26 (1944); J.L. Nelson, 'The Rites of the Conqueror', *Battle*, 4 (1982); G. Garnett, '*Franci et Angli*: The Legal Distinctions between Peoples after the Conquest', *Battle*, 8 (1986); G. Garnett, 'Coronation and Propaganda: Some Implications of the Norman Claim to the Throne of England in 1066', *TRHS*, 5th series, 36 (1986); C.P. Lewis, 'The Norman Settlement of Herefordshire under William I', *Battle*, 7 (1985); J.F.A. Mason, William the First and the Sussex Rapes (1966); E. Searle, 'Women and Legitimization of Succession at the Norman Conquest', *Battle*, 3 (1981); J. Campbell, 'Observations on English Government from the Tenth to the Twelfth Century', *TRHS*, 5th series, 25 (1975); W.L. Warren, 'The Myth of Norman Administrative Efficiency', *TRHS*, 5th series, 34 (1984); J.A. Green, 'The Last Century of Danegeld', *EHR*, 96 (1981); J.A. Green, 'The Sheriffs of William the Conqueror', *Battle*, 5 (1983); D. Bates, 'The Land Pleas of William I's Reign: Penenden Heath Revisited', *BIHR*, 51 (1978); F.J. West, *The Justiciarship in England, 1066-1232* (1966); M Dolley, *The Norman Conquest and the English Coinage* (1966); S.P.J. Harvey, 'Domesday Book and Anglo-Norman Governance', *TRHS*, 5th series, 25 (1975); S.P.J. Harvey, 'Taxation and the Ploughland in Domesday Book', in P. Sawyer (ed.), *Domesday Book: A Reassessment* (1985); S.P.J. Harvey, 'Taxation and the Economy', in J.C. Holt (ed.), *Domesday Studies* (1987); J. Campbell, 'Some Agents and Agencies of the Late Anglo-Saxon State', in J.C. Holt (ed.), *Domesday Studies* (1987); S. Keynes, 'Regenbald the Chancellor (*sic*)', *Battle*, 10 (1988); D.M: Metcalf, 'The Taxation of Moneyers under Edward the Confessor and in 1086', in J.C. Holt (ed.), *Domesday Studies* (1987); R.A. Brown, T*he Origins of English Feudalism (*1973); E.A.R. Brown, 'The Tyranny of a Construct: Feudalism and Historians of Medieval Europe', *American Historical Review*, 79 (1974); J. Gillingham, 'The Introduction of Knight Service into England', *Battle*, 4 (1982); J.C. Holt, 'The Introduction of Knight Service in England', *Battle*, 6 (1984); J.C. Holt, 'Feudal Society and the Family in Early Medieval England: I. The Revolution of 1066', *TRHS*, 5th series, 32 (1982); R. Mortimer, 'Land and Service: the Tenants of the Honour of Clare', *Battle*, 8 (1986).

William and the Church

In addition to Gibson, *Lanfranc of Bec* (see General Section), the reader should consult: F. Barlow, *The English Church, 1000-1066* (1963); F. Barlow, *The English Church, 1066-1154* (1979); H.E.J. Cowdrey, 'Pope Gregory VII and the Anglo-Norman Church and Kingdom', *Studi Gregoriani*, 9 (1972); H.E.J. Cowdrey, 'Bishop Ermenfrid of Sion and the Penitential Ordinance following the Battle of Hastings', *Journal of Ecclesiastical History*, 20 (1969); H.R. Loyn, 'William's Bishops: Some Further Thoughts', *Battle*, 10 (1988); S.N.Vaughn, 'Lanfranc at Bec: A Reinterpretation', *Albion*, 17 (1985); F. Barlow, 'William I's Relations with Cluny', *Journal of Ecclesiastical History*, 32 (1981); W. Frohlich, 'St Anselm's Special Relationship with William the Conqueror', *Battle*, 10 (1988); E.M. Hallam, 'Monasteries as "War Memorials"; Battle Abbey and La Victoire', *Studies in Church History*, 20 (1983); E. Searle (ed.), *The Chronicle of Battle Abbey* (1980).

Index